America:
Exploration and Travel

America:
Exploration and Travel

Steven E. Kagle
Editor

Bowling Green State University Popular Press
Bowling Green, Ohio 43403
1979

Cover design by Victoria Heninger

CONTENTS

Preface
Ray B. Browne

Introduction
Steven E. Kagle

I.   **Travel and the American Identity**
The Idea of National Character:
Inspiration or Fallacy?   9
Lynn Altenbernd

Speaking and Touching:
The Problem of Inexpressibility in American
Travel Books   18
Wayne Franklin

II.   **Foreign Travelers in America**
Exploration and Creativity:
Chateaubriand's Travels in America   40
Frans C. Amelinckx

Travel Narratives of D.F. Sarmiento:
A Seminal Frontier Thesis   50
Cathryn A. Ducey

III.   **American Travelers Abroad**
Americans Abroad:
The Popular Art of Travel Writing in the
Nineteenth Century   68
Ahmed M. Metwalli

The Traveller as Antihero:
Richard Smith Elliott in the Mexican War   83
Nicholas T. Joost

Science in the Exploration Narratives Authored
by U.S. Naval Officers   92
V. Ponko, Jr.

IV.   **Exploration and the American Naturalists**
John Muir's My First Summer in the Sierra   102
Donez Xiques

John Muir, Emerson, and the book of Nature:
The Explorer as Prophet   113
   John Tallmadge

V.   **Travel & Exploration as a Theme in
American Literature**
Hawthorne's "Foot-prints on the Sea Shore"
and the Literature of Walking   127
   Roberta F. Weldon

Expatriation and Exploration:
The Exiled Artists of the 1920s   136
   Marjorie Smelstor

The Family Journey to the West   153
   Paul T. Bryant

The Incorporative Consciousness:
Levertov's Journey From Discretion to Unity   166
   Victoria Harris

"No Time for Fainting"
The Frontier Woman in Some Early
American Novels   191
   Edna L. Steeves

Exploration Studies and Popular Culture

Ray B. Browne

The popular culture movement broke upon the academic scene in 1970 with something of the enthusiasm and hope that must have sustained Cortés in his drive to explore Mexico to find the much-rumored gold there or Ponce de Leon in his search for the Fountain of Youth, for the proponents of this area in academic studies realized that great riches and vitalities of youth lay for the finding. Although some of the earliest movements in popular culture studies may have resembled to some people the pioneer's slash and burn policy, those individuals seriously interested in these studies realized that exploring popular culture meant discovering new materials—and this would be of immense importance and potential—but also in using the study of these new areas to probe for new meanings and new significances for the world at large and for the individual in particular.

In a way this new study was the classic Westward movement all over again, a thrust into uncharted lands seeking whatever treasures could be found. But, contrary to the physical pioneer, the student of popular culture recognized that as much as a venture into terra incognita this new movement was also a settling down in familiar land, an exploration rather than a march through an area, an investigation of a land covered with highways and television antennas with a newer and wider lens than had conventionally be used in the past. It was indeed a recharting of old and familiar lands.

Ten years after the beginning of formal popular culture studies, the enthusiasm of the scholars is by no means diminished; they still face the West and dream new dreams. They realize that there are still many lands that need to be explored or re-explored, and the riches reaped and understood. No area is too far from or to close to home, too seemingly insignificant, too esoteric. Academics owe it to themselves and to the humanities at large to explore all possibilities. But it is also a journey over well-traveled roads, a look homeward, a stirring of old ashes.

For those reasons the study of exploration and travel is of utmost importance at this time, both in its own right and as another probe into the larger field of popular culture. It is only logical that today as we complain that there are no new horizons for us to conquer, no new challenges, we realize that the challenge is in fact right under our noses, or our feet, and that is the understanding of where we have been and where we are—in other words the challenge of exploration and understanding rather of travel. Travel gets us from one place to another—often with wonderful attendant enjoyment—but exploration makes us understand our travel, the places we travel to—and ourselves.

The essays in this collection constitute a major step toward this understanding. They open up new areas for concern and draw many valuable insights and conclusions. But most important, perhaps, they demonstrate the viability of the study of these materials. Many more studies should follow this one.

Introduction

Unaccustomed Earth:
The Movement of Americans from Travel to Exploration

Steven Kagle

In his poem "The Gift Outright," Robert Frost wrote:

> The land was ours before we were the land's,
> She was our land more than a hundred years
> Before we were her people, She was ours
> In Massachusetts, in Virginia
> But we were England's, still colonials
> Possessing what we were still unpossessed by.

In these lines and those that followed them, Frost asserted that the colonists lacked more than the name "American" to belong, that we lacked an identification with the land that could only be achieved through struggle. Frost's poem not only argues for such things as the "Declaration," the battles of the Revolution, and the new political and social order set forth by the "Constitution" and the "Bill of Rights"; he argues that we needed to give ourselves "to the land vaguely realizing westward."[1] What was necessary was a shift in the direction of attention from East to West, a shift that involved a change from travel to exploration.

Of course the colonists had moved steadily westward as individuals, but as a society their eyes were still directed eastward. One possible reason for this eastward vision was the early colonists' dependence on Europe for supplies, but their behavior seems less conditioned by such physical concerns than by intangible attitudes.[2] In their consideration of the physical world these early colonists seemed to consider where they were going to be less important than where they had been. As a result though they bordered a wilderness, they were travelers before they were explorers.

There were men who explored the frontier during the colonial period, but most of these explorers were Europeans. As Turner points out, the Atlantic coastal frontier "was the frontier of

Europe." It was only later as the frontier moved west that it "became more and more American."[3] The early explorers came questing to the New World but returned to the Old. When examining the diaries and autobiographies of those who were born or who settled in America during the seventeenth and eighteenth centuries, one finds that they are far richer in accounts of travel than in those of true exploration. The colonists "traveled," visiting and writing about the known world—Europe and the coastal areas already settled. Geographical and political barriers were partly responsible for this situation, but they do not adequately explain the situation especially during the two decades after the Revolution. One can find works like those of Knight and Woolman after the eighteenth century, but one rarely finds ones like those of Pike and Parkman before the nineteenth.

One example of the colonial attitude can be seen in John Winthrop's "A Modell of Christian Charity." Here Winthrop declares that New England shall be a "City on a Hill," a model for Europe to follow. Thus rather than turning their backs on their native England, these colonists kept it as a major concern and were less attentive to the frontier than they might have been. As Perry Miller pointed out in his "Errand in the Wilderness," this attitude contributed to the failure of the Puritans' experiment, because their European audience neglected them, while the frontier they devalued caused economic and cultural changes which threatened their traditional social order.

The period of the Enlightenment saw Americans remain more interested in travel than in exploration. This era was still intellectually conservative accepting changes and even a revolution as long as that change was in the direction of the eternally consistent ideal that the society believed in. As the wild frontier was further from that ideal, it had little to offer. Consequently, the end desired and expected was the imposition of civilization on the frontier.

This attitude is still apparent in the journals kept by Lewis and Clark (1804-1806). While conveying a sense of the power and immensity of the western wilderness, these journals show the explorers imposing the order of civilization on their observations. The hours and minutes of a lunar eclipse are totaled in neat columns; new plants are placed in categories and described in appropriate botanical terms; the animals are skinned or caged for further study; and, when Lewis and Clark encounter an Indian tribe that believes a certain hill is the residence of devils, the explorers march directly to it and exorcize its demons by recording the hill's size, form and location in their notebooks.

However, while Jefferson sent Lewis and Clark out as scouts for the Age of Reason, they actually helped to open America to the romantic force of the West. Their writing was literature of exploration that helped to further the consideration of exploration in American literature. For example, in his novel *Mardi* (1849) Melville could announce the mystical force of the west that had so captured the attention of his society:

West, West! West west! Witherward point Hope and prophet fingers; Witherward at sunset kneel all worshipers of fire...witherward lie heaven and hell! West, west! Witherward mankind and empires—flocks, caravans, armies, navies—worlds, suns, and stars all went! West, west! Oh, boundless boundary! eternal goal.... Beacon by which the universe is steered! Like the north star, attracting all needles! Unattainable forever, but forever leading to great things this side thyself.[4]

Significantly in the chapter in which this passage appears Melville's protagonists sailing westward reach the orient. But as in the case of many of the writers of America during this period, Melville is more concerned with direction than location.[5]

This development is expressed in "Walking"; here Thoreau states his belief "that there is a subtle magnetism in Nature, which if we unconsciously yield to it, will direct us aright. It is not indifferent to us which way we walk. There is a right way." For him that way is west, for he feels that "the future lies that way." Thoreau reverses the assumptions of the previous age in America by declaring that wildness and not civilization "is the preservation of the world." Thoreau explains: "We go eastward to realize history and study the works of art and literature, retracing the steps of the race; we go westward as into the future, with a spirit of enterprise and adventure." He exhorts his fellow Americans to be explorers rather than travelers by considering that even if only symbolically eastward migration is "retrograde movement."[6]

Hawthorne in his "Custom-House" preface to *The Scarlet Letter* writes about the effect of his family's two and a quarter century residence in Salem, Massachusetts:

This long connection of a family with one spot, as its place of birth and burial creates a kindred between the human being and the locality, quite independent of any charm in the scenery or moral circumstances that surround him. It is not love, but instinct. The new inhabitant—who came himself from some foreign land, or whose father or grandfather came— has little claim to be called a Salemite; he has no conception of the oyster- like tenacity with which the old settler, over whom his third century is creeping, clings to the spot where his successive generations have been imbedded. It is no matter that the place is joyless for him; that he is weary of the old wooded house, the mud and dust.... The spell survives, and just as powerfully as if the native spot were an earthly paradise. So it has been in my case.... This connection, which is an unhealthy one, should at last be severed. Human nature will not flourish any more than a potato, if it be planted and replanted, for too long a series of generations, in the same worn out soil. My children have had other birthplaces, and so far as their fortunes may be within my control, shall strike their roots into unaccustomed earth.[7]

It is unlikely that a similar attitude could have been expressed by Hawthorne's Puritan ancestors for whom this "unaccustomed earth" was an adversary, not a source of hybrid vigor. They, like Hawthorne's Goodman Brown, were likely to enter the forest fearing "a devilish Indian behind every tree" and "the devil himself" right beside them.[8] Their salvation, they believed, lay in travel eastward toward Jerusalem, the known, the orthodox; exploration westward toward the unknown forest was heresy. These ancestors studied the Bible and might well, as Hawthorne suggests, have considered it "quite a sufficient retribution" for their own transgressions to have a descendant who was "A writer of story-books!"[9]

Although for Hawthorne the frontier was potentially dangerous, stagnation was a surer evil; therefore, exploration, even if only intellectual exploration, was essential. As traditional as Hawthorne may seem to the modern reader, he is still liberal in his acceptance of change. He is willing to experiment and to reject unsuccessful attempts.

Significantly, when Melville, Thoreau and Hawthorne wrote the passages quoted above, each author was living within a short distance of the Atlantic coast and from the Boston that had once been John Winthrop's. Clearly a change in the focus of attention, an acceptance of the "idea" of exploration, was more significant for them than a change in location. But whatever its type, exploration is still vital to the American identity. Americans have walked on the moon and, through the eyes of television cameras, explored the surface of Mars. Such events are possible, because the American identity includes the impetus to explore. As we examine exploration as fact and idea, so we become better able to understand the American identity. This situation offers one of the most important justifications for the continuing study of exploration and travel.

The original version of this paper and other papers in this book were part of a conference on America; Exploration and Travel held at Illinois State University in 1976. That conference was sponsored by *Exploration,* a journal of the literature of travel and exploration and by the Illinois State University Bicentennial Committee.

NOTES

[1] Robert Frost, "The Gift Outright," *Collected Poems of Robert Frost* (Garden City: Halcyon House, 1942), p. 445.

[2] Walter Allen, *Urgent West* (New York: E.P. Dutton & Co. Inc., 1969), p. 49.

[3] Frederick J. Turner, "The Significance of the Frontier in American History," Annual Report of the American Historical Association for the Year 1893, facsimile reprint (Readex Microprint, 1966), p. 201.

[4] Herman Melville, *Mardi* (Evanston: Northwestern University Press, 1970), p. 551.

[5] Edwin Russell, *Frontier: American Literature and the American West* (Princeton: Princeton University Press, 1965), pp. 175-191.

[6] Henry David Thoreau, "Walking," in *Excursions* (Boston: Houghton Mifflin & Co., 1863), pp. 176-185.

[7] Nathaniel Hawthorne, "The Custom-House," preface to *The Scarlet Letter* (Columbus: Ohio State University Press, 1962), pp. 11-12.

[8] Nathaniel Hawthorne, "Young Goodman Brown," in *Mosses From An Old Manse* (Columbus: Ohio State University Press, 1974), p. 75.

[9] Hawthorne, "Custom-House," p. 10.

Travel
and the American Identity

The Idea of National Character:
Inspiration or Fallacy?

Lynn Altenbernd

It took many generations to trim and comb and perfume the first boat-load of Norse pirates into royal highnesses and most noble Knights of the Garter; but every sparkle of ornament dates back to the Norse boat. There will be time enough to mellow this strength into civility and religion....

The mildness of the following ages has not quite effaced these traits of Odin;...The nation has a tough, acrid, animal nature, which centuries of churching and civilizing have not been able to sweeten.

That's Ralph Waldo Emerson in *English Traits*, published in 1847. Like most responsible travelers of his century, Emerson assumed that his duty was to record the national character of the people he visited. That assumption may well have been conscious; more likely unconscious—unquestioned because unquestionable—was the assumption that every nationality has an ascertainable national character. The idea was endemic in the nineteenth century, though it was not invented in that otherwise fertile age. It appears in the world's oldest literature, and may well have had its origins in preliterate times. In the rivalries between tribes and city-states and ultimately nations, every people who have left a record of themselves appear to have elaborated collective character portraits of their enemies, their friends and themselves. We hear of supersubtle Venetians, of perfidious Albion, of lascivious Frenchman, and a thousand other national types and stereotypes that populate the pages of the world's history books—and literature. Lest we smile too smugly at the naivete of more primitive generations, let's not forget the latest Polish joke.

Let me attempt a definition of the idea of national character as I propose to use the term: The idea of national character is the assertion that the citizens of a nation share widely a set of relatively stable traits of physique and personality, patterns of behavior, and attitudes. This apparently innocent idea went unchallenged so long as everyone knew what qualities characterize a nation. A nation has a shared ancestry; a common

9

history; a generally accepted tradition, including a religion, a myth and a literature; a national language; allegiance to a state; occupation of a territory; and—climactically—a national consciousness reflecting the joint possession of a national genius, soul or character. Well, a nation has at least some of these qualities, and the trouble really started when the world began to wonder whether a large, diverse and widely scattered people like the Americans of the early republic could in fact be a nation. They could claim only a dominant language, allegiance to a state, and a territory. They were acquiring a history at a great rate and presumably a culture would follow. But whatever the current rate of accumulation, they didn't really have very much history behind them, and they were diverse in tribal origins, religion and tradition. Under such adverse circumstances, did they already possess, or were they evolving, a national character?

A flat affirmative was given by Hector St. John de Crevecoeur in his *Letters from an American Farmer* of 1782. In the third letter he asked his famous question: "What then is the American, this new man?" This new man, he replied, "acts upon new principles; he must therefore entertain new ideas, and form new opinions." Crevecoeur's American is, in general, an individualist, an egalitarian and a practical idealist. Crevecoeur's description became and remained the dominant image of the national character; the assertion of Alexis de Tocqueville in *Democracy in America* of 1835 that the American is a conformist and a materialist ran a poor second in the generalization sweepstakes. But these two French observers and a host of other visiting and resident commentators agreed that there is an American national character, whatever its components. Hence the idea of national character had survived its sternest trial in the emergence of a new national type under the eyes of a watching world. The concept became an unquestioned commonplace of the writers of travel essays and of international fiction throughout the nineteenth century and on into our time. Let me offer a few examples drawn from novels, travel books, letters and journals.

Many of you will remember that in the first scene of *The Scarlet Letter*, Hawthorne characterizes the English-born women of seventeenth-century Boston as more robust and bold than their descendants were to be. Dealing with the contemporary generation in *Our Old Home* of 1863, Hawthorne still depicted the English woman as a fit spouse for John Bull:

It strikes me that the English woman of fifty is apt to become a creature less refined and delicate, so far as her physique goes, than anything that we Western people class under the name of woman. She has an awful ponderosity of frame, not pulpy, like the loose development of our few fat women, but massive with solid beef and streaky tallow; so that...you inevitably think of her as made up of steaks and sirloins.

In *A Chance Acquaintance* (1873) Willliam Dean Howells makes some remarkably fine distinctions in national physical types when he describes a Canadian girl:

The young girl was redeemed by her New World birth from the English heaviness; a more delicate bloom lighted her cheeks; a softer grace dwelt in her movement; yet she was round and full and she was in the perfect flower of youth. She was not so ethereal in her loveliness as an American girl, but she was not so nervous and had none of the painful fragility of the latter.

In *A Woman's Reason* (1883) Howells says of a young American male, "He was the sort of young American whom you might pronounce an Italian before you had seen the American look in his grey eyes."

Henry Adams had special reasons to dislike the English during his term as confidential secretary to his father in the American legation in London during the Civil War, but during the remainder of his life and despite close friendships with a number of English women and men, he never really repudiated the view of English attitudes which he expressed in a letter to *The New York Times* in December, 1861: "The phlegmatic and dogmatic Englishman...is seldom well informed on any but English subjects looked at from a national point of view; he is often sullen, dogged, and unsocial."

Howells's generalizations about the Italians in *Venetian Life* (1866) are rather more affectionate, but still tinctured with condescension. While he corrected his countrymen's misconceptions by denying that Italians display the carefree gaiety attributed to them, he did speak of their "passionate nature" and "their large, natural capacity for enjoyment." He found them childlike and simple in many ways, indolent or at best inefficiently industrious, and naturally dignified but willing to beg or cheat. Later in the same volume, Howells offers an explanation for the characteristic moral composition of the Italians:

There is that equality in Italian fibre which I believe fits the nation for democratic institutions better than any other, and which is perhaps partly the result of their ancient civilization. At any rate, it fascinates a stranger to see people so mutually gentle and deferential; and must often be a matter of surprise to the Anglo-Saxon, in whose race, reclaimed from barbarism more recently, the native wild beast is still so strong as to inform the manner. The uneducated Anglo-Saxon is a savage; the Italian, though born to utter ignorance, poverty, and depravity, is a civilized man. I do not say that his civilization is of a high order, or that the civilization is at all comparable to that of a gentleman among ourselves. The Italian's education, however profound, has left his passion undisciplined, while it has carefully polished his manner; he yields lightly to temptation, he loses his self-control, he blasphemes habitually; his gentleness is conventional, his civilization not individual. With us the education of a gentleman (I do not mean a person born to wealth or station, but any man who has trained himself in morals or religion, in letters, and in the world) disciplines the impulses, and leaves the good manner to grow naturally out of habits of self-command and consequent habitual self-respect.

The Italian possesses manners, form; the Anglo-Saxon, though self-taught and lacking in form, exhibits the essence of morality and civilization.

Finally, to bring in the French and to illustrate the high intellectual level on which the debate was sometimes conducted, let me recall an exchange between Mark Twain and the French novelist Paul Bourget. In his *Outre-Mer* of 1897, Bourget marveled over the great freedom allowed to unmarried young women in the United States. Similarly he was puzzled at the infrequency of attempts to seduce young married women; he supposed that the lingering effect of Puritan laws providing the death penalty for adultery and the ease of divorce accounted for this phenomenon. Mark Twain retorted that it had never occurred to the Frenchman that the young people were moral—that they were pure in their hearts. And Mark Twain topped this stunner by recalling Napoleon's slur on a democratic people notorious for their interest in discovering illustrious ancestors. If an American is ever without a pastime, Napoleon had said, he can occupy himself trying to find out who his grandfather was. A Frenchman, Mark Twain replied, can always put in his time trying to find out who his father was.

The idea of national character was never without its critics. Even Mark Twain, who was jingoistic and cosmically humane by turns, denied that it was possible to sum up so vast a nation as the United States in a single work. But the most serious assault on the concept grew out of the Nazi promulgation of the Aryan superiority lie during the thirties and forties of this century. Some critics sought to modify the idea into defensible form; others mounted an argument that there simply isn't any such thing as national character. An example of the latter tactic is Hamilton Fyfe's *The Illusion of National Character* of 1940. The argument of this English writer is impassioned and in many ways persuasive. On the theoretical side he contends that generalization about the charactistics of a large and diverse population is simply not possible; all nations are racially mixed, and the qualities of occupations, sexes, classes and other subcommunities are at least as important as national traits. On the practical side Fyfe argues that the idea of national character irresistibly becomes an idea of national superiority and eventually leads to international conflict instead of harmony.

Fyfe's book is in large part a rejoinder to a work of Sir Ernest Barker, first published in 1927, *National Character and the Factors in Its Formation*. Barker was not driven from the field, however; indeed, he revised his book shortly after the close of World War II and reiterated and strengthened his original insistence on the importance of national character. According to Barker, the factors in the formation of national character are these: race; territory and climate; population and occupation;

politics, law and government; religion; language, literature and thought; and ideas and systems of education. Barker's work is a curious mixture of almost mystical British patriotism and scrupulous scholarship; it too is in many ways a persuasive document.

Meanwhile on this side of the ocean the concept similarly went into eclipse during the Nazi period and gradually recovered respectability in a modified form after the War. The social scientists were perhaps more prominent than the humanists in this development. Ruth Benedict's *Patterns of Culture* (1934) and Margaret Mead's *And Keep Your Powder Dry: An Anthropologist Looks at America* (1943) were significant works in tribal and national characterization. After the War, Mead revised her book without fundamentally altering its position on national character. *The Lonely Crowd: A Study of the Changing American Character* by David Riesman, Reuel Denney and Nathan Glazer (1950), David M. Potter's *People of Plenty: Economic Abundance and the American Character* (1954), and Max Lerner's *America as a Civilization* (1957) were only the most prominent works in a substantial body of writing dealing with our subject.

These American essays considered the attacks on the idea of national character and responded with a modification and a defense. An important modification was accomplished by eliminating race as a source of national character. Max Lerner put the matter succinctly in *America as a Civilization*: "Much of the chauvinist and racist treachery of the term can be avoided if it is remembered that national character is a doctrine not of blood but of culture." In addition, David Potter found it necessary to offer an addendum to *People of Plenty* eight years after the book was published. In an article entitled "American Women and the American Character," he observed that most delineations of the supposed national character were really best applicable to adult white males. Rather than abandoning the enterprise, Potter proposed more meticulous attention to the diversity of the population.

The defense was curiously negative in its logic, though not necessarily false for that reason. Character is a product of culture, the social scientist argues; cultures are demonstrably different from one another; hence national characters must differ. One might properly add, I think, that a persistent and powerful subjective sense of national difference, felt by virtually all who travel abroad, has persuaded behavioral scientists and humanists alike to persist in efforts toward an acceptable and defensible theory of national character.

In effect, the social scientists have put in a claim to hegemony in the study of national character, and particularly American character. The case is effectively summed up in an excellent book of readings, Michael McGiffert's *The Character of Americans,* first published in 1964 and reissued in a revised edition in 1970. Anthropologists, sociologists and psychologists, McGiffert wrote in his foreword to the first edition, "have held up a mirror to America and, over the last two decades, have developed a formal theory for the analysis of national character as an enterprise of the behavioral sciences." The foreword to the revised edition speaks of "deepening misgivings about the applicability of the formulas of culture and personality to the explanation of large, complex, modern national societies," and the revision adds essays on sexual, racial, and regional varieties of American character.

If the humanists have been less articulate about theory and methodology than the behavioral scientists, they have nevertheless made significant contributions to the study of the American character. As early as 1931 Constance Rourke gave us *American Humor: A Study in the National Character.* In 1941 F.O. Matthissen's *American Renaissance* gave new vigor and a new direction to the study of American literature. R.W.B. Lewis jarred us awake once more in 1955 with *The American Adam; Innocence, Tragedy, and Tradition in the Nineteenth Century.* Leo Marx's *The Machine in the Garden: Technology and the Pastoral Ideal in America,* of 1964, added further momentum to the study. I note finally, though there are other titles that deserve mention, Roderick Nash, *Wilderness and the American Mind* of 1967, revised in 1973. Two objections can be brought against this list: Each of these works is more or less beside the mark; none of these authors—not even Rourke and Nash, who come closest— deals directly and explicitly with the issue of national character.

Secondly, these authors are concerned with myth as well as actuality. The first of these objections seems to me wholly valid: We should have more studies from humanists dealing with instances of national characterization, both American and other, and with theoretical analysis of the concept as it appears in literature. The second objection, that the authors listed have studied myth, represents an opportunity rather than a disqualification. Few phenomena are more important to a culture than its mythology, and the interplay of myth and actuality, where they diverge, is a fascinating and revealing study of human motivation and aspiration. The study should not be left to anthropologists alone.

Literature offers a concreteness, specificity and vividness that can usefully supplement the sometimes sweeping and abstract generalizations of the behavioral scientists. The latter are likely to object to literary works, and to the work of critics and historians of literature as well, that their evidence is "impressionistic" and "anecdotal." So it is; we might take courage from Max Lerner, who writes of Emerson's *English Traits* as "witness that literary insight may be worth more than all the paraphernalia of recent social science." We need more and more studies that demonstrate the value, if not the validity in the strictest scientific sense, of studies like those I named a few moments ago.

In thus seeking to hearten and challenge students of literature, I am not suggesting that we try to snatch the initiative from our colleagues in the social sciences and show their work to be deficient, but rather that we join forces with them, each group studying its chosen body of material through its distinctive methods, so that together we can carry forward the unfinished work. We need to collect many more citations than have yet been gathered, and we must face up to a number of issues: What are the sources of national character? Does it alter with time? How is national character influenced by the traits of subcommunities within a nation? What is the character of Americans and of other groups? Finally, it seems to me still an open question whether there is such a thing as national character. Certainly the idea of national character is an actuality worthy of study, whether the alleged phenomenon exists or not. And what a lot of travel such research will justify!

Speaking and Touching:
The Problem of Inexpressibility in American Travel Books

Wayne Franklin

Columbus and those who followed him to the Americas before 1600 often complain, in their narratives of travel and exploration, about the tendency of their *literary* precursors to use language not merely inaccurately but even with malice. Columbus himself rails at casual travelers who indulge their private fantasies at the cost of blinding themselves and their audiences to the public truth; and, though he has fantasies of his own regarding the presence of Paradise near the Orinoco, his criticisms of older travelers do reflect a sincere effort on his part to approach the discovered lands with a fresh eye, subordinating as much as possible in his age the preconceived to the literally seen. Yet perception alone is not the issue, in his case or in that of other travelers. His critique underscores the peculiar relation between word and thing which one often discovers in travel books; it accuses his predecessors, in effect, of constituting things by naming them—which is to say, of dealing in words rather than in those facts (whether fantastic or mundane) which it was the traveler's task to address and convey. As a man who had full knowledge of the intractable nature of reality—perhaps only as a sea captain in his age could know such things—Columbus apparently was irked by the ease with which imaginary or imaginative travelers could regard the world.[1]

One might pursue this opening distinction in many directions: as Columbus makes it, for instance, it points toward the growing rift between science and the imagination, and toward the debate over style which was to affect Francis Bacon, and which was to surface, later in the seventeenth century, as an issue of large dimensions for the British Royal Society. Then again, one might see in the distinction a certain obtuseness on the part of Columbus and others—an insensitivity to the creative nature of any act of writing, whether the text produced concerns "scientific" facts, "real" events, or deeds utterly within the writer's mind. Aware as he is of the need for close seeing and attentive writing, Columbus seems curiously dead to the difficulties of exposition; one wonders, as a result, if he ever found himself struggling with that other intractability—the one discovered when words and things fall asunder.

It is this question which I wish to pursue. One need not go very far, even in Columbus, before finding ample evidence that the struggle did take place. That, by his own account, he heard nightingales singing in the Caribbean provides a nice indication of the problem.[2] Are we to take this remark as a reflection of his lack of perceptivity? or, perhaps, as a mark that species names were not as rigid in his age as they have become in ours? or, finally, as a fundamental sign of the New World traveler's accommodating spirit when faced with a flora and a fauna (and a human world) for much of which few immediate resemblances could be found in European experience? Is this a case of misnaming through inattention, or of approximate naming motivated by a sharp attention to the abundance of unknown details?

All these explanations, and others, can throw light on the problem, but this last one will prove most fruitful here. Wherever they went, New World travelers were agreed about the inexpressibile quality of their visual, social, and—as I hope to show later—their spiritual life on this side of the Atlantic. Things, people and experiences all taxed the lexical equipment of these travelers, and they reacted to the challenge thus given them in similar, and highly interesting, ways. Hernán Cortés, almost literally rapt by the sounds, sights and human events of the Mexican world he was to destroy in his weirdly ritualistic conquest—perhaps the shock of newness itself recoiled at the natives in his own violence—Cortés writes to Charles V time and again about the beggarly power of his language in the face of this apparitional world. Montezuma's palace is "so marvelous that it seems to me impossible," Cortés writes, "to describe its excellence and grandeur. Therefore, I shall not attempt to describe it at all, save to say that in Spain there is nothing to compare it with."[3] Or, again, he relates how rich the native marketplaces are in appearance and in the goods exchanged in them; after listing a great many items regularly sold there—"lime, hewn and unhewn stone, adobe bricks, tiles, and cut and uncut woods of various kinds," runs one catalogue; "onions, leeks, garlic, common cress and watercress, borage, sorrel, teasels and artichokes," runs another one (*Letters,* pp. 103-104)—Cortés finds even this particularized vocabulary failing him, rich as it is in its own way: "Finally, besides those things which I have already mentioned," he concludes, "they sell in the market everything else to be found in this land, but they are so many and so varied that because of their number and because I cannot remember many of them nor do I know what they are called I shall not mention them" (p. 104).

There are rhetorical principles behind these passages, and the many others like them, to be sure: the need to convince Charles of his own purity, for one thing, forces Cortés quite obviously into a hyperbolic mood—for his legal standing as the subordinate of the Cuban governor, a man whom he had disobeyed pointedly at the start of his expedition, left him with the large burden of washing his spotted linen in the golden streams of the continent, and in the equally golden language of a man almost too fully overwhelmed by the territory he had discovered by what was, after all, an accident. Screw invention to its utmost stop, and the scurrilous becomes laudable. There is another rhetorical principle involved here, as well, what Faulkner might have called the *reducto parvum*: the conveying of a large field of objects or people or events by rendering a few in high detail and then suggesting how partial this recovered list is, how vast the unending list never quite encompassed by words.

But Cortés will not let us off with rhetoric alone: his sense of inexpressibility is real, even devastating at times—indeed, a source of embarrassment before the distant eyes of Charles, not of reconciliation. "Because I do not know the names of things," he admits to the Emperor, "I cannot express them."[4] Here is a European man, not highly educated perhaps, but able nonetheless, a man voluminous in his prose renderings of American experience; and yet a man up against the blank wall of what remains unnameable and hence unknown, incapable of the symbolic transit back to Europe through language. He is a little naked in Mexico, "unaccommodated" in King Lear's terms. Eager of eye and ear, he is confronted with a limit beyond which his curiosity cannot pass, and that outer limit rebounds against his own inner failures. Beneath the rhetorical flourishes, the traces of courtly politics which pervade his accounts and those of many other early Spanish explorers, one finds the bedrock of a nagging recognition that surpasses all merely European concerns. And that recognition, altered as it may become by later centuries of "converting" the American scene through word and deed—strewing the names and institutions of Europe over it— that recognition continues to exist at the center of the American travel book. It typifies the psychological shock of Westward discovery, and this points ahead to that sense of alienation which Octavio Paz has described in *The Labyrinth of Solitude,* and for which Philip Slater has provided Northern analogues in *The Pursuit of Loneliness.*

But I started with language, and I want to return to it. If the apparent failure of his language helps us to hear in Cortés the early rumblings of later cultural themes, the same failure points with even greater intensity toward later *literary* situations. The programmatic impulse in his own *Letters*—the desire to filligree the outer edges of a vacuum which itself remains unfilled—abides through the course of all subsequent American literatures, and this impulse takes (in Melville's *Moby-Dick*, for instance, as in the writings of Cortés) a markedly linguistic direction. Melville shares with the Spanish conquistador, as does Whitman, the deeply felt urge to fill empty space with a torrent of words, to name and codify reality as a means of self-expression and self-knowledge.

We must begin here with lexical concerns, and then move on to grammatical ones. The first level of literary reaction to what I have called the "inexpressibility" of America is diffident. Random items must be named, either with utterly new terms—as when John Winthrop dubs one Massachusetts hill "Cheese Rock" after he and his fellow explorers discover that they have only cheese for summer, "(the governor's man forgetting, for haste, to put up some bread)"—or with terms imported directly or by analogy from the Old World.[5] In cases where fortuitous events or imported words would not work, recourse was had to native terms, or, less frequently in the early years, to pure invention.

Columbus supplied, even from the voyage of 1492, a surprisingly large number of native borrowings, some of which—like *canoa*—entered quite quickly into the major European tongues. Such acts of linguistic accommodation have more than a lexical interest, however. They point, to be sure, toward lexical needs, and toward that larger need for bridging New World experiences and Old World audiences which forms the rhetorical core of American travel accounts. But to take over Indian terms, and to do so for lexical convenience, is to raise a further problem: the puzzling fact of a language existing already in the land, of a linguistic field causing almost as many problems as it solves—and problems analogous to those voiced by Cortés in his attempt to describe the indescribable artifacts or natural products or institutions of the culture with which he had contact. Far from enjoying the simple position of an eyewitness, the traveler becomes an interpreter as well; and as his roles diversify, his task as a writer becomes more difficult. Added to the failures of close observation are the failures of cultural misunderstanding. More "foreign" at times than American objects, the native words which describe them may interpose another barrier between self and world.

The nature of native American languages excited much speculation among early travelers and among the proto-anthropologists to whom their reports gave such impetus. In the debate over the supposed origins of the American tribes which Lee E. Huddleston has recreated, for instance, the nature of native languages (or even their presumed absence in some cases) was regarded as a key piece of evidence, and the diversity of spoken tongues clearly seemed, to European minds accustomed to a relatively unified linguistic world, a piece of accidental or even intentional deviltry. Gregorio García, who along with Joseph de Acosta was the most influential theorist of Indian origins in the early period, blamed Satan outrightly for the diversity of languages: as the New England Puritans regarded America as the devil's final refuge, so Garcia saw as a primary weapon in Satan's fight against God the invention of new tongues faster than the missionaries could learn them. The latters' spreading of *the Word* thus was frustrated by the devil's spreading of countless words, and systems of words, among the infidels.[6]

One has, on the opposite side of such fantasies, the theory of
Fernando de Montesinos, who referred to the New World as
"Hamerica," for he apparently believed that its name did not
stem from Amerigo Vespucci, but rather from an anagram of
"Hec Maria" ("Behold Mary, Mother of God")—so clearly had
God indicated, against the schemes of Satan, the true destiny of
European efforts in the West. For this writer, one solitary word
uttered in the Old World, and simply reordered for the New,
contains a complete solution to the vexing problem of American
"Newness." Or, to put the idea another way, the making sacred of
America's name can make sacred, and thus consoling, all that it
embraces.[7]

Broaching the topic of native tongues, even as modestly as
Columbus and other explorers did, thus opened up between the
would-be travel writer and his chosen subject a further
perspective which increased rather than diminished the
vexations caused by unworded terrain. Most writers could retreat
from this new threat, and from the danger of linguistic alienation
which it posed if one pursued native resources too far, by
exploiting adeptly the analogies and comparisons which I have
noted already. Even Cortés, confronted with the palace of
Montezuma, would pursue this route if he could, but no ready
analogue from his Spanish experience occurred to him. Hence he
left that object undescribed, mentioned in his text only for the
sake of being dismissed. Other writers were more ingenious:
Magellan, for example, rendered the bananas which he saw as
"figs a foot long"—certainly a rather curious instance of the
practice.[8] And beyond such botanical or zoological analogies, one
has, even into the nineteenth century—and in places far removed
from one another, though sharing a great literal and cultural
distance from Europe and from European America—more
puzzling and potentially more dangerous instances of analogical
naming. Captain James Cook, an astute observer and a highly
scientific voyager, as well as a systematic tester of older, more
fantastic hypotheses, labored under a cultural burden which
forced him to seek out "kings" among the Pacific islands, and
thus misled his perceptions about native political and cultural
structure.[9] In this sense, his observations were warped by the

"words" of his own origin; the limit placed on his understanding of native cultures did not come from his lack of Pacific experience—for Cook was enormously experienced in that ocean, more so than any European before him—but rather from the linguistic biases of his past, and from the values which those biases in part formed and in part reflected. The "things" of Europe, freighted in his mind as surely as the trade objects he carried were freighted in his ships, provided him with a lexicon which subtly caused him to misperceive, and to misrender, the "things" of Pacific culture. Closer to home, one may point to the persistent failure of white Americans, even to this day, to understand the roles and powers of those native figures whom *we* call "chiefs." Even adopting native terms, such as the Spanish "*cacique*," first used in December, 1492, by Columbus, was no protection against lexical misunderstandings.[10] The root of many subsequent tragedies in American history lies in language misappropriated or misapplied; and the root of such misapplications and misappropriations lies less in wilful or lazy habits of seeing and listening than in the strong desire to codify American sights and sounds as quickly as possible in written language.

Much more could be said about these lexical problems, about their origins, about their cultural and literary consequences. But we must turn now to the second level of linguistic reaction to the problem of inexpressibility—away from lexical and toward grammatical solutions. The first, and simplest, such solution has been demonstrated already in the case of Cortés: for the catalogues which one finds throughout his prose are not merely lexical lists, but rather rudimentary attempts to organize events and objects into groups—that is, to form "sentences" which do not just name, but put into relation whatever they contain. Most of these sentences do not have verbs, to be sure; like the simple act of naming, they seek to freeze whatever they point to. But once the shift away from naming has been made, once the possibility of more complex kinds of statement has been discovered, action and the words which suggest it are bound to follow. The progression I shall outline now thus moves from isolated words and phrases toward collections of terms, and finally toward something like a

"native" form of narrative. This development is a logical one, not
a historical one; it is found in a number of books from a variety of
literary periods, and no one stage of it ever is lost from the
tradition.

Perhaps the best list or catalogue which Cortés gives us is
appended to the first letter. An inventory of objects sent to the
Emperor, the list describes fifty-two separate items, or groups of
items, with admirable attention to detail. "First," it begins, "a
large gold wheel with a design of monsters on it and worked all
over with foliage"; then it goes on to featherwork fans, a jewelled
mirror, a gold alligator's head, scepters, miters, "imitation" birds
(made of "thread and feather work," with gold quills and claws
and eyes and beaks).[11] It is a virtual abstract of the exotic cultures
already seen by Cortés, or soon to be discovered, a linguistic
model not merely of the things sent to the Emperor, but also of
that larger collection of peoples and objects of which the things
conveyed to Spain themselves are a tangible abstract. If one can
picture the loading of these objects onto the ship, the image thus
evoked provides a perfect expression of the linguistic act
performed in his letter by Cortés. Sending word and thing alike to
the Old World, Cortés gives one an early example of those
"cabinets of curiosities" which Margaret Hodgen has described
in her book on early anthropology, and which often contained
substantial numbers of American artifacts or natural products.[12]
If the attempt to name single items elsewhere in the writings of
Cortés may be likened to the fine New World paintings of John
White (to those which treat natural objects, not those which are
concerned with native life), or to the finer paintings of Jacopo
Ligozzi, based on that Italian's experience of animals and plants
in European collections, then such lists as the one referred to here
find their own analogues in the kind of illustration exemplified in
the early seventeenth-century engraving of Ole Worm's
"Museum" in Copenhagen.[13] In place of merely giving us a single
object, or term, against the background of a blank page or an
artist's blank ground, the cataloguers and the collectors begin to
create a grammar, principles of subordination and coordination,
or of relation and difference. The aesthetic principle of
composition does not enter into the former acts of rendering,

while it is crucial to the latter.

As a guide to scientific understanding, the catalogue predates New World exploration—Aristotle's *Parts of Animals,* or even Pliny's *Natural History* clearly employ the device, for instance, and one may speculate that language itself rests in large part on the human need to catalogue, and thereby to understand, the myriad objects of human curiosity. Yet in the case of New World travel books the general principle becomes of acute significance: for one must see such books against the background of a long period of relative stability in European culture, and hence as literary attempts to catch up with the sudden loss of that stability in the face of rapid physical expansion. Certainly the word always lags behind the thing, but this principle is exemplified with particular force in the two centuries following the discovery of America. In strictly linguistic terms, to be sure, Europe had had a good deal of experience during the late medieval period with the entrance of new words and new ideas from the Arabic world; but that world never had been so completely unknown as the American landmasses were, and if a certain exoticism attached itself to the former exchange, and hence a certain inexpressibility arose in it, both these traits entered much more crucially into the Western excursion of European in the sixteenth and following centuries. Never before, in its relation to other peoples, had Europe relied so heavily on the word alone, or on those few objects which, like the shipment sent by Cortés in 1520, made their way to the Old World. As Hodgen argues, for instance, the connections of Europe with the Near and even the Far East relied on commercial contacts built up over a long period of time; its connections with the West, however, began quite suddenly, and this sudden rise of another, radically different perspective accounts for many of the differences between the *Letters* of Cortés and, say, the *Travels* of Marco Polo.[14] At its outer reaches, to be sure—as Columbus complains— Polo's book touches on worlds quite as exotic as those described by Cortés some two centuries later. But Polo's *Travels* remains, on a grander scale, the medieval version of Gilbert White's *Natural History of Selbourne*—a close account of the known— whereas the *Letters* of Cortés stands in the line which leads finally to the radical "travels" of Darwin in South America and among the Galapagos Islands. Venerable as the catalogue tradition was when the first American travelers turned toward it; established as the form of the travel account was by that time; aware as Europe had been of regions far severed from itself—yet the essential and abiding newness of the Americas made all these hackneyed facts and themes into something equally new. The catalogue was not merely a convenient form of expression: it bore, for Cortés and for other New World travelers, a crucial importance as a means of knowing the unknown, and as a means of impressing upon it—and upon the traveler's psyche—the gridwork of old and comforting assumptions.

To list details becomes, in these works, a way of domesticating them, and of giving to them an order that is both linguistic and more broadly intellectual. As one discovers it in John Lawson's *A New Voyage to Carolina* (published in 1709), for instance, the catalogue aspires toward a full anatomy of the landscape, of flora and fauna, of social life among white settlers and among the Indians. After giving the "Journal" of his own travels in the Carolinas, Lawson goes on to discourse minutely on the landforms and the rivers, the trees and wild animals, the birds and the fish, the domestic animals and crops and finally on the customs and beliefs of the native inhabitants. Both his "Journal" and the later sections of his book report on the same body of experience—the former organizing it by means of space and time, the latter, by means of logical categories. The catalogues thus become an attempt to go back through the undigested events and sights described earlier, and to lift them above the level of merely private (and hence arbitrary) life in the New World—to insert between the traveler's mind and his experience a series of reassuringly general frameworks. Starting with the bald statement of his travels, Lawson moves toward a higher plane of description and analysis, and thus is able to escape from the limits of actual space and time both as conditions of life and as grounds of expression. His initial grammar is narrative; his second means of relation, however, pushs away from action and toward contemplation. It is a movement from feet to head, from touching the region to speaking about it in increasingly abstract ways.

Lawson's catalogues serve, by this movement, a definitely scientific purpose, as well as a mildly propagandistic one. The need for generalization springs, in other words, from public as well as private considerations. The balance between such differing drives can be assessed by comparing Lawson's work with another one inspired by it,[15] the promotional tract written by Samuel Jenner, Swiss agent for William Byrd II, as an inducement to emigration. *Neu-gefundenes Eden* (1737) uses Lawson's natural history less as a way of organizing the American scenes which it describes than as a way of inciting action within those scenes—its catalogues *imply* a journey in the future rather than build on one from the past. Contemplation yields to motivation; the organization of detail points toward the feet, not toward the head. Though Lawson himself is not adverse to adding succulent details to his own lists, or to inserting the facts of his personal experience into the description of any animal or plant or locale, he adheres generally to an aesthetic which limits such intrusions. Jenner's book, on the other hand, is almost pornographic in its aesthetic: it resembles a harangue delivered to a hungry army of emigrants about to pounce on the plenty which he salaciously describes. "*Herring* are not as large as the European ones," he writes, "but better and more delicious." Lawson says of this fish: "The Herrings in *Carolina* are not so large as in *Europe*. They spawn there in *March* and *April,* running up the fresh Rivers and small fresh Runs of Water in great shoals, where they are taken. They become red if salted; and, drest with Vinegar and Oil, resemble an Anchovy very much; for they are far beyond an *English* Herring, when pickled."[16] Jenner embroiders on this description in his own prose, for he continues: "After being salted they become red. If one prepares them with vinegar and olive oil, they then taste like anchovies or sardines, since they are far better in salt than the English or European herring. When they spawn, all streams and waters are completely filled with them, and one might believe, when he sees such terrible amounts of them, that there was as great a supply of herrings as there is water. In a word," he concludes, though he uses three words, "it is unbelievable, indeed, indescribable, as also incomprehensible, what quantity is found

there. One must behold [the sight] oneself."[17] Lawson is not blind
to the culinary uses of his catalogue, or of the items it describes;
but he evinces much more balance than Jenner, more distance
and objectivity. The Swiss writer transforms the catalogue
technique from its function in the *Voyage* as an anatomizing
device into a less intellectual, more tangible—and yet not naively
tangible—vehicle. It is as if his words are virtually one with the
things they describe, and hence as if reading his book is an act of
consumption. In one sense, of course, this transformation rests on
Lawson's own usage, and thus points to a practice common
among travel writers. Hard and clear in its details, a catalogue
conveys the sense of a world touched, and a world inviting our
own touch in return. Yet the kinds of experience which can be
rendered by the catalogue are severely limited. One never "feels"
the scenes described as complete landscapes, multi-dimensional
and complex, but rather as a collection of objects to which one's
relation remains simple. That relation is one-way: traveler and
reader alike are in control of the objects, never at *their* mercy—the
author and his audience possess a fund of verbs which determines
the grammar of New World action. One can discover, to be sure,
catalogues of "discommodities" (as in the account of Frobisher's
second voyage by Dionise Settle, found in Hakluyt)—and one can
discover, as in Just Girard's *Adventures of a French Captain*
(American translation, 1876), the touching description of a Texas
river "as wide as the Seine, but full of alligators."[18] Yet the
cataloguer remains, despite these subversions of his form, a man
whose attributions to the world he describes appear to have the
warrant of the land's own "text," and whose prose elides
wherever possible the suggestion that this given text may include
distressing passages—objects beyond the control of *our* language
and hence of our selves. His basic pretense is that he "gives voice"
to the country, not that he lays his words over its surface.

The catalogue device thus becomes a form of insidious
predication which extends the acts of naming into newer, more
evaluative fields. The nature of New World items remains of
interest to the cataloguer; but far more important is their
potential meaning, defined most usually through the listing of
their uses. Grammatically, this shift involves the addition of

implied or uttered verbs of the sort already mentioned. To the nouns of the namer are added the terms of the possessor, terms which bridge the gap between mere economic interest and vaguely emotional satisfactions. Whereas Cortés, despite his own economic drives, and his need to possess Mexican things by word and deed, rests most typically at the level of enumeration, promotional writers like Jenner transform the inventory into a true bill of lading—one which, unlike that supplied by Cortés at the end of his first letter, has more to do with worldly gain than with exotic delight. Under the pressure of this sort of language, the traveler's New World becomes a vast storehouse of goods on which every act of writing resembles a requisition. Though Jenner himself protests about the "unbelievable, indeed, indescribable, as also incomprehensible"nature of American herring, he is in fact unmoved by the naive sense of inexpressibility which keeps even Cortés slightly innocent. His lists of commodities—as well as his redundant section on "What one generally eats and drinks in Virginia"—become a frenzied means of ignoring silence, of filling it with the greedy words of a mind less stated by the bombardment of details than deranged by the possibility that any one detail might prove intractable—or, God forbid, inedible. That his America is so fully worded proves how attuned this man who never came to the New World is to the abiding mystery of a region beyond the power of received language. Jenner's predications aim, like the simpler lists of Cortés, or the single words of other travelers, at lining in a canvas all-too-blank.

Those predications were heard, and responded to, by a group of Swiss citizens who set sail for Byrd's supposed Eden, only to die in shipwreck off the American coast, or to survive that disaster only to encounter failure on the land. Responding to a world constituted by Jenner's language, these men and women were testing, in effect, the supposed congruence of word and thing in America—or, more precisely, the relation of European word and American thing. Experience in the New World often has become such a test, an act of practical criticism which compares some invented text with the hard text of reality. One may say that the "anatomy" as a New World form of writing has helped us to imagine a static universe, and then has caused us to enter—and to touch—the field of an actual universe which requires rather a physiological than an anatomical imagination. The failure of the catalogue as a linguistic (and a cultural) device springs from its limitation of relations—its tendency to suggest that the most important bearing of any rendered detail is that which it has on us, rather than on other details existing in its own natural environment. As a grammer, it is woefully inadequate (its inadequacy accounts, perversely enough, for its ready acceptance by writers); it allows for subordination only along a single axis, and for action only in one direction. American things are named in the catalogue merely as objects for our own desire, as passive subjects yielding all to their imported beneficiaries. Almost never do the objects interact with each other; even less rarely do they acquire the power of aggressive action over those who have named them and have set out to appropriate their virtues.

Yet that power is sensed even within the catalogue, is, in fact, the reason for the great popularity of this static means of rendering the New World scene. The movement in Lawson's book away from the narrative approach—the presentation of experience within the spatial and temporal terms in which it actually occurs—and toward more categorical forms of language, reflects something other than his scientific bent, reflects as well the abiding pressure in American travel books to discover alternate means of organization. There is in human experience here, as in the abundance of sights and sounds encountered in that experience, something inexpressible: some sense of alienation and displacement, and the traveler often retreats from this fact, as from the unnameable objects around him, by adopting a language which minimizes such evanescent and yet potentially frightening things. Lawson, accomplished traveler and sage observer, was captured by the Tuscaroras in 1711— never mind his marginal comment in the *Voyage,* "Natives are docile," or his assertion later in that book that Carolina is "not a frontier"—and he died in the hands of his captors, while, ironically enough, his fellow captive and colonial promoter, Christopher de Graffenried, escaped by his powers of persuasion.[19] At the crucial moment of his life, Lawson's language failed him: prescient as his *Voyage* might have been, inclusive as it sought to be, there is no place in the linguistic universe of his book for the experiences he later endured, or rather failed to endure. His language in the book acts as a barrier to such events, in fact; nowhere do we sense the possibility that the "observer" may be swallowed in the world he is naming and ordering—even though we may sense that his rage for giving name and shape to the American objects or places he has seen springs indeed from a subliminal awareness of just this chance.

This sort of inexpressibility I have in mind finally, then, is like that which Conrad's Mistah Kurtz manages to indicate in that vaguest of last words—"The horror! the horror!" I am thinking, too, of all the lost travelers, and all the rumors and legends concerning them. The roster begins with the natives borne back to Spain by Columbus—most substantial of New World "objects," brought back as if no words imaginable can convey their meaning home as well as their own flesh can—and it goes on, through the alienation of Columbus himself ("in spiritual things," he writes in reporting the fourth voyage, "I have ceased here in the Indies from observing the prescribed forms of religion.... Weep for me, whoever has charity, truth, and justice!"); through the marooning of those Spanish sailors one begins to hear about in the conquistadors' records, some of them happy in their isolation, others lost in spirit as in body, forgetting their native tongues; on through the countless lost settlers (the Roanoke people, first among the English, rumored to be off with the Indians for twenty years after John White the painter, governor of the colony and grandfather of the famous, and lost, child, Virginia Dare, sought for them, and failing to find them—finding in fact only their ruined dwellings, their scattered possessions, and three large letters carved on a tree, "C R O," suggesting the settlers' departure for the island of Croatoan—renounced all his interest in the New World, his last words on it extracted only by the insistent curiosity of Hakluyt); on, too, through the list of explorers lost at sea (most touching among the English, the case of Sir Humphrey Gilbert, whose small ship disappeared at night after he had spent the day before sitting on its deck quoting vaguely from More's *Utopia,* book in hand, "We are as neere to heaven by sea as by land"; and lost with him, too, the Hungarian humanist and poet Stephanus Parmenius, who had gone along with the Newfoundland voyage to capture the New World in his verse); on, finally, through the senseless destruction of native cultures in all parts of the Americas, the temples destroyed and the memories effaced in the South, whole tribes extirpated in the North with nagging but false sadness; and on through the present crisis of extinction and exhaustion with which we have visited the land—so efficiently that we have lost the things, and keep now only the words for them, and we must make catalogues of our depredations. Once more we may say, as the chronicler of Gilbert's end did, that we can "not observe the hundreth part of creatures" here; but we cannot mean by this, as he did, that the abundance of life forms outruns our attention—rather, that we have cursed that abundance by applying to it too insistently the consumptive terms of our cultural, and our linguistic, traditions.[20]

Oblivion, forced or freely coming, has been one of the constant muses of America, and in its face all lesser inexpressibilities seem trivial. As a single example of this theme, and of the place of language in it, I would point to *La Relacion* of Alvar Núñez Cabeza de Vaca, first published in 1542, and telling an incredible story of almost eight years of wandering in the American South from Florida to Mexico. Cabeza de Vaca was second in command to Pamfilo de Narvaez on an expedition sent out to conquer Florida—Narváez, whom the Cuban governor had sent to arrest Cortés years before, but whom Cortés put in jail— and his commander's incapacity quickly brought the party of four hundred men to ruin. Forging inland in search of a golden city, Narváez left his ships coasting North, but failed to find them again when his men reached the panhandle region. Building makeshift vessels, Narváez and the rest embarked on the Gulf; a storm soon separated them, however, and the commander himself never was seen or heard from again. Cabeza de Vaca and the others were wrecked off the Texas coast late in 1528, and it is from that point that their overland journey, ending finally in Mexico City in July, 1536, began. They survived famine and storm, slavery among the natives, loneliness and extreme psychological stress (at one point, for instance, Cabeza de Vaca himself performed a risky operation on an Indian, removing an arrowhead from his chest and then patching him up successfully, knowing the probable result of failure all the time); and yet the tale which Cabeza de Vaca tells shifts its attention, and ours, away from such surface details, harrowing as they are, and points instead toward precisely that more ample grammar missing from Lawson or Jenner or Cortés, a way of arranging facts and feelings which preserves their complex relations, which does not remove the empty spaces of America from our consideration, but rather makes of them (and of their cultural analogues) the prime subject of inquiry and expression. It is in such books that a truly native form of language first emerges, a language responsive to the strange amplitude of emotion and experience in the vast reaches of the New World, a language which does not minimize but stresses this amplitude; and which draws us into it as readers, forcing us to see how inadequate any mere formulas, of feeling or of words, must be in a true attempt to render the traveler's life in America. More fully than any of his contemporaries, Cabeza de Vaca touched America, and was touched by it. *La Relación* records the shifts of viewpoint which resulted. Its central theme is the wilful embrace of "nakedness," both literal and cultural, and the development in this state of nakedness of new ways of seeing and feeling. When Cabeza de Vaca adopts Indian dress; when he begins to render time according to the native sense, rather than the European; when he emerges at the end of the book as an advocate for Indian rights against Spanish corruption and mistreatment—we find, at last, a traveler who has entered the American world fully, and who has responded to that world on its own terms. At the end of his wanderings, we see him *within* the Indian circle, dressed as his hosts dress, sharing in their customs and even their beliefs. And we thus can see in him the threat which he posed for the Spanish overlords whom he accuses, in his final pages, of gross cruelties: the threat of complete alienation from imported ways, and that chance for personal and communal growth which that threat carried with it. It is highly appropriate, almost ritualistic, that the Spaniards on whom Cabeza de Vaca stumbled in upper Mexico should regard him with a horror to match Mistah Kurtz's, with a sense of imminent dread generated by his endurance. Seeing Spanish artifacts among one tribe, Cabeza de Vaca is enthusiastic; but when he finds those who have left them there, he is taken by them as an enemy, is put in chains by the countrymen from whom his own separation has been such a long trial. Even though he later is freed and exonerated, other troubles intercede: appointed governor in Paraguay, he leads an expedition in search of the golden city of Manoa—one begins to wonder how much he had learned, after all, on the Narváez expedition, but these doubts evaporate as one learns more, learns, for example, that his attempt to enforce humane policies toward the natives in the South causes the settlers to rise up against him as an enemy to their own interest, to depose him and send him home to Spain in disgrace. After eight years of exile in Africa, he is pardoned and given a judicial position. He was not a man untouched by delusions, but he remains in the catalogue of American travelers as a permanent reminder of the challenge to an open bearing on New World experience, a bearing unencumbered by the typical anxieties and false ideas—as well as the false words—which hampered so many of his contemporaries. Unlike most of those others, except for the fully lost, he touched the continent, and the act of touching it gives his prose, as it gave his mind, a life beyond the formulas imported so greedily from Europe. Perhaps no one is equal to the challenge—even Cabeza de Vaca, one must be amused to learn, forced his men to carry a fine camp bed for him from stage to stage during his delusive South American odyssey—but much more than most, this Spaniard found in the terms of his confinement and shipwreck resources of emotion and of tongue that bring back to us even today, across multiple barriers, sharp words from what remained for so many others not only inexpressible but also unsensed. In the fifty years which separate his narrative from the first voyage of Columbus, a tremendous flexibility has been wrung from countless bitter lives and the tales which record or fail to record them—a flexibility of vast consequences for the future of American narrative art. All the stages in the development which I have sketched here survive—one finds, on the first page of Gabriel García Márquez's

One Hundred Years of Solitude, for instance, the following rune freshly rendered for our own century: "The world was so recent," he writes, "that many things lacked names, and in order to indicate them it was necessary to point."[21] Such survivals provide continually rich resources for the New World writer, whether the book to be written is actually a work of travel or not. A good many of the best American novels employ the typical devices of the traveler, in fact—much more so than do the contemporaneous novels of English authors—and the same may be said of such American classics in other forms of Crèvecoeur's *Letters from an American Farmer,* Thoreau's *Walden,* or Aldo Leopold's *Sand County Almanac.* In such works, as in our novels, one continually finds runes like those exhibited in *One Hundred Years of Solitude,* old snatches of language and idea first developed in the contact of American scene and European words. But the example of Cabeza de Vaca is not simply a local or particularized one: the gift which he and other, similar writers bequeathed to later American literature entails much more than single terms or even single linguistic strategies. It is the "mixed" nature of his art that matters—the invention of a language suitable to a world of wonders and things unknown, of events and sufferings and delights beyond imagination, a language which thrives on the destruction of older forms and older awarenesses, which reaches out like Melville's prose or Whitman's poetry not simply to catalogue but to engage a universe particolored in its appearance and bewildering in its sense and its implication. American travel books, and the literary forms to which they have given so much, have been created out of the clash of a language like a palisade, a form of blindness rather than sight—and a language as expansive as the New World scene, as open and rich as the possibilities of life, and of death, beyond the pale. Of this latter language no one provides a better example than Cabeza de Vaca when he tells, near the end, of the efforts of his "rescuer," Diego de Alcaraz, to convince the native Mexicans that the wanderers and he himself are men of the same race, and that *he* is a man of greater importance than any of the castaways. "Alcaraz bade his interpreter tell the Indians," Cabeza de Vaca writes, "that we were members of his race who had been long lost; that his group were the lords of the land who must be obeyed and served, while we were inconsequential. The Indians paid no attention to this. Conferring among themselves, they replied that the Christians lied: We had come from the sunrise, they from the sunset; we healed the sick, they killed the sound; we came naked and barefoot, they clothed, horsed, and lanced; we coveted nothing but gave whatever we were given, while they robbed whomever they found and bestowed nothing on anyone." Cabeza de Vaca himself is anxious for the natives to understand this linkage—or says he is—but his full reporting of the native response, as well as his own adoption, as a term for the other Spaniards, of the derogatory word "Christians," shows how deeply into his mind, and into its language, the burden of his long experience in the wilderness has impressed itself. Neither native nor colonizer, he occupies as a man and as a writer a mediate position which remains for us a challenge to full perception and matured belief. And his prose remains as an allied challenge—a call upon us to abandon categorical language, and to respond to the amplitude of life in what still is a New World if we only have the power of sight, and of word, required for its imagination.[22]

NOTES

[1]The issue of Columbus as an "observer" is a complex one: whereas, in the account of his first voyage which he prepared in Lisbon during March, 1493, he boldly contrasts his own attentiveness with the fantasies of earlier travelers to the "East" (surely he is thinking of Marco Polo here), he evinces in the full record of all four voyages a growing mysticism born partly of his failures but partly also of his own imaginative biases. In terms of language, this tension becomes most interesting when, in the "History" of his third voyage which he wrote in Hispaniola and sent to Ferdinand and Isabella, he subtly shifts away from verbs of "discovery" and employs in their place verbs of speculation—shifts away, in other words, from a language of experience and toward a language of thought, supposition, and deduction. (See *Select Letters of Christopher Columbus,* ed. R.H. Major, and published in London by the Hakluyt Society in 1847, esp. pp.127-146).

[2]Major, p.5.

[3]Hernán Cortés, *Letters from Mexico,* trans. and ed. A.R. Pagden (New York: Grossman, 1971), p.109.

[4]This confession is quoted, without citation, by Jean Franco, *An Introduction to Spanish-American Literature* (London: Cambridge Univ. Press, 1969), p.viii.

[5]*Winthrop's Journal,* ed. James Kendall Hosmer (New York: Scribner's 1908),

I, 74. Three helpful articles on the problems of language in America can be found in *First Images of America: The Impact of the New World on the Old,* ed. Fredi Chiappelli (Berkeley: Univ. of California Press, 1976), II, 561-611 (Stephen J. Greenblatt, "Learning to Curse: Aspects of Linguistic Colonialism in the Sixteenth Century"; Yakov Malkiel, "Changes in the European Languages under a New Set of Sociolinguistic Circumstances"; and Edward F. Tuttle, "Borrowing versus Semantic Shift: New World Nomenclature in Europe").

[6]Lee Eldridge Huddleston, *Origins of the American Indians: European Concepts, 1492-1729* (Austin: Univ. of Texas Press, 1967), p.66. Margaret T. Hodgen, *Early Anthropology in the Sixteenth and Seventeenth Centuries* (Philadelphia: Univ. of Pennsylvania Press, 1964), also deals with the problem of native languages.

[7]Huddleston, p.82.

[8]J.C. Beaglehole, *The Exploration of the Pacific,* 3rd ed. (Stanford: Stanford Univ. Press, 1966), p.32.

[9]Beaglehole, *The Life of Captain James Cook* (Stanford: Stanford Univ. Press, 1974), *passim.* Beaglehole's humorous account of the naming practices of Samuel Wallis and Philip Carteret *(Exploration,* pp.200-21) is also worthy of consideration here. Wallis began his voyage in the Pacific by seeding the ocean with names derived from members of the Royal Family; exhausting this supply, "he was obliged to fall back on the royal navy" (p.206).

[10]Tuttle, *First Images,* II, 596, lists such terms.

[11]Cortés, *Letters,* pp.40-46.

[12]Hodgen, *Early Anthropology,* pp.111-206.

[13]Hugh Honour reproduces the Worm engraving, many John White works, and several of Ligozzi's, in *The New Golden Land: European Images of America from the Discoveries to the Present Time* (New York: Patheon, 1975), *passim.*

[14]Hodgen, pp.80-81.

[15]Percy G. Adams, *Travelers and Travel Liars, 1600-1800* (Berkeley: Univ. of California Press, 1962), pp.144-57, discusses Lawson, Jenner, and Byrd. He provides convincing proof that Jenner relied heavily on Lawson's work.

[16]John Lawson, *A New Voyage to Carolina* (London: 1709), p.158.

[17]*William Byrd's Natural History of Virginia or The Newly Discovered Eden,* ed. and trans. Richmond C. Beatty and William J. Mulloy (Richmond: Dietz Press, 1940), pp.78-79.

[19]*New Voyage,* pp.84, 88; see *DAB* for Lawson's fate.

[20]Major, p.203; John White, *Hakluyt* (London: Everyman's Library, 1907), VI, 211-27; Gilbert's death, described by Edward Haies, *Hakluyt,* VI, 35; More's *Utopia* is identified by S.E. Morison, *The European Discovery of America* (New York: Oxford Univ. Press, 1971-74), I, 577; Haies on the creatures, *Hakluyt,* VI, 23.

[21]I quote from the translation of Gregory Rabassa (New York: Avon, 1971), p.11.

[22]*Adventures in the Unknown Interior of America,* trans. by Cyclone Covey (New York: Collier, 1961), p.128.

Originally published in *Exploration,* IV:1, December 1976. Reprinted with the permission of the editor and the author.

Foreign Travelers in America

Exploration and Creativity: Chateaubriand's
Travels in America

Frans C. Amelinckx

From the time of its discovery, America has excited the European imagination. To some, it has appeared as a Utopian dream, with its promises of freedom and opportunity; to others a land of unexplored frontiers, and natural, unspoiled man.

All of these aspects attracted a young French officer whose career in the army had been frustrated by the political upheaval. Francois-Rene de Chateaubriand wanted to leave his mark on the world around him. Young and ambitious, he sought to acquire fame by becoming an explorer. He had been enthralled by Cook's voyages and the search for the Northwest passage. He hoped to find the passage by exploring the region by land. His plan was to cross the North-American continent, staying close to the Great Lakes, going down the Mississippi valley to the fortieth parallel and from there to go west. Upon reaching the Gulf of California, he planned to go north following the coast to a river discovered by Cook and from there up to Copper River near the seventy-second parallel west. If his search for the Northwest Passage proved unsuccessful, Chateaubriand planned to return to the United States through Hudson Bay and Labrador.[1]

The young man's enthusiasm was fueled by Malesherbes, the scholarly secretary of the court of Louis the sixteenth, and the grandfather of Chateaubriand's sister-in-law. Malesherbes, member of the French Academy and the Academy of Sciences and Letters, had a passion for natural history and travels. His personal library, which had an exceptional collection of travel books dealing with the New World, became a resource center for Chateaubriand. In his *Memoirs,* he recalls fondly the time spent in conversations and in making plans: "M. de Malesherbes excited me on the subject of this voyage. I went to see him in the mornings: we sat, with our noses glued to maps, we compared the different plans of the Artic Circle; we calculated the distances between Behring's Straits and the furthermost part of Hudson Bay; we read the different narratives of the travellers and navigators, English, Dutch, French, Russian, Swedish, Danish; we enquired into the roads to be followed on land to reach the shores of the Polar Sea; we discussed the difficulties to be overcome, the precautions to be taken against the rigors of the climate, the attacks of wild animals, the scarcity of food."[2] Apparently Malesherbe's encouragement was not purely scientific. According to an article by George Colas, Malesherbes, in conjunction with Chateaubriand's family, wanted to get the young man away from the nefarious indolence of Parisian life.[3]

Chateaubriand left for America in April, 1791, arriving in Baltimore on the 11th day of July. His stay in the New World was rather short, as he returned to France at the end of November in the same year.

His grandiose project, conceived in the comfortable surroundings of Malesherbes's library, came to naught in America. In Buffalo, the young man contacted a fur trader, named Swift, who, upon hearing of the project, simply laughed it off. He recommended that the young Frenchman prepare for his undertaking by acquainting himself with life in the American wilderness while learning several Indian languages and spending time with some of the Hudson Bay agents. Swift further suggested that after a training period of about 4 or 5 years, with the financial backing of the French government, he might be ready to begin his search for the Northwest Passage. This very wise advice did not set well with the impatient young man. He had wanted to go to the North Pole as one would go from Paris to Pontoise.[4] Later, he mentioned in his *Historical Essay* that his trip to the United States was to have been purely exploratory.[5] He had planned to submit a more definite project to Malesherbes who would in turn have requested governmental subsidies for its undertaking. Of course, this too was never realized because of the political turmoil in France and Malesherbes's execution under the Reign of Terror.

Although the exploration was never realized and his stay in the United States was very short, the American experience was for Chateaubriand a lasting one in terms of creativity. Rene Bazin in *Chateaubriand et l'Amerique* notes that for Chateaubriand it was the journey par excellence, one which exerted on his sensibilities and on his genius the most decisive influence and which made him one of the giants of literature.[6] And certainly this is true, for the American experience in one form or another, apeared in Chateaubriand's writing from his first work—*Historical Essay*—in 1797, to his last—*Memoirs from Beyond the Grave*—published in 1848.

Generally the American influence is considered in terms of descriptive poetry such as the beautiful settings of Chateaubriand's novels. Even more, perhaps, his own experience of life. My contention is that the American travels influenced the writer in terms of his vision of the world expressed through the main themes of his writings: Conflict between cultures and glorification of the past. In terms of Chateaubriand's creativity, his American experience opened him to the possibility of transforming reality and disillusion into poetic beauty, and taught him that imagination is the mainspring of human experience and literature. As Richard Switzer in his introduction to Chateaubriand's *Travels in America* comments, "America, as Chateaubriand portrayed it, was much more a product of his reading and his imagination than of his actual visit."[7]

The first result of Chateaubriand's reading and imagination was the itinerary of his travels. So intertwined was reality and imagination that it has been a subject of debate since 1827.[8] Most scholars agree on two itineraries, one factual, the other fictional. The former appears less exotic than the latter, and it reveals the fact that the young traveller remained mostly in the Northeastern part of the United States. He visited Baltimore, Philadelphia, and New York, probably Boston, and Lexington, then Albany, following the Mohawk Trail to Niagara Falls. After the Falls his itinerary is uncertain. He claimed visits to Pittsburgh and on the warpath. Since Chateaubriand makes no mention of the Indian troubles nor of the French settlement of Scioto, which at that time had received much publicity in France, it appears that he did not actually visit that region. We may presume that he spent most of his time around Niagara Falls.

The fictional itinerary covers the whole length of the United States. According to Chateaubriand, after his visit to Niagara Falls, he went down to Pittsburgh, then down the Ohio and the

Mississippi, visited the Natchez, making a side trip to Florida. After visiting the Southern part of the United States, he returned to Ohio. While there he read about the flight of Louis the sixteenth and decided to return to France. This itinerary was obviously the product of Chateaubriand's imagination; during his brief stay in America, he could not possibly have travelled so extensively, even under the best of circumstances and certainly not when there were Indian troubles in the Ohio valley. In fact, the fictional itinerary developed only after the publication of *Atala and Rene* ten years after the actual visit.

In his *Historical Essay,* published in 1797, the only reference made to his American voyage is with regard to the Northeastern part of United States. In describing what he did not really see, Chateaubriand followed the tradition of early travel literature. Great travellers, aware that their travel narratives could not be checked on, added an element of fantasy and imagination—a poetic veneer to their narratives. Chateaubriand himself mentioned that in America the poet overcame the traveller and promised to poetry what had been lost for science.[9]

The transformation of reality by the use of imagination is a particular characteristic of Chateaubriand. We find it again in another travel narrative, the *Itinerary from Paris to Jerusalem.* In this narrative of Chateaubriand's journey to the Middle East, the factor of disillusion with reality is one of the processes of creativity.

In his *Travels in America,* Chateaubriand shares with his readers his experiences in America. He had been overwhelmed by the scenic beauty and had experienced an exhilarating feeling of complete freedom in the wilderness, but was disappointed by the American cities, the people and his first meeting with Indians. He described Philadelphia in these terms: "The aspect of Philadelphia is cold and monotonous. In general the cities in the United States are lacking in monuments, especially old monuments...almost nothing at Philadelphia, New York, Boston, rises above the mass of walls and roofs. The eye is saddened by this level appearance."[10] As for the people, he had imagined them as being the new Romans, full of virtue and probity: "A man landing as I did in the United States, full of enthusiasm for the ancients, a Cato seeking everywhere for the rigidity of early Roman manners, is necessarily shocked to find everywhere the elegance of dress, the luxury of carriages, the frivolity of conversations, the disproportion of fortunes, the immorality of banks and gaming houses, the noise of dancehalls and theaters" (15). And his long-awaited introduction to the "noble savage" might well be termed one of the greatest disappointments he had ever felt. He described it in great detail: "In the midst of a forest, there could be seen a kind of barn; I found in this barn a score of savages, men and women, daubed like sorcerers, their bodies half naked, their ears slit, raven's feathers on their heads and rings in their noses. A little Frenchman, powdered and curled as in the old days, with an apple-green coat, brocaded jacket, muslin frill and cuffs, was scraping on a miniature violin, having these Iroquois dance Madelon Friquet..."(22). The writer concludes sadly "it was a rather strange thing for a disciple of Rousseau to be introduced to primitive life with a ball given for Iroquois by a former kitchen boy of General Rochambeau" (23). The Indians no longer conformed to the image of the natural man which Chateaubriand had envisioned before his departure. The traveller sadly notes: "I inquired into their usages [those of the Indians]; in return for small presents, I was given representation of their former customs, for the customs themselves no longer exist" (230).

The mental image which Chateaubrand had formed in Europe of the American people and of the Indians was rapidly dispelled when he came in contact with reality. The disenchantment which resulted from it led to a creative process of reconstruction of the former glory of the Indian nations, of a return to the past through imagination.

Chateaubriand, in his contacts with the American Indians, was greatly impressed by the decadence he saw within the tribes. As a disciple of Rousseau at the time of his travels, he had sought the natural man only to find him corrupted by civilization. The following remark shows clearly that the decay was already in progress: "The Indian has become perfidious, selfish, lying and dissolute; his cabin is a receptacle for filth and dirt. When he was nude or covered with animal skins, there was something proud and great about him; today European rags, without covering his nudity, merely attest to his misery: he is a beggar at the door of the trading post; he no longer is a savage in his forest" (182).

In his analysis of the causes of the decay of the Indian nations, Chateaubriand very carefully points out that, contrary to what many colonists believed, the Indians were not savages but had already attained a highly sophisticated level of culture which was incompatible with that of the Europeans: "...the European civilzation did not act on the pure state of nature; it acted on the rising American civilization; if it had found nothing, it would have created something; but it found manners and destroyed them because it was stronger and did not consider it should mix with those manners" (178).

Several factors combined to speed up the annihilation of the Indians: religious, political, economic, psychological and sexual. As Chateaubriand sees it, the native religious traditions have become confused, through the mixing of foreign ideas with those of the Indians. However, he feels that the Catholic religion is more appropriate than Protestantism to the education of the Indians, and praises his native countrymen—the early French missionary priests—for their exemplary lives and generosity to the Indians, while criticizing the Protestant governments for having been more interested in trading with the Indians than in caring about them as human beings.

In the area of politics, Chateaubriand feels that the delicate political structures of the Indian tribes were subverted by the European presence. He adds that "our presents, our vices, and our arms bought, corrupted, or killed the individuals who made up the several powers" (180-181).

Economics between Indians and Europeans was weighted heavily in favor of the latter. The fur traders were responsible for a subtly corrupting influence: "Pursued by the European avidity and by the corruption of civilized people even in the depths of their forests, the Indians exchange at these trading posts rich furs for objects of little value but which have become for them objects of prime necessity" (181-182).

The psychological cause for the decadence was even more subtle, for it attacked the dignity of man and put to question the intrinsic worth of the Indians. The commanders of American and English military posts assumed that they had authority over the Indians and treated them as minors with no rights to the land they occupied. Thus "the savage ends up believing he is not the real possessor of the land disposed of without his being consulted; he becomes accustomed to look upon himself as a species inferior to the white; he consents to receive orders, to hunt, to fight for masters" (181).

The final reason for the slow destruction of the Indian nations was the sexual contacts between white adventurers and Indian women. Chateaubriand felt that the half-breeds possessed the vices of both parent races. They were the businessmen and the brokers between the tribes and the fur-trading companies. For Chateaubriand, they had no past and no culture and they were the incarnation of the economic and political evils. He describes them thus: "These bastards of civilized nature and savage nature sell themselves now to the Americans, now to the English, to deliver to them the monopoly of the pelts..." (182).

If reality and the present are so disappointing, and the Indian culture has become decadent, there remains the possibility of returning to the past. Chateaubriand casts himself in the role of the spokesman for the Indians, as their historian: "the roll of the indigenous peoples of that part of the New World has not been called: I shall do it. Many men, many tribes will fail to answer: a last historian of these peoples, I shall open their death register" (174). This desire which corresponds so well to Chateaubriand's personality and character, stems in part from his own concept of the past and of literature. Its function is to preserve the past and to set it against the devalued present, to contrast glory and decay. The idea of preserving the past as a living monument to former grandeur can only be accomplished through literature. The Indians, because of their culture have only an oral tradition which can disappear under the impact of cultural strife. For Chateaubriand, the written word has the power to keep and to preserve: "Civilized people have monuments of letters and arts to preserve the memories of their homeland; they have cities, palaces, towers, columns, obelisks; they have the furrows in the field they have cultivated; their names are engraved on bronze and marble; their actions are preserved in chronicles. The savages have nothing of all that: their names are not written on the trees of the forests; their hut, built in a few hours, perishes in a few moments; their simple plowing stick, which has only grazed the earth, has not even been able to raise a furrow; their traditional songs vanish with the memory that retains them, with the last voice that repeats them" (231).

Thus in recalling the religion, the political institutions, the mores and customs of the Indian nations, Chateaubriand preserves their past glory. In every instance the writer's purpose is to show that the Indian culture was not inferior to that of the Europeans, it was simply different and that, in fact, it had many traits of the ancient culture of Greece and Rome. At the same time, he attempts to make a balanced presentation. He notes that there are two ways of portraying the native population, neither of them correct: "one is to speak only of their laws and their manners, without entering into the details of their bizarre customs and their habits which are often disgusting to civilized men. Then all you will see will be Greeks and Romans. . . the other way consists in representing only the habits and customs of the savages, without mentioning their laws and their manners; then you will see only the smoky, filthy cabins to which retires a kind of monkey endowed with human speech" (81).

Chateaubriand also attempts to give a complete picture of the Indian culture as it had once been, including marriage customs, education of children, funerals, feasts, dances and games, medicine, languages, hunting, war, religion and political institutions. The presentation is made not by a trained anthropologist, but by a poet who finds grace and poetry in the Indian customs. Consequently, he points out the intrinsic value of these customs and makes it clear that the people called savages were indeed very much advanced in the art of languages and the combination of ideas. In other instances, he refers to the similarities between Indian customs and those of Europeans. He feels there is even a superiority in some of their customs, such as those of the Muskogees who have slaves but with whom slavery is not hereditary. Chateaubriand remarks on this subject: "the misfortune of the parents is not passed on to their posterity; the

Muskogees did not want servitude to be hereditary: a fine lesson that savages have given to civilized man" (164).

The task of the historian ends with the recording for posterity of what constitutes the grandeur of natural man. The Indian nations are no longer: "pushed by the European population toward the Northwest of North America; the savage population comes by a singular destiny to expire on the very shore on which they landed in unknown centuries to take possession of America. In the Iroquois language the Indians give themselves the name of 'men of forever'—*Ongoueonoue*. The 'men of forever' are gone, and the foreigner will soon leave to these legitimate heirs to a whole world, only the earth of their tombs" (178). The saga of the Indian nations ends in death.

But for Chateaubriand, death can be conquered. For him it is a literary theme which sustains his inspiration. By the power of the written word he has succeeded in creating a world where his "natural man" can live and remain forever free from the contamination of civilization. And, in the building of this new world, he has at the same time erected a kind of monument, not only to the Indian nations, but to his own creative genius as well.

Notes

[1]The project is first mentioned in the *Essai historique sur les revolutions anciennes et modernes,* published in London in 1797, and reprinted in the *Oeuvres completes* in 1826. It also appeared in the preface of *Atala* published in 1801, and in *Travels in America,* trans. by Richard Switzer (Lexington: University of Kentucky Press, 1969), p. 6.

[2]*Memoires of Francois Rene Vicomte de Chateaubriand,* trans. by Alexander Teixeiros de Mattos (London: Freemantle, 1902), I, p. 180.

[3]Georges Colas, 'L'Embanquement de Chateaubriand pour l'Americaque," *Nouvelle Revue de Britagne,* No. 2 (1947), p. 129.

[4]*Memoirs,* p. 218.

[5]*Essai sur les revolutions, Oeuvres completes* (Paris: Furne, Jouvet et Cie, 1880), vol. I, pp. 304-305.

[6]Rene Bazin, *Chateaubriand et l'Amerique* (Paris: La Table Ronde, 1969), p. 39.

[7]Switzer, p. xvi.

[8]cf. Richard Switzer, edition critique du *Voyage en Amerique* (Paris: Didier, 1964), pp. xxvi-xxxi.

[9]R.-R. de Chateaubriand, *Memories d'Outre-Tombe,* edition du Centenaire (Paris: Flammarion, 1948), I, pp. 287-288, 328.

[10]F.-R. de Chateaubriand, *Travels in America,* trans. by Richard Switzer (Lexington: University of Kentucky Press, 1969), p. 14. Subsequent references will be indicated in the text.

Originally published in *Exploration,* IV:1, December 1976. Reprinted with the permission of the editor and the author.

Travel Narratives of D.F. Sarmiento:
A Seminal Frontier Thesis

Cathryn A. Ducey

Until the relatively recent (1970) publication of Michael Rockland's translations of Domingo Faustino Sarmiento's *Travels,* interest in the Argentianian theorist and statesman has been practically nonexistent. Although some writers mention him as an advocate of public and progressive education in South America, and some economic and political studies deal with him as a liberal Latin-American President, Sarmiento's interest in the frontier development in Argentina are largely ignored. His *El Facundo* is read by some undergraduate and graduate students, with an emphasis upon the attacks, political and personal, on Rosas and other of the "barbarous" dictators.[1] Neglected, overlooked aspects of *Facundo* must be examined, along with his *Travels,* as presaging the frontier thesis of Frederick Jackson Turner, for Sarmiento theorized, generalized and applied concepts of the frontier based upon travels and observation.

Faustino Valentin Sarmiento was born February 15, 1811, in the Argentinian frontier town of San Juan de la Frontera. Located between the Andes and the Pampas, it had a population in 1811 of about 3,000. His family was poor, as were most of the inhabitants of San Juan. Early in life the young man took the name of his patron saint and became known as Domingo Faustino Sarmiento. He attended the first established school in the frontier province of San Juan; in 1825 he left school to become apprenticed to a French engineer; he next accepted the offer of his priest-uncle, Jose de Oro, to travel far outside the province and to study; in 1827 Sarmiento returned home to San Juan and began work as a shopkeeper in his aunt's store.

Somehow copies of Benjamin Franklin's *Autobiography* and of some works by Thomas Paine came into his hands. These books led him to decide that a "rationally ordered and understandable universe should exist."[2] Yet he saw no evidence of it on the Argentine frontier. Instead he saw only poverty, ignorance and a chaotic political situation. *Caudillo* (strongman) leaders like Manuel Rosas and Juan Facundo Quiroga were unconcerned about organized programs to combat poverty, illiteracy and uncertain political conditions.

As civil dissension became widespread, Argentinians were forced to choose between bending to the will and whip of the caudillos or following revolutionaries in the hopes of bringing reform to the government of Argentina. Sarmiento fought the caudillos and was forced into exile during the years 1828 to 1832.

While in self-imposed exile in Chile he began writing for newspapers, expressing his bitter disgust for the Federalists who were raping his country and undertaking what was to become a life-long role: teacher and advocate of public education.

He learned English, became caught up with the fever of the Chilian silver rush, became a mine worker and then a foreman. Such work must not have been fully satisfying, even if physically tiring, for he also gave English lessons, wrote assiduously, and began to develop his first full reform work—a program to colonize the Colorado River Valley.

From 1832 to 1839, while political equilibrium in Argentina was shakily maintained, Sarmiento zealously applied himself to personal development and to reforming some of the conditions in San Juan. The soldier-miner-fledgling teacher phases of his life were over. While earning a sketchy living as a journalist, he also founded a literary society and edited reform newspapers. Sarmiento set out to become a European in education, a North American in politics and a South American in loyalty.

Sarmiento began his best known work, *Civilization and Barbarism: the Life of Juan Facundo Quiroga* (popularly known in South America as *El Facundo* and in the United States as *Life in the Argentine Republic*), during the 1840s. This pseudo-biography was a vehicle for his attack on caudillo government and an analysis of the social and political causes of Argentina's problems. Primarily for this work Sarmiento is considered the major reformer of South America and the "Father of Spanish-American sociology."[3]

With the exception of particular passages dealing solely with the tyrant Juan Facundo Quiroga most of Sarmiento's *El Facundo* presages in tone, style and content both Mark Twain's

Roughing It and Turner's thesis. Sarmiento granted that he was not writing an unbiassed history of Argentina; he intended, rather, a study of "national antecedents, the features of the soil, in the popular customs and traditions."[4]

It is difficult to tell that it is Sarmiento writing of Argentina rather than Turner of the United States in the following passage from the end of *El Facundo:*

...Our future destiny is foretold in our numerous rivers, the boundless pasturage of our plains, our immense forests, and a climate favorable to the production of the whole world. If we lack an intelligent population, let the people of Europe once feel that there is permanent peace and freedom in our country, and multitudes of emigrants would find their way to a land where success is sure.[5]

A strong faith in Argentina's future is clear throughout *El Facundo.* The primary concerns trace the geographical and political conditions which transformed Argentina and describe individuals, both specific and archetypal, who influenced change.

Of the fourteen provinces in Argentina all except San Juan and Mendoza were pastoral; the city-dwellers of Buenos Aires were Europeanized and civilized, while the plains-frontier people recognized only the brutishness in life:

supremacy of the strongest, the absolute and irresponsible authority of rulers, the administration of justice without formalities or discussion.

Rule by force, whether by the leaders of cattle trains and caravans or by local gauchos (cowboys), is accepted and respected, as it was in the American West. Emigrants to the plains, enduring long journeys by caravan, learned to

acquire the habit of living far from society, of struggling, single-handed with nature, of disregarding privation, and of depending for protection against the dangers ever imminent upon no other resources than personal strength and skill.

Although Sarmiento continues to emphasize the self-sufficiency of the pampas pioneer/frontiersman, he finds the frontier traits only half-admirable. He contends, unlike Turner, that the lack of a stable, unified government, the isolation of "self-concentrated feudal" families, the roving nature of the gaucho, the lack of public schools and lack of tolerance for religious differences, and the "dearth of all amenities of life induces all the externals leading to barbarism."

The continual struggle of "isolated man with untamed nature," the constant "defying and subduing of nature," develops the "consciousness of individual consequence and superior prowess," but for Sarmiento it does not foster those principles of concern for the common good and progress which he believed so necessary for the development of a republic.

Life and customs on the pastoral pampas contrasted sharply with life in the commercial, water-based cities:

distinct, rival and incompatible forms of society, two differing kinds of civilization existed in the Argentine Republic: one being Spanish, European, and cultivated, the other barbarous, American, and almost wholly of native growth. The revolution which occurred in the cities acted only as the cause, the impulse, which set these two distinct forms of national existence face to face, and gave occasion for a contest between them, to be ended, after lasting many years, by the absorption of one into the other.

Sarmiento saw the struggle between Hispanic European civilization and native barbarism as a struggle between "mind and matter" quite different from anything else in the world.

Sarmiento's thesis is that the way of life on the pampas, the individualism, independence and anti-European traits of the gaucho, and the isolation from centers of culture, led directly to a confrontation of values culminating in the revolution.

It is important to note that the same traits which Turner cites as leading to democracy on the American frontier, as supportive to the principles of liberty and responsibility, are pointed to by Sarmiento as leading to precisely opposite goals and conditions. Just as these traits strengthened the North American Union they fractured Argentina.

Embarking on a fateful trip to the United States in 1847, arranged as a public relations gesture by his government, Sarmiento began a series of letters which later were published as his *Viajes,* translated as *Travels in the United States in 1847.*[6] Always perceptive and inquisitive, Sarmiento's discussions of and observations on American life in mid-century anticipate the personalistic reportorial genre of Mark Twain's *Roughing It* and *Life on the Mississippi.* Rambling, sympathetic, humorous, often disconnected, descriptions are recorded with the intention of suggesting some insights to the American character.

On his initial trip he visited twenty-one states and was impressed by the technology, the industrial growth of cities, and by the order resulting from a federal republic based upon allegiance to ideals.

> On the other side of the Alleghenies, the New World begins.... In the west, Yankee genius has more room to move about and expand to try new things that would seem impossible in the older states. In the West they try things which are superhuman, inconceivable, seemingly absurd.[7]

In his *Travels* the various stages in frontier development which he describes in *Facundo* are re-established and a model of the frontier is expanded. On the American frontier, he says, the first pioneer is the "Indian Hater" who persecutes the native inhabitants of the lands so that they will desert them. Then come the Squatters, "who are misanthropes looking for solitude in which to dwell, danger for excitement, and the work of felling trees...." The real pioneers come next, "opening the forests, sowing the earth, and spreading themselves over a great area." Once they are established, the "capitalist impresarios" follow, nearly on their heels, along with immigrant laborers and fortune-hunting youth. Finally are established the proprietary class, the cities, and the commercial routes.[8] Sarmiento suggests that the availability of free and open land partially contributes to the prospering western development of the United States. But he asks, "...then why in South America, where it is just as easy if not easier to take up new land, are population and wealth not increasing?"[9] There, with a greater amount of virgin land than in the United States "have the backwardness, poverty and ...ignorance" continued unabated. The reason why the mere existence of free land cannot be accepted as the major impetus for prosperity is clear:

> The American is a man with a home or the certainty of having one, a man beyond the clutch of hunger or desperation, a man with hopes for the future as bright as the imagination can invent, a man with political sentiments and needs. He is, in short, master of himself with a spirit elevated by education and a sense of his own dignity.[10]

These are attributes the Hispano-American lacks, and until they can be developed through education the free land of the Pampas will remain uncultivated, the masses of people will remain in poverty, and the nation of Argentina will not prosper. "...Being a new country does not mean anything if action is wanting."[11]

Americans, in contrast, are "free men and not disciplined prisoners whose lives are administered," and they are energetic and active.[12]

The North American frontier land belongs to the Union and is sold for a dollar an acre to any man; while in Argentina, says Sarmiento, the system of land distribution is different. There land concessions are granted first to the conquistadors

> ...who established earldoms for themselves, while soldiers, fathers of the sharecropper, that worker without land who multiplies without increasing the number of his buildings, sheltered themselves in the shade of their improvised roofs. The passion to occupy lands in the name of the king drove men to dominion over entire districts, which put great distances between landowners so that after three centuries the intervening land still has not been cleared. The city, for this reason, has been suppressed in the vast design, and the few villages which have been created since the conquest have been *decreed* by presidents."[13]

On the other hand, the American takes possession of his lands "in the name of the kings of the world: Work and Good Will."[14]

Sarmiento's view of the American seeking to tame the wilderness is admittedly romantic. He sees the Yankee as "a born proprietor," dreaming of conquering the forests. The western wilderness is tamed by "American Alexanders, who wander through the wilds looking for points that a profound study of the future indicates will be centers of commerce. The Yankee, an inventor of cities, professes a speculative science which leads him by deduction to the divination of a site where a future city must flourish."[15] Unhampered by the stigmas of ignorance or poverty and unimpeded by governmental regulations he accepts the land as his. His is a free "colonizing spirit," untrammelled by outside forces. Thus do

Americans cross six hundred leagues of wilderness for an ideal....They sacrifice themselves for the future of the nation....These people carry with them, like a political conscience, certain constitutive principles of association. Political science becomes moral sentiment, perfecting the man, the people, even the mob. The municipality is converted into a phenomenon dependent upon spontaneous association. There is liberty of conscience and of thought. There is trial by jury.[16]

How different are the Americans from the Argentinians of any class, who are unable to conceive of voluntary association for the common good, unable to consider a political system based upon the principle of liberty, unable to forget the strictures of both religion and class. For they, their revolution not withstanding, assume that government exists because of the necessity to regulate the actions of individuals according to a predetermined code. And, says Sarmiento, without a system of universal education, the Argentine Republic will not be able to provide man with the means to develop fully his moral and political conscience.

In his *Travels* Sarmiento is concerned with actions and attitudes and customs of people throughout the United States, although his recurring emphasis is upon the westward movement and progress. Various customs are a source of both interest and amusement. Lack of attention paid to leisurely eating is somewhat disconcerting to the fastidious Sarmiento: "The American has two minutes set aside for lunch, five for dinner, ten for a smoke or to chew tobacco....The Yankee *pur sang* eats all his food, desserts, and fruit from the same plate, one at a time or all together."[17]

Lack of respect for privacy is rife in America: "In the reading rooms [of large hotels] four or five parasites support themselves heavily on your shoulders to read the same tiny bit of print you are reading.... If you are tranquilly smoking your cigar, a passerby will take it out of your mouth in order to light his own."[18] If certain niceties of manners are not observed as they are in Europe or in South America it is perhaps because the trappings of civilization are unimportant in a burgeoning, apparently classless society. More to the point, for Sarmiento, is the acceptance by the American of man by man, whatever he may be lacking in the social graces.

Tolerance for men, and for their vagaries and differences, impresses the Argentinian visitor. As a Hispano-Catholic, reared with the rigid authority of the Spanish church ubiquitous in his country, Sarmiento is amazed by the American acceptance of the number and variety of religious sects. Although some of the frenetic, enthusiastic, or faith healing sects are both strange and unusual, he is impressed by the tolerance among the people he meets of and for religious differences.

Related to the tolerance of religious attitudes and practices is the American development and support of philanthropic and improvement organizations, an interest unheard of among South Americans. That individuals would give away capital to help their fellow man, that others would crusade against drunkenness, that anyone would freely donate money to establish institutions for the sick, the insane, or for the education of orphans—these are aspects of the uniquely North American way of life which so intrigues Sarmiento, and of which he approves. Groups and individuals seeking the improvement of society, with nothing to gain personally, he believes are a reflection and product of the American's overwhelming interest in mass education.[19]

Even if he sees much of the country and the lives of its inhabitants through the proverbial rose-colored classes, even if he can believe that all the mill girls in Lowell are "educated...conscientious and devoted to their work."[20] one comes to understand that such seemingly naive conclusions and his almost child-like acceptance of anything American are understandable. He reaches conclusions because he almost desperately wants to believe that somewhere in the world an ideal state for all men could exist.

Such was his dream for his homeland. If the North American model could be imposed upon, or accepted by, Argentina then there was reason to hope and dream that his country could one day be as settled, as prosperous, its lands as cultivated, its people as free as in the United States.

The United States progressed rapidly because Old World values were cast off, because Americans continually searched for ways of improving the land and society. Thus, Sarmiento reflects bitterly about South America. In his own country he deplores what the Spaniards had not done in three centuries compared to what had been acomplished in less time in the United States.

Sarmiento remains optimistic that there will be a change, for he believes that in the expansion and "mixing and juxtaposition" of peoples that someday all America will be "homogenous." He firmly accepts the idea of the "melting pot," although slavery was a jarring note.

Sarmiento sees slaves as unassimilated and suppressed, describing slavery in the United States as "the deep ulcer and the incurable fistula which threatens to corrupt the robust body of the Union!"[21] He believes that the Founding Fathers made a "fatal error" in allowing the injustice of man's subjugation to man to exist in a country founded on diametrically opposed principles. He astutely remarks that had slavery been abolished with the Declaration of Independence or the Constitution at a time when the number of slaves was relatively few that it would have been a much more acceptable act then than in the nineteenth century. He suggests that a "racial war within a century" will take place, for he sees the division between slave and free states and the increasing numbers of Negroes as portents for a dire future.[22] He is concerned that slavery is a blight upon a fruitful democratic nation.

In spite of such weaknesses in the North American system, by and large Sarmiento sees only good. As a thoroughly curious traveller he remarks upon the many freedoms that Americans have. Among these is the freedom to travel at will. "Since everyone travels, there is no impossible or unprofitable enterprise in the field of transportation. . . . The great number of travellers makes for cheap rates, and cheap rates in turn tempt those who have no precise object in mind to go somewhere."[23] Even in 1847 Sarmiento was aware that the peripatetic American was unique in the world.

As he moves about the country, Sarmiento observes that in this dynamic society "the hotels will be more important than any other kind of public construction." Not only do the hotels which accommodate the increasing number of travellers impress him with public and private appointments, but so also do other buildings, such as banks and municipal edifices. The eclectic attitude of the American architects suggests: "If the Americans have not, then, created a new kind of architecture, they have at least developed national applications, forms, and a character influenced by their political and social institutions."[24]

The "melting pot," adaptability, and ingenuity in architecture, manners, and customs contrast with differences in his own country. In the Argentinian population centers public and private architecture was solely Spanish-inspired, modified only by availability of materials. Country adobe huts were crude, built from available materials. Hispanic class and national attitudes were reflected in architecture. In the United States, however, the buildings reflect pride in monuments, a penchant for echoing styles of past, republican, ages, and general experimental uses of forms and materials.

As population moved restlessly the need for railroads and varieties of internal communication and transport systems developed. The westward movement and attendant growth of industrial cities Sarmiento attributes, partially, to "the infallible Yankee instinct for sensing places which will produce wealth. . . ."[25]

Sarmiento judged the adaptability of the new westerners to be important, but recognized that even as emigrants from the East Coast and immigrants from Europe and the Orient adapted to new conditions so also

the land soon puts its stamp upon them. . . . So the fragments of old societies are coming together in the flood of immigrants, mixing and

forming the newest, the youngest, and the most daring republic on the
face of the earth.[26]

The words foreshadow Turner's assertion that the land makes an
impression on the people who set out, initially, to conquer it;
"Americanization" takes place.

Portents for success on the frontier include, says Sarmiento,
not only the adaptability of the new westerners and their inherent
native ingenuity, but also the development of towns. Sarmiento
describes "the village, which is the center of political life, just as
the family is the center of domestic life...the essence of the
United States is to be found in its small towns. This cannot be
said of any other country."[27]

Even in the poorest of villages, he notes, North Americans
repect and use manufactured items (locks, kitchen utensils,
plows, axes) rather than local, crudely crafted items. Amenities
lacking in South American villages (signposts, hotels,
newspapers, banks, churches, post office, streets) are
omnipresent in even the newest of American villages. What he
sees as a basic difference between life in semi-isolated areas on
the two continents is "widespread distribution of civilized ways
in the towns as well as in the cities and among men of all
classes."[28]

Sarmiento is quick to accept, however, that the signs of
"civilized ways" do diminish the further west one moves.

"Westward, where civilization diminishes," he writes, "and in the
FAR WEST, where it is almost non-existent because of the sparseness of
the population, things are, of course, different. Comfort is reduced to
what is strictly necessary.... But even in these remote plantations there
is an appearance of perfect equality among the population in their dress,
in their manners, and even in their intelligence. The merchant, the
doctor, the SHERIFF, the farmer—all look the same.... Americans do
not wear jackets or ponchos, but have a dress common to all and a
universal roughness of manner which gives an impression of equality in
education."[29]

How different are these views, of dress and attitudes, from
appearances on the Argentinian frontier! There class differences

in clothing and manner are readily apparent. The peon would be recognized by poncho and hand woven garments, the cleric by black robes, and if perchance a wealthy merchant or doctor travelled through a farm region the European cut in jackets, trousers and imported linens would be signs of wealth.

Beyond the superficial similitude in clothing and roughness of manner what Sarmiento finds most characteristic of Americans

Is their ability to appropriate for their own use, generalize, popularize, conserve, and perfect all the practices, tools, methods, and aids which the most advanced civilization has put in the hands of men. In this the United States is unique on earth. There are no unconquerable habits that retard for centuries the adoption of an obvious improvement, and , on the other hand, there is a predisposition to try anything. . . . You would have to wait a century for something like this to happen in Spain, or in France, or in our own part of America.[30]

In his continuation of a seminal "frontier thesis" Sarmiento says that civilization is comprised of "moral and physical perfection or the abilities which a civilized man develops in order to subject nature to his desires."[31] Such perfection and abilities exist on only one frontier in the world and only among the men who forge their way through that frontier. Only the American is able to adapt to conditions easily, accept man as man, believe in his own ability to conquer nature, to use technology, to rely on his own native gifts of intuition and intelligence not only to survive in the wilderness, but to succeed. The ability and the willingness to try new things, new ways, new lands, is intrinsic to the American: ". . . If you want to know if a machine, an invention, or a social doctrine is useful and can be applied or developed in the near future, you must test it on the touchstone of Yankee knowhow."[32] The pragmatic and utilitarian and ingenious American "far from barbarizing, as we have, the elements which European civilization handed him when he came as a settler, has worked to perfect them and even improve upon them."[33]

With the attributes Sarmiento describes he finds it understandable that American inventions, products, and business forms rapidly displace those of Europe. But America's greatest potential for development lies in the citizen's "possession of the land which will be the nursery of his new family,"[34] in the small free-hold system.

Again and again Sarmiento recalls the points first made in *El Facundo:* that an inevitable confrontation occurs when civilization and barbarism meet and that the outcome decides the future of a nation. At the beginning of *El Facundo* he writes:

If any form of national literature should appear in these new American societies, it must result from the description of the mighty scenes of nature, and still more from the illustration of the struggle between European civilization and native barbarism, between mind and matter— a struggle of imposing magnitude in South America....[35]

In North America only Cooper, Sarmiento suggests, was able to capture the sense of the struggle:

by removing the scene of the events he described from the settled portion of the country to the border land between civilized life and that of the savage, the theatre of war for the possession of the soil waged against each other, by the native tribes and the saxon race.[36]

As he pursues these points as journalist and statesman he repeatedly affirms his frontier thesis.

Although the cultural historian Henry Nash Smith asserts Turner's

most important debt to his intellectual tradition is the idea of savagery and civilization that he uses to define his central factor. His frontier is explicitly 'the meeting point between savagery and civilization.'[37]

Clearly Sarmiento's location of the scene of man's struggle as "the border land between civilized life and that of the savage" and his emphasis upon the battle between "European civilization and native barbarism," nearly fifty years before Turner, is equally, if not more, important to the intellectual tradition.

What makes Sarmiento unique is the background from which he writes. He was neither a semi-trained political theorist as was a de Tocqueville, nor was he a transplanted—but seemingly thoroughly adapted "American" as a de Crevecouer. Nor was he a native-born, self-made, thoroughly new-world, North American as was Franklin. Although he could assess and accept the vagaries of American frontier life, he was not the native satirist, or the "adaptable" American that was a Mark Twain. Nor, indeed, was he a Ph.D. trained historian, a product of the West, of the East, of universities, of the Germanic "school" of analysis as Turner was. He was not the interesting romantic novelist, as Cooper was, nor an intellectual like Emerson, nor a politician-statesman like T.R. Roosevelt. He was none of these and yet all of them.

Sarmiento is examined, although rarely at length, by historians who concern themselves with developments in Latin and South American history and political theory. He, Echeverria and Mitre and Rivadavia, as Argentine political theorists and presidents, belong in histories and analyses of South American development. But only Sarmiento can be considered as an instigator of changes in Argentina based upon analyses of a North American model. For it is he alone who could look at his own country and decide that he needed to assess analogues before he could set forth possible changes. He alone looked to a North American model as a total possibility for a means to develop a free and prosperous Argentina.

Beyond and above all else, it is the traveller-statesman D.F.V.Sarmiento of Argentina who formulates a thesis concerning the American Frontier as coherent and complete—if not more complete—as that of Frederick Jackson Turner of the United States.

Many contemporary historians have dismissed Turner's thesis for its generalizations, its roots in a romantic view of the American West, and its over-emphasis upon individualism. Others have questioned his lack of emphasis upon economic changes and his over-emphasis of the frontier as a decisive factor in shaping American life and thought. Few argue, however, about his definition of the frontier as a meeting point between civilization and savagery as being uniquely American. And historians credit Turner with being the first commentator to approach the concept of the American frontier from an analytic viewpoint. It seems almost futile to dismiss his "Frontier Thesis" as unimportant in analyses of American culture. If nothing else, he precipitated arguments about the nature of American development, and thus prompted other historians to delve into reasons for what shaped "the American Character."

Turner wrote, primarily, in the late nineteenth century, and he is especially important for: 1) precipitating historiographical inquiry based on New World, not Old World, models; and, 2) attempting a definition of New World development unlike any previously recognized by the North American academic world. He wrote within a context; he was a westerner, a man brought up on the frontier past—its realities and myths. His was an "insider's" interpretation.

Turner was nurtured on generalizations about the American frontier. It was the "safety-valve," a place where Huck Finns could "light out," to, if necessary, to build a new life. Frontier life produced archetypal political characters in Daniel Boone and Andrew Jackson. Controversy over slavery was promoted because of the Territories. Travellers continually commented about the New American produced on the frontier. Many of the frontier aspects celebrated by Turner existed in a Tidewater Virginia or a Puritan Massachusetts; de Tocqueville and de Crevecouer described many of the same concepts of the American Character as "foreigners" observing life in the New World. Turner wrote out of his understandings and experience about frontier attributes psychologically accepted by most nineteenth century Americans. He solidified concepts, myths and psychological viewpoints.

In contrast, D.F. Sarmiento's interpretation of the frontier arises from a different set of experiences and background. He is the "outsider," a Hispanic-American, self-educated, relatively uninformed about North America. His knowledge was very limited when he finished *Facundo* in 1845. Yet from that limited knowledge he expresses in *Facundo* and later in the *Viajes* some startling insights: 1) a redefinition of the frontier as a meeting place between barbarism and civilization; 2) a celebration of individuality as it develops away from the cities; and, 3) an elaboration of the several phases of frontier social development.

Sarmiento, like Turner, sees the frontier as a step in the development of a nation and a national character. From a totally different psychological, social and educational background he arrives at similar definitions. His travels in the United States solidified his impressions and interpretations, but did not create them.

Notes

[1] *El Facundo* is best known in the English translation by Mary Peabody Mann, *Life in the Argentine Republic in the Days of the Tyrants; or, Civilization and Barbarism.* (New York: 1960). All quotations from *El Facundo* will be referenced hereinafter as *Life in the Argentine Republic....*

[2] Allison Williams Bunkley, *The Life of Sarmiento* (Princeton: 1952), p. 63.

[3] Bunkley, pp. 179-80.

[4] *Life in the Argentine Republic,* p. 4.

[5] *Life in the Argentine Republic,* p. 247. Unless otherwise noted all successive quotations from Sarmiento are from this source.

[6] Michael Aaron Rockland, Sarmiento's *"Travels in the United States."* (Princeton: 1970).

[7] Quoted by Rockland, pp. 64-5, from "Hacia el Oeste."

[8] Rockland, p. 190.

[9] Rockland, p. 153.

[10] Rockland, p. 153.

[11] Rockland, p. 155.

[12] Rockland, p. 158.

[13] Rockland, p. 165.

[14] Rockland, p. 165.

[15] Rockland, p. 166.

[16] Rockland, p. 171.

[17] Rockland, pp. 147-8.

[18] Rockland, p. 148.

[19] Rockland, p. 244, and elsewhere in text.

[20] Rockland, p. 246.

[21] Rockland, p. 304.

[22] Rockland, p. 305.

[23] Rockland, pp. 133-4.

[24] Rockland, p. 145.

[25] Rockland, p. 123.

[26] Rockland, p. 124.

[27] Rockland, pp. 126-7.

[28] Rockland, p. 131.

[29] Rockland, pp. 131-2.

[30]Rockland, pp. 132-3.

[31]Rockland, p. 133.

[32]Rockland, p. 144.

[33]Rockland, pp. 162-3.

[34]Quoted in Edmundo Correas, *Sarmiento and the United States* (Gainesville: 1961), p. 19.

[35]*Life in the Argentine Republic,* p. 25.

[36]*Life in the Argentine Republic,* p. 25.

[37] Smith, p. 293.

American Travelers Abroad

Americans Abroad:
The Popular Art of Travel Writing in the Nineteenth Century

Ahmed M. Metwalli

Almost every prominent American literary figure of the nineteenth century has written one type or another of travel book or based some of his literary output on his experiences of travel in foreign lands. And yet the travel literature of the century has not been adequately studied and, so far, books of travel have never been universally accepted as a literary genre. More than twenty years ago, Thomas H. Johnson underscored the undeserved neglect that was and still is the lot of this genre: "And discussion of the literature written to interpret foreign countries," said Johnson, "must at present be very incomplete, for few investigations of the subject have been undertaken."[1] Yet the value of this literature in interpreting the Old World to America in the nineteenth century, especially on the level of popular interest, the vital role it played in mass culture,[2] and the impact it had on some cultural trends of the century cannot be overestimated.

The "cultural" orientation of the age was responsible for the increased production and dissemination of books of travel. During the nineteenth century, almost every literate and zealous traveler managed to avail himself of one or more, and sometimes all, public media, to excite, entertain, or instruct the masses with his own experiences in foreign lands. Public lectures in the increasingly popular Lyceums, serialized travel letters, serialized articles, and books were available organs of expression. The romantic adventurer, the explorer, the missionary, the merchant or mercantile agent, the diplomatic and military envoy, as well as the man of letters, were all able to reach and influence the public in one way or another.

The interest and avidity of a reading public aware of its deficiency in knowledge and information encouraged this kind of composition. The cultural milieu was certainly ripe. Moreover, since it was the fashionable thing to do and also the most lucrative financially, almost every individual who left home—

even for a hike in the mountains—committed his impressions and experiences to paper and inflicted them on the reading public. Most of these producers of travel yarns lacked what Matthew Arnold calls "the power of the man," which, combined with "the power of the moment," produces a work of literary merit. The very few nineteenth-century travelers who possessed this "power" and who concern us here, were submerged in an interminable sea of mediocrity. And though their travel books were instrumental in the ultimate shaping and vitality of their literary artistic lives, these books were engulfed in oblivion—the oblivion which is almost always the destiny of whatever is written for the level of popular rather than intellectual interest—by the indiscriminate and uncritical taste of the contemporary reading public which made an instant success of almost every travel book.

All kinds of books of travel, a large number of which were mere hasty collections of unedited letters or article serials, sold by the tens of thousands. Many ran into tens of reprints and were in constant demand for decades after their first publication. Because they almost always succeeded in satisfying the immediate cultural and nationalistic needs of the reading public, they were among the best sellers of the day. Publishers encouraged authors to write accounts of their travel experiences at home and abroad; they knew well that travel narratives needed very little promotion and almost no puffing.[3] Six editions of Bayard Taylor's first book of travels, *Views Afoot,* plublished in 1846 when he was barely twenty years old, were sold in the first year; and in less than a decade twenty editions were printed.[4] His royalties from *Journey to Central Africa* (August, 1854) and *The Lands of the Saracens* (October, 1858), had mounted to $2,650 by the first of the new year.[5] He must have anticipated the success of his volumes of travel and the sums that would accrue from their immediate sale. Attuned to the needs and demands of the reading public, Taylor, in a casual and business-like manner, stated in the preface to the first edition of his second volume of travel, *Journey to Central Africa,* that his "reasons for offering this volume to the public are, simply, that there is room for it." Indeed, there was "room" enough not only for his personal accounts, but for a *Cyclopedia of Modern Travel* and a whole *Illustrated Library of*

Travel, both of which he edited.

Nor was this instant success and popular favor Bayard Taylor's lot alone. The travel books of other literary figures were similarly, if not as spectacularly, blessed. The first edition of 2,500 copies of George William Curtis's book, *Nile Notes of Howadji* (1851) was exhausted within six months.[6] His second book, *Howadji in Syria* (1852), met with the same success. Significantly, the sale of Melville's books declined as he moved away from the domain of popular travel literature which he had considered at the onset of his career to be his literary field. The first edition of some 3,000 copies of *Omoo* (1847), which is a melange of fact and fiction based on Melville's travel adventures in the South Seas, was selling out so rapidly in its first week of publication that a new printing was immediately planned. On the other hand, the more intellectual and subtle *Moby Dick* (1851) sold only 2,500 copies in its first five years, and only 2,965 in its first twenty.[7]

Emerson was also graced by this same popular favor. The first printing of 3,000 copies of his *English Traits* (1856), which is actually more an essay in cultural anthropology dealing with ideas and institutions than a travel book of intinerant wanderings and recorded experiences, sold immediately. Within a month, a second edition of 2,000 copies was printed. Mark Twain's *The Innocents Abroad* (1869) established his fame as a popular author. A little over thirty thousand copies were sold during the first five months after publication, and by the end of the first year 67,000 copies were bought at $3.50 each.[8]

The demand for travel literature was not restricted to the printed word. Lyceums and the popular lectures which grew out of the Lyceum system were other media used by travelers to entertain, instruct and satisfy the curiosity of the public about ancient and faraway places. Enterprising lecture booking-agents, such as James Redpath and his successor, James B. Pond, guided and catered to the needs and tastes of the new national audience; and travelers and travel writers were their most profitable assets. Much could be learned about the popularity of travel literature from the fact that while Emerson could earn as much as $2,000 for a season of lecturing after a considerable effort, Bayard Taylor often made $5,000 from his travel lectures.[9] These travel lectures were derived mostly from the lecturer's own travel journal or book; sometimes, the lecture room functioned as a useful proving ground for materials intended for publication. In either case, the lecture podium was utilized by the travelers to promote their already available or forthcoming travel books, augmenting their sales considerably.

These figures provide us with ample evidence of the phenomenal popularity of travel literature. But the question that needs to be answered is why were nineteenth-century books of travel the best sellers of their time?

Geared for the masses, popular literature in all its infinite variety—and American popular literature included such diverse types as travel books, tall tales of the Near and Far East and the American West, sea-lore adventures, popular journals and magazines, almanacs, dime or best-selling novels—mirrors the intellectual complex of an age, reflecting its ideas, activities, and motivations to action; in short, it sums up its culture. It also reveals the "cultural dialects" which may exist side by side in the writings of representative men in any given period, and which may appear, especially if divested of their historical and intellectual contexts, as puzzling or paradoxical. Arthur E. Christy aptly described popular literature as the "weathercock which points the direction of all winds of opinion that blow."[10] An understanding of these "winds of opinion" is essential in comprehending the *raison d'etre* of the bulk and popularity of books of travel in the nineteenth century. It was the remarkable increase in the number of travel books as the century progressed that prompted James Grant Wilson to note in 1886 that "American books of Old World travel" were appearing in "battalions."[11] Stanley Williams pointed out the necessity of tracing the real roots of this pehnomenal growth and popularity of travel books, which rivaled those of history and fiction, when he observed:

To ascribe the increase of travel books, expanding from a rivulet at the beginning of the century to a gigantic river at its close, to the growing number of travelers and these to the enlarged facilities of transportation is too simple a logic.[12]

The not too simple logic behind the phenomenal growth and popularity of travel books could be traced to two seemingly opposed traits in the American temperament, which were markedly reflected in the American literary scene. The one was the conscious need for a past with its established values, institutional continuity, and stable traditions. The other was a similarly strong conscious need for national identity and the establishment of the definable American "Self," the creation of the "New Adam" entirely based on the exclusively American vistas of democratic experience. The pull of the past and the push of the present formed the nucleus of this double consciousness, and most travel books of the nineteenth century did indeed embody it.

Culturally, America was still an unhistorical land, a land which had neither a childhood replete with romantically lovable experiences nor a youth confirmed in exemplary patterns. The short historical past that the Americans possessed was not yet crystallized in terms of popular "traditions" or "myths," which are needed psychologically for man's sense of stability. A large number of Americans who were entering upon the life of the mind for the first time during the first half of the nineteenth century had a strong romantic bent. This bent expressed itself in a serious interest in the past, in faraway places, and in the vast treasures of knowledge that they contained. The strong obsession with the past was partially, yet vehemently, stirred by the public's acute consciousness of the wide chasm that separated it from old stable traditions. A large segment of the new reading public was aware of what it lacked and also was concerned about the danger of both intellectual and cultural insularity that 3,000 miles of ocean could lead to.[13] The measure of the awareness and concern of this new class evinced itself in the response of the literary figures. American men of letters were obliged to satisfy the needs of increasing millions of new readers. Lacking a past, the literary figures in the United States had to look to the other side of the Atlantic and more often than not cross the Atlantic itself in their endeavor to meet their obligations. Inevitably, the development and growth of an indigenous literature were hampered in proportion to the success of the literary figures in their attempts to satisfy these needs; for the outcome was largely a derivative literature.

The strong need for national identity and the desire to trace and establish an identifiable American "Self" was the other facet of this double consciousness. It had its roots in the political experiment of the new nation, which demanded a break with the past and an assertion of the sovereignty of the present. Such sentiment was forcibly conveyed in the declamation of the *Democratic Review* in 1839: "Our national birth was the beginning of a new history...which separates us from the past and connects us with the future only."[14] Declamations like this had their repercussions in the literary scene; and as R.W.B. Lewis has pointed out, such "a manifesto of liberation from the past" meant a more vigorous demand "for an independent literature to communicate the novelty of experience in the New World."[15]

Furthermore, since the beginning of the century, the question of a native literature was constantly confused with the issue of patriotism; and patriotism was rampant in a nation that had won its political independence only a few decades earlier, and whose viability was further tested in the War of 1812. In the eighteen twenties and early thirties the British reviews, the *Quarterly* and *Blackwood's*, carried on a campaign of invective in which they "decried and insulted America as a barbarous land," intending, as Van Wyck Brooks remarked, to "discourage emigration and arouse a republicanism in the rising English masses."[16] Accounts written by English travelers who visited America in the eighteen thirties and forties contributed to igniting the patriotic zeal of Americans, for a goodly number of these accounts depicted the new nation as uncouth and vulgar. Americans were hypersensitive to criticisms leveled against them in such books as Mrs. Frances Trollope's *Domestic Manners of the Americans* (1832), Harriet Martineau's *Society in America* (1837), Captain Marryat's *A Diary in America* (1837), and, the unkindest of them all, Charles Dickens' *American Notes* (1842). These and various other accounts of travelers nurtured what Washington Irving termed "the literary animosity daily growing up between

England and America." To him, as to most of his contemporaries, these accounts seemed "intended to diffuse error rather than knowledge."[17] Such unfair treatment of the new nation by the British reviews and travelers confirmed patriotic Americans in their detestation of the imitative quality of their literature, and in their rejection of what they regarded as toadying to the Old World, and especially to England.

But despite Emerson's teachings, particularly in "The American Scholar," and the zeal of such representative Americans as Bryant, Thoreau and Whitman, most men of letters persisted in relying on European ideas, literary traditions and intellectual habits as sources of inspiration.[18] They realized that the total American experience had no rich local accumulation of character, legend or lore, sufficient to ignite originality or sustain the creative imagination. To be sure, such figures as Irving, Cooper and Hawthorne were indubitably successful in their determination to grasp the "usable truth" defined by F.L. Matthiessen as "the actual meaning of civilization as it had existed in America";[19] yet they were nonetheless aware of the scantiness of native sources and frequently voiced their concern.[20]

Nineteenth-century authors' awareness of the lack in America of what Henry James called "the items of high civilization"[21] was rendered much more acute by their sense of obligation to satisfy the need of the growing reading public for knowledge and for a romantic past with all its traditions. Since the past could not be invented, most of the authors persisted in facing eastward, in borrowing and recreating. Similarly, since "items of civilization" could not be imported, most men of letters crossed the Atlantic to plunder the riches of old-world cultures.

Almost all of the well-known American authors of the nineteenth century traveled extensively: Irving, Bryant, Cooper, Hawthorne, Dana, Melville, Emerson, Longfellow, Howells, DeForest, Lowell, Mark Twain, Bret Harte, Henry Adams, James, Crane—and this is only a partial list of major writers. It does not include authors who were well known and influential during their lifetime but who are regarded now as minor: N.P. Willis, John Lloyd Stephens, George William Curtis, Bayard

Taylor, Charles Dudley Warner, Charles Warren Stoddard—to mention only a few. As travelers they were all in a sense pilgrims on a quest—a quest for both knowledge and experience.

However, there was the other facet of the double consciousness that characterized the American temperament throughout the century, namely, the patriotic, the conscious need for national identity and the assertion of the rising American "Self," which paradoxically enough regarded dependence on Europe and the Old World as sycophantic and unpatriotic, and demanded dispensing with the past and all that it connoted. The American men of letters found themselves caught in a dilemma. On the intellectual and literary level the dilemma emanated from this double consciousness could not be resolved. Despite the growing utilization of native materials, literary traditions and forms remained largely foreign. It was on the popular level and most notably in the multifarious forms of the travel book that the American author was able to resolve the dilemma. No other literary genre was as successful as the travel book in providing the author with a medium by means of which he could fulfill some of his literary and personal aspirations, and, most importantly, the conflicting demands of this double consciousness.

Written chiefly for those who, in Bayard Taylor's words, "can only travel by their fireside"[22]—and most Americans, especially in the years before and during the Civil War, were unable to enjoy the pleasure of foreign travel—the travel book, in its fluid, undefined shape enabled its author to give the growing reading masses what they needed, when they needed it. Everything that was old enchanted Americans. They shared this romantic bent with their European counterparts of the first half of the nineteenth century; yet the enchantment of Americans was more poignant and lasted longer because their country was all so new. They cherished the relics of the European past, the memories and culture of their "Old Home."[23] The newness of their country was an underlying factor in the persistence, almost permanence, of an important ingredient of the romantic movement throughout the century, namely the craving for remoteness both in space and time. The hunger of the reading public for every crumb of knowledge about the lands of the oldest civilizations was

satisfied by the vicarious tours of these lands. To the average
American the words of the travelers who had beheld with their
own eyes the ancient sites of London, Paris, Rome,
Constantinople, the Holy Land or Cairo were more authentic
than the words of the poets, historians or translators which were
secondhand and remote. And as Willard Thorp has pointed out,
even amateur travelers "often returned home better instructed
than the scholars and critics whose profession it was to interpret
European civilization."[24]

The authentic element in books of foreign travel was largely
engendered from the desire to convey information and
communicate firsthand personal experiences and impressions.
This authenticity was further enhanced by the personal
approach employed by most travel writers in the retelling of their
experiences. The reader is almost always addressed in the second
person. He is often called upon to join the traveler in touring a
famous monument or exploring an ancient site. Nonetheless,
when carried to an extreme, this personal approach rendered the
travel writer more of a tourist guide in the modern sense of the
term; and his account can be legitimately described as not written
but told. Moreover, the emphasis on authenticity caused most of
these travel accounts to become anecdotal rather than analytical,
and hence not very demanding intellectually. They were easy
reading material for the new literate class. Dry information,
whether historical, geographical, cultural or statistical, was often
made alive and palatable by the inclusion of vignettes of native
exoticism. The fact that they conveyed information of various
kinds in an entertaining context gave travel books much
prominence and popularity in an age which was not only thirsty
for knowledge but intent on disseminating it.

Travel books also satisfied vicariously the general readers'
craving for the romantic associations of adventure. Some of the
actual experiences of the travelers were exaggerated in the
retelling to make them assume the dimensions of real adventure.
Even the sophisticated travelers who criticized this bent among
some of their predecessors and made fun of the anticipated
adventure that never came did not tone down accounts of
incidents involving encounters with danger. A touch of

adventure, factual or fanciful, gave the vicarious experience of
the general reader an added measure of charm.

Similarly, the reading public found in books of foreign travel
a gratification of their patriotic zeal, and an assertion of their
national identity. In spite of all the interest in the Old World and
its culture, many Americans still considered the vogue of foreign
travel unpatriotic. Traveling abroad was declared unhealthy for
all young men. It was even thought that travel corrupted them
and weakened their patriotism; that the experience of visiting or
staying in foreign countries made Americans worse instead of
better, for it led them not only to praise but to adopt some foreign
manners and habits. Washington Irving, for instance, was
frequently chided for his long sojourns abroad. Howells, in later
years, spoke contemptuously of those American romancers who
tried to be "little Londoners."[25] For this reason, many authors did
not spare the chance when it offered itself on the pages of their
accounts of travel to reveal to their readers the great value of
foreign travel to the American national character. They
constantly reassured their countrymen that their stay abroad
had increased their faith in their country, and strengthened
rather than weakened their patriotism and loyalty to America.[26]
They demonstrated that in addition to the acquisition of the
knowledge and culture which the Old World offered them—and
which were essential to the gradual education of the American
masses themselves—they were also able to gain new insights into
the traditions and institutions of the Old World. By contrasting
the traditions and institutions of the Old World societies with
those of the New, the travelers contributed significantly toward
fulfilling the need for national as well as cultural identity. They
exhibited and interpreted the American way, its republicanism
and the virtue of its free institutions in the light of European and
Eastern history. In this juxtaposition the readers were made to
perceive the intrinsic values of the democratic traditions of their
nation and the salutary effects they had on the ultimate
betterment and happiness of the individual. It was repeatedly
pointed out in books of foreign travel that if the Old World
excelled in the cultural and historical riches of the past, America
had a better present and certainly a more promising future.

The appeal to the patriotic and national impulses of the reading public was often sentimental and in some instances verged on the chauvinistic. The sight of the Stars and Stripes flying from the tallest of poles in some remote corner of the world was always declared to be a source of unexpected delight to the traveler. On learning that Bayard Taylor was ready to leave the town of Berber in the Sudan, the Governor sent word to him that he would bring a company of his soldiers down to the banks of the Nile and salute his flag; and, Taylor wrote,

Truly enough, when we were all embarked and I had given the Stars and Stripes of the Ethiopian winds, a company of about fifty soldiers ranged themselves on the high bank, and saluted the flag with a dozen rattling volleys.[27]

The flag was much more than a mere symbol in books of travel. There was always the satisfaction of identifying with it. Physically, its presence was an assertion of the eminent place the young nation occupied in the world community and an evidence that other peoples recognized and respected that place. Psychologically, the flag was a source of inner security; the American's sense of his personal value and importance was largely derived from his feeling of belonging to America, the favored land, rather than from an inner conviction of his worth as a well-rounded individual. He was acutely conscious of what he lacked: culture, experience, and cosmopolitanism—the qualities that his European counterparts possessed. He could not vie with them on those grounds. But by posing as a representative of America, which he believed to be morally and politically superior to the Old World, he could bolster his own ego and extract a deep sense of pride in his identity. Simultaneously, the loyalty of the traveler was assured; and the reader, by experiencing the vicarious thrill, could identify with the writer and share his feelings.

In the same patriotic vein, the travel book was frequently used as a weapon of retaliation. American authors found in books of travel a conveniently fitted platform for rebutting the criticisms and misrepresentations of European, especially

English, travelers in the United States. (Cooper's *Notions of the Americans* [1828] is a good case in point.) The virtue of American traditions and free institutions was reiterated vis-a-vis the current evils and injustice inherent in the European and Eastern societies. Patriotic Americans who were incensed by the condescending attitude of European and English observers read with great approbation the pages of the travel books that vindicated their country. Some American authors went so far as to give European and English travelers a taste of their own medicine. Usually assuming an air of superiority, they singled out and conspicuously framed the vulgarities of the European and English travelers, especially those who made claims to nobility, whom they encountered on neutral grounds—for example, in the Levant. With a streak of sarcastic glee, in *My Winter on the Nile* (1876) Charles Dudley Warner gibed:

I hear the natives complain that almost all the English men of rank who came to Egypt, beg, or shall we say accept? substantial favors of the Khedive. The nobility appear to have a new rendering of *noblesse oblige*. This is rather humiliating to us Americans, who are, after all, almost blood-relations of the English; and besides, we are often taken for *Inglese,* in villages where few strangers go.

Inwardly, readers must have revelled in sharing Warner's conscious snobbery, and relished the connotations of such words as "complain," "beg" and "substantial favors"; and the more so because these words were used in direct reference to English nobility—the standard-bearers of tradition with all their civilized embellishments—in an attempt to mark a low ebb in their values and codes of moral behavior. Self-righteously and with an added degree of pride, they must also have winced at being often branded in faraway lands as *"Inglese"* and thus suffering what they considered an undeserved humiliation.

Significantly then, the travel book gave the growing reading masses all they needed when they needed it. The two poles of nineteenth-century American temperament, the conscious need of the public for knowledge, specifically that of its ancestral heritage and of the stable traditions and institutions of old civilizations, and its conscious need for national identity, inspiring confidence and pride in being American, were reconciled in books of foreign travel. Knowledge of European and Eastern civilizations was disseminated in America to satisfy the insatiable appetite of the reading public. Yet the travelers never portrayed the Old World as the exemplary or redeemed society to the American Man. This Old World was seen and criticized from a peculiarly American point of view. Furthermore, by seeing in juxtaposition the structures and textures of both the Old and the New societies, the American reader was able to perceive the intrinsic value and virtues of the democratic traditions and free institutions of his society. This was ultimately the logic behind the phenomenal growth and popularity of travel books in the nineteenth century. They were triumphantly American, written by Americans exclusively for Americans.

Notes

[1] *The Literary History of the United States,* third revised edition, ed. Robert E. Spiller, Willard Thorp, Thomas H. Johnson and Henry S. Canby (New York: The Macmillan Co., 1963), III, 356. Johnson's list of the American writers who traveled abroad and "whose works have literary merit" is incomplete. It is beyond the scope of this article to list all books of travel or books based on travel experience that were written by the literary figures of the nineteenth century. For such a list to be adequately complete it should begin with Washington Irving and end with Henry James, and should embrace almost every major writer of the century. However, for the sake of emphasis we should mention that the "international novel," exemplified in Hawthorne's *The Marble Faun* (1860) and later perfected by Henry James in his novels that deal with Americans abroad and the confrontation between the Old and New, is an important offshoot of travel literature.

[2] The word "culture" is used here to mean, according to Webster's *Third New International Dictionary,* the act of developing the intellectual and moral faculties especially by education. This was largely what the word "culture" meant to the nineteenth-century reading public.

[3] Why books of foreign travel were particularly successful and needed little publicity campaigning on the part of the publishers will be shown later in some detail. For an excellent discussion of the tradition of puffing in the mid-nineteenth century see *The Profession of Authorship in America, 1800-1870: The Papers of William Charvat,* ed. Matthew J. Bruccoli (Columbus: Ohio State University Press, 1968), particularly chapter ten, "James T. Fields and the beginning of Book

Promotion, 1840-1855." Hereafter cited as *The Papers of William Charvat.*

[4]Albert H. Smyth, *Bayard Taylor,* American Men of Letters (Boston and New York: Houghton, Mifflin & Co., 1896), p. 51.

[5]Richard C. Beatty, *Bayard Taylor, Laureate of the Gilded Age* (Norman: University of Oklahoma Press, 1936), p. 180.

[6]Edward Cary, *George William Curtis,* American Men of Letters (Boston and New York: Houghton, Mifflin & Co., 1894), pp. 59-60.

[7]*The Papers of William Charvat,* pp. 240-241.

[8]James D. Hart, *The Popular Book: A History of America's Literary Taste* (Berkeley: University of California Press, 1963), p. 147. In 1869 one edition often contained over 20,000 copies as contrasted to smaller editions of 3,000 or so each, more than a decade earlier. The increase in number of copies in each edition should be considered here also as indicative of the concomitant increase in the number of the reading public.

[9]*The Papers of Willliam Charvat,* p. 306. Taylor's dashing figure was partly responsible for his popularity as a lecturer. He was given to a certain degree of exhibitionism and frequently appeared on the podium in Arab garb. In contrast, Melville, who also delivered some lectures based on his travels, was not an exciting figure. He was considered a dull lecturer.

[10]*The Asian Legacy and American Life,* ed. Arthur E. Christy (New York: The John Day Co., 1945), p. 51.

[11]James G. Wilson, *Bryant and His Friends: Some Reminiscences of the Knickerbocker Writers* (New York: Fords, Howards, & Hulbert, 1886), p. 235.

[12]Stanley T. Williams, *The Spanish Background of American Literature* (New Haven: Yale University Press, 1955), I, 51.

[13]This national trait is evinced in the overwhelming desire of many European immigrants, once they are comfortably established in the United States, to return to the old continent as American tourists.

[14]Quoted in R.W.B. Lewis, *The American Adam: Innocence, Tragedy, and Tradition in the Nineteenth Century* (Chicago: The University of Chicago Press, 1965), p. 5.

[15] Ibid., p. 20.

[16]Van Wyck Brooks, *The World of Washington Irving* (Philadelphia: The Blakiston Co., 1945), pp. 248-249.

[17]Washington Irving, *The Sketch Book* (Philadelphia: David McKay, Publishers, 1893), p. 62.

[18]For the battle of words that raged on the New York literary stage "in the era of Poe and Melville" between those who advocated the importance of the past and of continuity and those who preached the gospel of national identity and the sovereignty of the present, see Perry Miller, *The Raven and the Whale* (New York: Harcourt, Brace & World, Inc., 1956).

[19]F.O. Matthiessen, *American Renaissance* (New York: Oxford University Press, 1964), p. 235.

[220]Cooper complained of what he called "the baldness of American life" in *Notions of the Americans Picked Up By a Travelling Bachelor* (New York, 1863),

II, 108. Irving who, like Cooper and Hawthorne, did his share in creating an American *mythus,* wrote on August 1, 1841, to his niece, Sarah Storrow, then in Paris: "Good Lord, deliver me from the all pervading commonplace which is the curse of our country," (quoted in *The American Writer and the European Tradition,* ed. Margaret Denny and William Gilman [New York: McGraw & Hill Book Co., 1964], p. 45).

[21] Henry James, *Hawthorne* (New York: Doubleday and Co., 1879), p. 43.

[22] Bayard Taylor, *The Land of the Saracens; or, Pictures of Palestine, Asia Minor, Sicily and Spain* (New York: G.P. Putnam & Co., 1856), p. vi.

[23] Until recently Americans made little effort to preserve their old cultural shrines as objects of veneration belonging to times past. If America is not privileged enough to have a Stratford-on-Avon, it still has a Concord; if it does not have "Abbotsford" or "Dryburgh Abbey," it has "Sunnyside," and "Idlewild." Therefore, how important it would have been for the cultural history and heritage of America if a native or a foreign visitor had been able to tour the house where Melville lived on Market Street in Albany, N.Y! That is but one example, and is as culturally and historically valuable as sites of Battlefields, Forts and old Warships! No small wonder that some Americans feel that they have no alternative other than to worship at the cultural shrines of the Old World.

[24] Willard Thorp, "Pilgrims' Return," in *Literary History of the United States,* ed. Robert E. Spiller, *et. al.* revised edition in one volume (New York: The Macmillan Co., 1955), p. 830.

[25] *Literary History of the United States,* p.621.

[26] From Frankfort Bayard Taylor wrote his relative Hannah M. Taylor: "The more we see of other lands the more we love our own." In another letter to the same relative he wrote: "I must say that with us (he was traveling with his cousin), as with all Americans who go abroad, everyday but proves that the free States are far, far beyond any other nation in the world, though it is foolish to suppose we can learn nothing from others." (*The Unpublished Letters of Bayard Taylor,* ed. John R. Schultz, *The Huntington Library Publications* [San Marino, California, 1937], pp. 9-11).

[27] Bayard Taylor, *A Journey to Central Africa; or, Life and Landscapes from Egypt to the Negro Kingdoms of the White Nile* (New York: G.P. Putnam & Sons, 1866), p. 218.

[28] Charles Dudley Warner, *My Winter on the Nile* (Boston: Houghton, Mifflin Co., 1904), pp. 389-390. *Inglese* (Ingliz) is the Arabic word (pl.) for British. It was used by the populace generally to refer to foreigners who spoke English.

Originally published in *Exploration,* IV:1, December 1976. Reprinted with the permission of the editor and the author.

The Traveller as Antihero :
Richard Smith Elliott in the Mexican War

Nicholas T. Joost

Six years ago, in a long essay on Keemle and Fields's newspaper the St. Louis *Weekly Reveille,* I wrote about a young Pennsylvania lawyer named Richard Smith Elliott and his part in the war between Mexico and the United States of America. My purpose here is not so much to recapitulate what was said six years ago but to expand those remarks with a brief sketch of Elliott's character as a traveler through regions then as exotic and dangerous as they were little known

Fortunately Elliott wrote a memoir, *Notes Taken in Sixty Years,* which he published himself in 1883 in St. Louis, and which usefully supplements his letters and other writings in the *Reveille.* Thus we learn that he was born in Lewistown, Pennsylvania, on 10 July 1817, that like millions of other Americans young Elliott started for the West at the age of twenty, "going to Texas" to join the "Texian campaign," that he abandoned that scheme in Louisville, where he briefly essayed acting and dutifully repaid his enlistment fee of six dollars, and that he returned home to Pennsylvania, where he helped run once again his father's rural paper and engaged himself as a "jour. printer" and then as an editor to sundry employers. Elliott married a local girl in 1838 and read for and was admitted to the bar. Also he dabbled in Whig party politics with the result that he received through the help of President John Tyler, early in 1843, from his "old friend, Mr. Potts, chief clerk of the Indian Bureau...'a little sub-agency' at Council Bluffs, $750 Salary." Mr. Potts kindly explained the difference between an agency and a subagency: the latter was an "agency except in title, salary, and mode of appointment. Same duties as those of an Agent, who gets $1,500. The Council Bluffs sub-agency is east of the Missouri river, and disburses over $40,000 a year. The bond is $20,000. The Secretary of War appoints the sub-agents—the President appoints the agents." Because the prospective subagency might lead to something, Elliott decided, for the second time, to go West:

"I had a vague idea that something might come of it."

There proved to be several things. Because he was in law, Elliott dabbled in politics, for which he had little heart, however; but by an osmotic process, because he was in politics, he became interested in the future of the American railroad system, then just entering its golden age of expansion and rapacity. And since he was interested in the railroads and the law and politics, Elliott became interested in land speculation, and where else but in the West? As early as 1838, he dabbled—the *Notes* become imprecise here—in the building of a "continuous railroad to the city of St. Louis," from Pennsylvania.

When he went West in 1843, St.Louis was still the center of the American fur trade and accordingly was the major entrepot for that great enterprise as well as the American-Mexican trade across the Sante Fe trail and on to Chihuahua; St. Louis merchants also took the lead in outfitting emigrants then beginning to settle the lands west of the Mississippi. Eventually Elliot would settle in St. Louis; the title page of his *Notes* would describe him as "Richard Smith Elliott of St. Louis, Missouri, U.S.A."

When he first arrived in St. Louis on 13 May 1843, Elliott found himself in a city of "probably 25,000 people," which had been, he avers, a town of merely 2,000 in 1822. Elliott did not tarry, apparently. He took his younger brother Joe with him and they walked and rode to what is now Council Bluffs, Iowa, to attend to the affairs of the Indian subagency and to raise corn on a plot where the brothers built of cottonwood logs the first house ever erected in the city of Council Bluffs by a white man not connected with Indians (p. 171). For 1843 and 1844, the reader of Elliott's *Notes* must work his way through some addled chronology: Elliott now has an infant son; back in St. Louis, Judge Bryan Mullanphy grants him a license to practice law after a few casually put questions; the three Elliotts journey *en famille* to the farm and subagency at Council Bluffs; Mrs. Elliott and "little John D." go back to Pennsylvania, whence she returns with John D. and "his wee sister," plus an aunt, this event occurring not until the spring of 1845.

During the months that he lived alone in his log cabin,

Elliott's "greatest enjoyment was vocal and instrumental music," and he began to read—at any rate, as regularly as the frontier mails permitted—the St. Louis *Weekly Reveille*. In return, the *Reveille* printed his first contribution in its issue for 12 August 1844. We now have a second source for getting to know Richard Smith Elliott. The grandfather of 1883, the white-haired and full-bearded old gentleman peering wistfully into the unimaginable distances of 1976, whose memory of the past is precise for one occasion and vague for another, contrasts to the ebullient young frontiersman, with his gift for doggerel and playacting and for the casual, easygoing cameraderie of the great western waters.

Elliott's first contribution to the *Reveille* was a letter that he signed as "John Brown"; the pseudonym was a common device of the day, whether in journalism or in less ephemeral writing. The *Reveille* was also a vehicle for the new American humor of the frontier, and "John Brown" was an exponent of that humor. Under the title of "What's in a Name?" "John Brown" wrote that

At the present writing, I have not seen *The Reveille*. I may never see it. I am only mortal, like its editors (the paper, too, perhaps!) and may die, as others have done. But I am assured by good authority, that *The Reveille* is seen and felt every morning, Sundays not excepted, by the good people of St. Louis, and that its rub-a-dubs are directed by good *Field* officers. Seen and felt! *Reveille!* But there's no telling what will come next, as the old lady said when told of the new way to hatch eggs by steam. "Dear me," says she, 'I suppose the next thing"—and here she muttered something— "but for my part, I would prefer the old way!"

"John Brown" added a postscript to the effect that if editors thought his letter worth a place in their columns—"your name is so military that I can't keep war-like thoughts down"—they should "place it among the *rank* and *file*. Just *say* if you please, it is very humorous and good, or your readers may not discover its merits." Elliott's writing for the *Reveille* is characterized largely by the quizzical, pawky tone of that first letter, whether in the verse he published in the paper—with which I am not concerned here—or in his travel letters and news dispatches.

For Elliott, 1845 was largely taken up with various negotiations in Washington, for the Potawatomies, and he was away from Council Bluffs and St. Louis part of the year. He continued, nevertheless, to report back to the paper, whether an account of his activity as subagent for the Otoes, Pawnees, and Potawatomies or an entry from his "Hibernian Log-Book—A Trip to Galena."

Early in 1846, Elliott left his subagency and moved himself and his family to St. Louis, where he set himself up as an attorney-at-law, in an office on the second floor of a building opposite what he called the "old Court House." Shortly thereafter, however, his legal career ended for the duration of the war with Mexico. During May and June of 1846, after President Polk declared war on Mexico, the "decisive call on Missouri" came, and, as Elliott remarked ironically in his *Notes,* "the air was full of patriotism." Another St. Louis attorney, Thomas B. Hudson, began to organize a company, with Elliott acting as first lieutenant. The hundred men of the company rapidly enlisted, as cavalry soldiers, calling themselves the "Laclede Rangers." The Laclede Rangers formed part of the Regiment of Missouri Mounted Volunteers in June 1846 and elected William Alexander Doniphan as their Colonel. Unofficially but vitally for our topic, Elliott was their most important reporter; there were other men in Doniphan's regiment who wrote accounts for the *Reveille* as well as other newspapers printed in St. Louis; Elliott, however, is by all odds the most important reporter of the group, sending back upwards of seventy dispatches printed in the *Reveille* between June 1846 and July 1847, when he returned to St. Louis at the disbanding of the Regiment of Mounted Volunteers.

As I have mentioned elsewhere in some detail these dispatches by Elliott that were printed in the *Reveille,* I need not dwell here on their content. What is of further interest is that Elliott's *Notes* contain a complementary account of his experience as a horse soldier in 1846 and 1847. The obvious value of the dispatches is their freshness, their immediacy, their careful regard for fact, and their omission of jingoist propaganda. The value of Elliott's complementary account in Chapters 32 through 37 (pp.214-257) of his *Notes* lies in their being a retrospective

account, a story matured and composed and mulled over for many
years. These chapters are the most vivid pages of an uncommonly
entertaining and kindhearted autobiography. They show,
morever, how sharply one's youthful enthusiasms may differ
from one's elderly qualifications regarding the very experience
about which as a young man he had been so enthusiastic.

That the war with Mexico was a bitterly divisive war—as
indeed have been the majority of the conflicts our nation has
waged—remains part of the historical record. Every student of
American culture recalls the energy with which such men as
Emerson and Thoreau inveighed against what they regarded as
the enormity of our collective action. But what most of us fail to
recall is that, by and large, divisive though the war may have
been, it was one of our more popular wars. Emerson and Thoreau
were disgruntled intellectuals. The slave-owning group that still
dominated the Congress, adventurers on the make, such as
Fremont, his father-in-law Senator Benton, the incumbent
president, Polk, bankers, railroad magnates, manufacturing
interests outside Massachusetts (which has traditionally been
isolationist)—all these were in an expansionist mood, and they
carried the great mass of Americans with them. The youthful
Richard Smith Elliott cheerfully allowed himself to be carried
along, too. After all, he helped organize a company of cavalry, all
of them volunteers.

The elderly Richard Smith Elliott held rather different
opinions regarding that youthful experience riding through the
deserts and mountains of the Southwest. He admits as much in
his *Notes*:

Not the least animosity had I felt towards the Mexicans, nor did I
wish to kill anybody; but as the war seemed to be taking so much of the
Government's attention . . . and as, by volunteering I would acquire a sort
of right to talk against war in the future—I had decided that I might as
well be one of the 'Army of the West,' which I had a notion would be
recalled before we should get half way to Sante Fe. The narrow strip of
country between the Nueces and the Rio Grande, which Texas had only
conquered constructively, did not appear to be worth fighting for; and I
supposed the Governmeent would occupy it with large armies, and then
negotiate, as the cheapest way of acquiring title. I even imagined the St.

Louis Legion marching up and down along the Rio Grande, scaring away any Mexican troops that might want to come over.

But President Polk, who declared in his message that war existed 'by the act of Mexico,' had views differing from mine, as I had not risen above plain common sense, and he had got up to statesmanship. The upshot was, that before the dispute was settled, millions on millions of wealth were wasted, thousands of good lives were sacrificed, unutterable distress brought to many homes, and a crop of veterans left to solicit in vain for pensions. Mr. Polk's policy, thanks to the soldiers, added to the national domain nearly all of what are now Colorado, Utah, New Mexico, Arizona, and California. We took them as 'indemnity for the past and security for the future'; and then, in the Gadsden Purchase, we bought a strip to straighten our southern boundary, just as we might have bought the land between the Nueces and Rio Grande, and had no war at all. But the general sentiment was, that the Mexicans were a half-barbarous set anyway, and had no business to send their greasy and ragged soldiers over the Rio Grande, into a territory always owned by them but constructively conquered by the Texans, who were the advanced guard of our superior civilization; and we taught the successors of Montezuma the infallible maxim that justice and right are always on the side of the strongest armies. Abraham Lincoln, Thomas Corwin, and a few others in Congress regarded the war as cruel and unjust, but once begun it had to go on.

I find this passage (p. 218) a curious mixture of disingenuity and sincere feeling. There is an unpleasant cynicism about the admission that "by vounteering I would acquire a sort of right to talk against war in the future"—and it simply does not square with Elliott's known course of action at the time, as we learn of it from his dispatches in the *Reveille* as well as from the *Notes* themselves. Missouri at the time of the war with Mexico was at least nominally one of the "Southern" states dominated by the slave-owners and their representatives. Missouri, in addition, was one of the states that were strongly in favor of westward expansion; many of the so-called "Texans"—an identity appropriated by the Americans of dominantly Anglo-Saxon culture (ironically, many of them were Celtic in their origins) who settled in Texas early in the nineteenth century—had migrated from Missouri. Richard Smith Elliott went along with the tide of public opinion and in fact even helped to channel it in a particular direction.

Both Elliott's dispatches and his *Notes* emphasize certain aspects of the war peculiar to New Mexico. Curiously, he does not emphasize the remarkable nature of Doniphan's expedition as half travel, half exploration. Rather, Elliott discusses at length the turning over of New Mexico and its capital of Santa Fe to the Americans and the consequent intrusion and dominance of novel concepts of law, governance, and social conduct. He has many an anecdote illustrating local Latin-American manners and working habits, and it is pleasant to note that Elliott seems not to have had in his make-up the racial snobbery that still characterizes the North American relationship with Latin America. It is true, however, that Elliott commented often and invariably unfavorably on the technology of the Mexican inhabitants of the newly conquered territory, as when he alluded in passing to "the miserable little axes now used by the Mexicans, which resemble in shape and size the wedges used by our farmers for splitting rails." His relations to several New Mexican families, on the other hand, were of a socially friendly nature, and he describes with evident approval how the officers of the occupying force regularly attended the nightly *fandangos* or dances, some of them accompanied by local *senoritas*.

The occupation of Santa Fe had been bloodless, but relations with both the Navajos and the Pueblo Indians (i.e., those Indians dwelling in their own villages) were eventful. At length a treaty with the Navajos was concluded, but the Indians of one of the villages in the valley of Taos began rioting over the jailing of three of their number who were "notorious thieves" (p.247), and several Americans were massacred, including the territorial governor, Bent. In the spring of 1847, matters came to a head because of the many outrages "committed by Indians on the plains, and even on the borders of New Mexico" (p. 251). Elliott was one of a force of seventy-five men sent out "to hunt Indians, and if possible recover stolen animals" (p. 252). At one point the Indians cleverly ambushed the soldiers in a deep canyon of the Canadian River. In an engagement lasting four or five hours, several men were wounded and one "man from Callaway

County" was killed—as Elliott wrote in italics: *"The Indians were charging after us."* At nightfall the Americans dispiritedly bivouacked and reached their camp the next day. Their haversacks of provisions and some other property had been lost in the melee, and even though reinforcements arrived, with a small howitzer, the nine officers leading the group decided to hold "a council of war on a proposal to go back to the canyon." The passage here is one of the most revealing in Elliott's *Notes*:

...four ayes and five noes. I voted no. We had neither provisions nor ammunition to continue the campaign. Besides, I had been in the canyon, and, on reflection, did not like it. I did not want to hear any more bullets singing. It was afterwards ascertained that the Indians had left the same night and gone a long march in another direction. They had greatly outnumbered us, and their loss was estimated at forty killed.

The most wonderful thing to me in the fight was, the entire absence of fear. In crossing the creek, a possible bullet in my back suggested the thought, that after my body should be found people might impugn my courage; but there was no other dread of that possible bullet. But at the council next day the scare that I ought naturally to have felt in the fight came on, and I was not at all sorry that with over two hundred men, no provisions, and no ammunition, my negative vote was a matter of duty as well as inclination. I have never been in a fight since, but have held bravery during battle in low estimation. If a man with a big bump of caution could be as cool and self-possessed as I was during our Indian fight, those with little bumps may easily be heroes. To deliberately go into battle requires courage; but once in, excitement seems to swallow up fear.

And with that comment Elliott proceeds abruptly to the sentence in which he tells his readers that he and the Rangers in his command were honorably discharged from the service of the United States and "on 13th June we started for 'home'." Despite a couple of alarms, the return journey was peaceful, even though the Santa Fe trail, Elliott reports, was always dangerous for travelers until "private capital had put a railroad in the Arkansas Valley! It seemed that there never was capacity in the government to deal with the wild Indian question" (p. 255).

So, as Elliott tells us, he "quietly subsided to private life." It is a remarkable story, whether read in *Notes Taken in Sixty Years* or in the discontinuous dispatches printed in the St. Louis *Weekly Reveille*. Not the least remarkable aspect is its having been lived and recounted by a man who explicitly considered himself an antihero. Here is a man who volunteered to go on one of the most reckless adventures in American military history, a feat that, as Senator Benton first told Doniphan himself, exceeded that of the Ten Thousand; yet when Elliott could have been elected Major in the Regiment of Missouri Mounted Volunteers,he decided to stand and in 1883 was still moaning, "The bump of 'Caution' lost me the rank of Major" (P.221). Elliott deliberately adopted the nearly anonymous name and attitude of "John Brown," the pawky frontiersman, in an age of gaudy flamboyance and grandiloquent oration. In Santa Fe he became so ill that he nearly died and his attending physician saved his life, says Elliott, only by giving him a massive dose of sixty grains of calomel. He had hoped to go with the body of Doniphan's regiment to take part in the major battles down in Mexico, and to report them back to the *Reveille*; instead he was relegated by his illness to the life of a soldier in an army of occupation. Gambling at *monte* alternated with evenings of quadrilles and waltzes. His one brush with violent death seems to have been rather disappointing, for the experience taught him to "hold bravery during battle in low estimation." The mystery to me is why this remarkable man firmly resolved to relate his life, both in youth and in age, in terms of the antihero "John Brown" with the bump of caution, cracking his mild jokes in the mildest of tones. It is as though a John Wayne Western thriller were being filmed in tones of grey and mauve!

Science in the Exploration Narratives Authored by U.S. Naval Officers

V. Ponko, Jr.

At the end of the nineteenth century there were few areas of the world yet to be explored. Humboldt had completed his travels in South America and, in North America, Mackenzie had journeyed from the St. Lawrence River to the Pacific coast. In Africa, Mungo Park had gotten to the Niger River while Bruce returned to the sources of the Blue Nile. Further east, the modern exploration of Arabia had begun with the work of Niebuhr and the foundations of the Indian surveys had been established by Rennel. In Australia, the nineteenth century witnessed the first settlements and the first inaland exploration expeditions; in the latter part of the century, exploration was particularly vigorous in Central Asia, Central Africa, Central Australia, the East Indies, New Guinea and the Arctic. Although it was not until the twentieth century that such prized objectives as the North Pole and the South Pole were reached, it is reasonable to agree with J.N.L. Baker that the nineteenth century had left relatively little in the way of discovery for the twentieth century to accomplish.[1]

In this work of filling in the last unknowns, the navies and naval officers of many nations were active participants. The Navy of the United States, for instance, in the years before the Civil War, conducted major exploring expeditions in at least eleven, sometimes overlapping but yet distinct, areas of the world. These forays were purposely planned and aimed not only at surveying, charting and, in general, increasing the world's geographical knowledge, but also at the advancement of other aspects of scientific inquiry and discovery. After the Civil War, the intensity and scope of the Navy's role in exploration was not as great, but it did not die. Officers of the U.S. Navy, for example, explored South America, Africa, the Arctic and other areas of the globe.

In addition to the reports, charts, maps and other items such as natural history specimens which were deposited with various governmental agencies, this activity also resulted in the production of books through which the exploits of the explorers and the results of their expeditions became known to the general public.

Science, both in relation to its general meaning of knowledge gained by study, as well as in its more restricted connotation as knowledge acquired by the study of natural and technical matters, constitutes an integral part of these presentations. In them scientific inquiry and the results of such investigations range from the study of music in the Samoas to the dissection of the ocean floor; from the examination of Penguin habits in the Antarctic to the life of whales in the Arctic. The areas and topics studied are broad and, one is tempted to say, almost all encompassing.

To substantiate this assertion one need only read such works of general circulation as Herndon, William Lewis, and Gibbon, Lardner, *Exploration of the Valley of the Amazon, Made Under Direction of the Navy Department* 2 vols (1854); Kane, Elisha Kent, *The U.S. Grinnell Expedition in Search of Sir John Franklin, A Personal Narrative* (1853) and *Arctic Explorations; The Second Grinnell Expedition in Search of Sir John Franklin in 1853, '54, and '55* 2 vols (1856); Lynch, William F. *Narrative of the United States Expedition to the River Jordan and the Dead Sea* (1849); Page,Thomas J. *La Plata, The Argentine Confederation and Paraguay* (1859); Wilkes, Charles, *Narrative of the United States Exploring Expedition During the Years 1838, 1839, 1840, 1841, 1842,* 5 vols (1845).[2]

Agreeing that the books noted above contain words about science vital to their purpose and structure is not, however, the point at which one should leave any discussion about science in the exploration narratives authored by United States Naval Officers. One might, for instance, ask how these officers evaluated science as an activity in their narratives, what sort of style they used in writing it, and how they viewed the knowledge gained through their efforts in relation to the climate of opinion in their eras. However, I am not a literary critic and I do not want to venture into the field of literary criticism under false colors. Neither do I intend to give a full assessment of the scientific achievements of these expeditions about which these naval officers wrote.[3] I think it worthy of note that the narratives under consideration were tales not only of heroic individual and team efforts at survival and recognition from a personal point of view, but also of heroic endeavors for the advancement of science in an impersonal way made all the more detached by deft touches of humor. These works associate knowledge and seekers of knowledge, i.e., science and scientists, as worthy of being considered heroic not only in terms of a particular problem, but also in a manner speaking of an eternal and universal justification independent of the local situation being described. As an example one might cite the following passages from Elisha Kent Kane's *Arctic Exploration in the Years 1853, 1854, 1855* on the subject of gathering magnetic data in the far north:

March 7, Tuesday.—I have said very little in this business journal about our daily Arctic life. I have had no time to draw pictures.

But we have some trials which might make up a day's adventures. Our Arctic observatory is cold beyond any of its class, Kesan, Pulkowa, Toronto, or even its shifting predecessors, Bossetop and Melville Island. Imagine it a term-day, a magnetic term-day.

The observer, if he were only at home, would be the "observed of all observers." He is clad in a pair of seal-skin pants, a dog-skin cap, a reindeer jumper, and walrus boots. He sits upon a box that once held a transit instrument. A stove, glowing with at least a bucketful of anthracite, represents pictorially a heating apparatus, and reduces the thermometer as near as may be to ten degrees below zero. One hand holds a chronometer, and is left bare to warm it; the other luxuriates in a fox-skin mitten. The right hand and the left take it "watch and watch about." As one burns with cold, the chronometer shifts to the other, and the mitten takes its place.

Perched on a pedestal of frozen gravel is a magnetometer; stretching out from it, a telescope: and, bending down to this, an abject human eye. Every six minutes, said eye takes cognizance of a finely-divided arc, and notes the result in a cold memorandum-book.This process continues for twenty-four hours, two sets of eyes taking it by turns; and, when twenty-four hours are over, term-day is over too.

We have such frolics every week. I have just been relieved from one, and after a few hours am to be called out of bed in the night to watch and dot again. I have been engaged in this way when the thermomenter gave 20 degrees above zero at the instrument, 20 degrees below at two feet above the floor, and 43 degrees below at the floor itself: on my person, away from the stove, 10 degrees above zero. "A grateful country" will of course appreciate the value of these labors, and, as it cons over hereafter the four hundred and eighty results which go to make up our record for each week, will never think of asking, "*Cui bono* all this?"

But this is no adventure. The adventure is the travel to and fro. We have night *now* only half the time; and half the time can go and come with eyes to help us. It was not so a little while since.[4]

In this passage the uncomfortableness of the local situation, the surmounting of which is heroic in itself, acts as the foil to the depiction of a process which, for all its aggravations, is given as one to be followed as a matter of course. Here science is depicted as exacting but heroic in relation to its demands; the person gathering the data suborinates his comforts to a large universal purpose and, in this respect, is a hero.

This presentation of science as a process independent of man's whims and desires, but at the same time as a laudatory enterprise demanding uplifting sacrifices of an heroic kind of advantage to the indivduals concerned, may be found in many of the other exploration and travel narratives authored by U.S. Naval Officers in the nineteenth century. Moreover, it was a popular theme as far as the general public was concerned and in most instances it was presented as a section of readable, sometimes exciting prose, which gave it even greater appeal. Consider, for example, the following passage from William Herndon's *Exploration of the Valley of the Amazon*:

Though not yet sixty miles from the sea, we had crossed the great "divide" which separates the waters of the Atlantic from those of the Pacific. The last steps of our mules had made a striking change in our geographical relations; so suddenly and so quickly had we been cut off from all connexion with the Pacific, and placed upon waters that rippled and sparkled joyously as they danced by our feet to join the glad waves of the ocean that washes the shores of our own dear land. They whispered to me of home, and my heart went along with them. I thought of Maury, with his researches concerning the currents of the sea; and, recollecting the close physical connexion pointed out by him as existing between these—the waters of the Amazon and those of our own majestic

Mississippi—I musingly dropped a bit of green moss, plucked from the hill-side, upon the bosom of the place lake of Morococha, and as it floated along I followed it, in imagination, down through the luxurious climes, the beautiful skies, and enchanting scenery of the tropics, to the mouth of the great river; thence across the Caribbean sea, through the Yucatan pass, into the Gulf of Mexico; thence along the Gulf-stream; and so out upon the ocean, off the shores of the "Land of Flowers." Here I fancied it might meet with the silent little messengers cast by the hands of sympathizing friends and countrymen high upon the head-waters of the Mississippi, or away in the "Far West," upon the distant fountains of the Missouri.

It was, indeed, but a bit of moss floating on the water; but as I mused, fancy, awakened and stimulated by surrounding circumstances, had already converted it into a skiff manned by Fairies, and bound upon a mission of high import, bearing messages of peace and good-will, telling of commerce and navigation, of settlement and civilization, of religious and political liberty, from the "King of Rivers" to the "Father of Waters"; and, possibly, meeting in the Florida pass, and "speaking" through a trumpet louder than the tempest spirits sent down by the Naiads of Lake Itaska, with greetings to Morococha.

I was now, for the first time, fairly in the field of my operations. I had been sent to explore the Valley of the Amazon, to sound its streams, and to report as to their navigability. I was commanded to examine its fields, its forest, and its rivers, that I might gauge their capabilities, active and dormant, for trade and commerce with the states of Christendom, and make known to the spirit and enterprise of the age the resources which lie in concealment there, waiting for the touch of civilization and the breath of the steam engine to give them animation, life and palpable existence.[5]

Passages such as the foregoing made Herndon's *Exploration of the Valley of the Amazon* a very popular book. Even Mark Twain read it and there is some indication also that it influenced him in the preparation of his Huckleberry Finn stories.[6]

In the midst of general acceptance, however, there were critics. Some British periodicals claimed that Herndon had not contributed anything new to geographical knowledge about the region. The *Spectator,* for instance, pointed out that Herndon followed generally the route taken in 1834 by Lieutenant William Smyth of the Royal Navy.[7]

Lack of originality in the selection of routes was not the only criticism leveled at the exploration efforts of the United States Naval Officers. Lynch's *Narrative of the United States' Expedition to the River Jordan and the Dead Sea* was criticized particularly with regard to its style. Fairly early in his presentation, for example, Lynch described two metallic boats used by the expedition in the following way: "The boats 'Fanny Mason' and 'Fanny Skinner,' of nearly equal dimensions, were named after two young and blooming children, whose hearts are spotless as their parentage is pure. Their prayers, like guardian spirits, would shield us in the hour of peril; and I trusted that, whether threading the rapids of the Jordan or floating on the wondrous sea of death, the 'Two Fannies' would not disgrace the gentle and artless beings whose names they proudly bore." This passage the *Boston Post* called well-meant but "fudge-like."

Also, in the first chapter of his book, Lynch writes about sickness which had afflicted one of his officers and he noted that the man "must naturally have longed to exchange his hard and narrow berth, and the stifling atmosphere of a ship, soon to be tossed about, the sport of the elements, for a softer and more spacious couch, a more airy apartment, and, above all, the quiet and the better attendance of the shore." The *Boston Post* characterized this observation as "one of the clearest examples of bathos, common-place and downright twattle extant." In the end, however, the *Boston Post* evaluated Lynch's product as being:

...really interesting and instructive, and is really and obviously the work of an able, well-educated man. How such silly defects of style should coexist with the more essential merits of the text is almost unintelligible, and, indeed, were we upon oath for our opinion at this moment, we should say that one man must have written the twattle, the triteness, the bad grammar and the bad taste, while another furnished the learning and narrated the facts.[8]

The somewhat harsh literary criticism of Lynch's work must be considered in relation to the fact that Lynch, as well as other officer authors, was writing for at least three audiences. Not only were these authors interested in winning acceptane from the general reader, they hoped for a favorable reception from their official superiors, as well as recognition for their achievements from the scientific community. In Lynch's case, whatever disappointment he might have had with regard to criticism of his presentation, was compensated by the fact that the work of the Dead Sea expedition "became the foundation on which all subsequent knowledge of the river and its valley was built and until the 1930s remained the main source of technical information on both the Jordan and the Dead Sea."[9]

In bringing this short excursion to a close, I think it worthy to note that science in the travel and exploration narratives authored by U.S. Naval officers was, at least in the first half of the period, accompanied by a pride in the achievements of the United States and confidence in the future.

These officers who traversed unknown regions or foreign soil took pains to see that the Star Spangled Banner was carried appropriately while on the march or flew correctly while in camp. Lynch, for instance, entered Damascus with the flag of the United States at the head of his group:

Before entering the city, we were advised to furl our flag, with the assurance that no foreign one had ever been tolerated within the walls; that the British Consul's had been torn down on the first attempt to raise it, and that the appearance of ours would excite commotion, and perhaps lead to serious consequences. But we had carried it to every place we had visited, and, determining to take our chances with it, we kept it flying. Many angry comments were, I believe, made by the populace, but, as we did not understand what our toorgeman was too wary to interpret, we passed unmolested.[10]

Too much, however, should not be made of these displays of patriotism. They were, I believe, nationalistic rather than imperialistically chauvinistic and were spurs to scientific achievement rather than representations of warlike propensities or blatantly imperialistic ventures. Moreover, they did not prevent Lynch and other U.S. Naval Officers from sharing their knowledge with explorers from other countries that they met, so to speak, on the road, and giving full credit to the work of other explorers. (In at least one instance this generosity formed the basis of an attack by the person to whom it was extended against the scientific integrity of the U.S. Naval officer concerned.) Pride and confidence in the United States did not conflict with an appreciation of teamwork relative to increasing the world's stock of knowledge.

Science in the exploration and travel narratives authored by U.S. Naval officers in the nineteenth century is a laudable, perhaps even a romantic, activity. Even apart from the increase in knowledge it brings in its own right to the reader, science in the exploration and travel narratives authored by U.S. Naval officers acts as a spur and model for human conduct. From a military service based on precedent the reader is advised to engage in the pursuit of truth rather than lolly or languish in the mire of tradition. The U.S. Naval officers who wrote exploration and travel narratives in the nineteenth century believed, to paraphrase Steven Marcus,[11] that science encompassed problems to be solved and that solutions could be found through hard work and courage. From this point of view their attitude toward science is both Victorian and modern. Their books can—and are— recommended to be read from these different but similar viewpoints. They have a lot to offer the contemporary reader. They should be edited and reprinted.

NOTES

[1]J.N.L. Baker, *A History of Geographical Discovery and Exploration,* New Edition Revised (New York: Cooper Square Publishers, Inc., 1967), p. 490.

[2]William Lewis Herndon and Lardner Gibbon, *Exploration of the Valley of the Amazon, Made Under Direction of the Navy Department,* 2 vols. (Vol. I, Herndon,Washington, D.C.: Taylor & Maury, 1854; Vol. II, Gibbon,Washington,D.C.: R. Armstrong, 1854); Elisha Kent Kane, *The U.S. Grinnell Expedition in Search of Sir John Franklin, A Personal Narrative* (New York: Harper & Bros., 1853); *Arctic Explorations, The Second Grinnell Expedition in Search of Sir John Franklin in 1853, '54, and '55* 2 Vols. (Philadelphia: Lea and Blanchard, 1849); Thomas J. Page, *La Plata, The Argentine Confederation and Paraguay* (New York: Harper & Bros., 1859); Charles Wilkes, *Narrative of the United States Exploring Expedition During the Years 1838, 1839, 1840, 1841, 1842,* 5 Vols. (Philadelphia: Lea and Blanchard, 1845).

[3]This topic deserves the attention of a full scale monograph.

[4]Kane, *Arctic Exploration in the Years 1853, 1854, 1855.*

[5]Herndon, *Exploration of the Valley of the Amazon,* p. 63.

[6]Charles Neider, ed., *The Autobiography of Mark Twain* (New York: Harper Brothers, 1959), p. 98.

[7]Smyth's account was published in 1836 as Frederick Lowe and William Smyth, *Narrative of a Journey from Lima to Para, Across the Andes and Down the Amazon: Undertaken with a View of Ascertaining the Practicability of a Navigable Communication with the Atlantic by the Rivers Pachitea, Ucayoli, and Amazon* (London: 1836).

[8]*Littell's Living Age,* Vol. XXII (July, August, Sepltember, 1849), 160.

[9]Robert St. John, *Roll Jordan Roll: The Life Story of a River and Its People* (New York: Doubleday and Co., Inc., 1963), p. 360.

[10]Lynch *Narrative,* pp. 147-48.

[11]Steven Marcus, *The Other Victorians, A Study of Sexuality and Pornography in Mid-Nineteenth Century England* (New York: Basic Books, Inc., c. 1966), p. 2.

Exploration
and the American Naturalists

John Muir's
My First Summer in the Sierra

Donez Xiques

John Muir is usually remembered for his accomplishments as an explorer and for his role as founder of the Sierra Club. However, his work as an author is less well-remembered. During his lifetime, John Muir published a number of books and articles relating to his experiences as a naturalist and conservationist; these and some posthumously published works fill ten volumes in the Sierra edition of his writings.[1]

Although the present ecological crisis provides good reason for a return to John Muir's books, his writing also invites attention because of its intrinsic merit. His prose reflects his incredible spirit of self-reliance and his great reverence for nature, qualities which serve to place him well within the tradition of nineteenth century American Romanticism. In addition, Muir's writing invites our attention because it often embodies features which are characteristic of exploration literature. This genre has been described by Jerome Rosenberg as follows: "Exploration literature depicts the discovery of self, of one's place in space and time, as one confronts the unknown, and as one confronts it under a particular set of personal, cultural, and historical contexts."[2]

A return to Muir as writer of exploration literature might well begin with *My First Summer in the Sierra,* a book he gleaned from notes made in 1869, but not published until 1911, more than forty years later. In this work Muir records in a series of chronological entries the impact of his first sojourn in the wilderness of the Sierra. He came to San Francisco by steamer in March 1868 and spent the summer of the following year in the Sierra earning a livelihood by overseeing some shepherds and a flock of more than two thousand sheep. During those months, Muir witnessed the ravages of unchecked grazing and the effects of man's domestication of the wild sheep.[3] That summer in the mountins of California was a turning point in his life. From that time onward he remained for almost twenty years amid the great outdoors: exploring the mountains, tracing the paths of ancient glaciers, and absorbing all in nature.

An interesting and appealing feature of *My First Summer in the Sierra* is the fact that Muir chooses to remain in the background. Even though his narrative is written in the first person, Muir is not anxious to tell what he has done, but rather what nature has done for him, an infinitely more important story.[4] Both the content of this book and its form reflect this focus. Nevertheless, the reader's interest is drawn to the narrator, John Muir, to his response to nature and the wilderness as it is revealed in this work: for in *My First Summer in the Sierra,* Muir really is describing his own awakening to his life's work.

Unlike some persons who set out in their explorations to conquer or subdue nature, Muir always endeavors to establish an harmonious relationship with nature. This is clear throughout *My First Summer in the Sierra.* He does not percive anything in nature merely as thing or object, but he ardently believes that everything that his senses apprehend is informed with life or spirit. He writes, "When we try to pick out anything by itself, we find it hitched to everything else in the universe. One fancies a heart like our own must be beating in every crystal and cell" (211). Elsewhere he notes, "the landscape beaming with consciousness like the face of a god" (113); and "the rocks, the air, everything speaking with audible voice or silent" (209).

The stylistic choices which Muir makes throughout *My First Summer* provide insight into the mind of this explorer. Rarely does the reader feel Muir strives to incorporate the artful phrase, finely balanced sentence or erudite allusion. On the contrary, one finds, for instance, abbreviated openings for sentences, such as the following: "Left camp soon after sunrise" (161); "Found a lovely lily" (22); "Have been sketching" (191). Other entries such as "Sundown, and I must to camp" (188) and "Saw a few Columbines Today" (52) lead one to feel that the published work retains the flavor and freshness of Muir's original jottings. In its own way this style is rather appealing. The reader is attracted by what sounds like an authentic voice. It is as if one is overhearing the dialogue of Muir with himself.

Over and over he remarks that the beauty of nature draws

him in some inexplicable way, "Beauty beyond thought everywhere, beneath, above, made and being made forever" (18). His delight in nature seems spontaneous and continuous. He can write, "Am delighted with this little bush" (44). The sunset can so excite him that he runs back to camp down slopes, across ridges and ravines, through avalanche gaps, firs, and chaparral (209). While treking along behind the herd of sheep, he sports a wild rose in the buttonhole of his jacket (26).

Amid those mountains Muir misses nothing. He observes the patterns made by the sunshine, writing, "How beautiful a rock is made by leaf shadows" (79). He is amazed even by the presence of the ordinary housefly (184) and in July, when the hemlock is in full bloom, he is not content simply to admire it; he climbs one of the trees to revel in the midst of the flowers (203).

Although the prose of a contemporary of Muir, the British naturalist Charles Darwin, also expresses wonder in the presence of nature, Darwin rarely displays the sense of exhilaration one finds in Muir's writings. That is a feature of his style which seems to be a consequence of his profound sense of God. For Muir, like Moses, was never quite the same after his journey to the mountain top. Those three months in the Sierra held a religious significance which he frequently alludes to and which colors his attitude toward his explorations. Lines such as the following are characteristic of *My First Summer:* "The place seemed holy, where one might hope to see God" (65); "A fruitful day, without measured beginning or ending. A terrestrial eternity. A gift of good God" (178). Muir is convinced that all in nature is part of the beneficient and wise handiwork of God. Nature, consequently, is something he respects, reverences, and seeks to understand. Product of God's thought and design it is not a threat to him. This attitude is apparent in *My First Summer* where his notes as naturalist indicate accuracy and attention to data, and also reflect his value judgments. Even when the weather is inclement or nasty, Muir avoids that sort of assessment. Writing on June 23, he simply says, "Our regular allowance of clouds and thunder" (82).The following month when there was an exceptionally heavy rain and thunder storm, he does not bemoan that, but is fascinated by it, commenting, "Now comes the rain with corresponding extravagant grandeur, covering the ground high and low with a sheet of flowing water, a transparent film fitted like a skin upon the rugged anatomy of the landscape" (166).

Muir would never concur with the Wordsworthian notion that nature teaches by a ministry of fear as well as beauty. In *My First Summer,* nature is never source or cause of fear. Even in its wild and unpredictable moments, Muir says, "We see that everything in Nature called destruction must be creation,—a change from beauty to beauty" (308). In an article on Yosemite he writes, "If among the agents that nature has employed in making these mountains there be one that above all others deserves the name of Destroyer, it is the glacier. But we quickly learn that destruction is creation."[5]

Muir's explorations, in fact, led him to conclude that then prevalent opinions were erroneous concerning the origins of the Drift (i.e., the vast layer of soil, sand gravel, and boulders derived from the far north which overlies eastern Canada and much of the United States to the 40th parallel). In the 1870's most American geologists were catastrophists who believed that a series of cataclysmic occurrences had caused the Drift. Muir rejects their theories, maintaining that the Drift is chiefly the result of gradual change, the action of glaciers, for example.

Although Muir believes change is constant in nature, he also believes that nothing is lost as a consequence of change. For him all that happens in nature is part of a larger harmony and unity. "How lavish is Nature," he writes, "building, pulling down, creating, destroying, chasing every material particle from form to form" (318-19).

This attitude that everything is in purposeful movement can be seen in *My First Summer.* By using verbs of motion as well as present participles, Muir conveys a sense of the vitality of all things and enables the reader to feel more like a participant and less like an observer. This effect is evident in the passages following: "Down over this ice-planed granite runs the glad young Tamarack Creek, rejoicing, exulting, chanting, dancing in white, glowing, irised falls and cascades on its way to the Merced Canon" (135). This emphasis on movement is characteristic of Muir's way of perceiving and relating his observations in *My*

First Summer in the Sierra. He speaks, for example, of shadows on rocks, "now gliding softly as if afraid of noise, now dancing, waltzing in swift, merry swirls, or jumping on and off sunny rocks in quick dashes" (79).

Although there is a sense here of vividness and immediacy, Muir's habit of personifying elements in nature tends to detract from the overall quality of some of his passages. When one reads of daisies "too small to fear" (177) and flowers leaning "confidingly" (35), it seems a bit too precious, at least for today's readers.

What does emerge very clearly, however, is the fact that amidst the mountains of California John Muir experiences a freedom of body and spirit that is exhilarating. At the end of his first month in the Sierra he writes: "This June seems the greatest of all the months of my life, the most truly, divinely free, boundless like eternity, immortal. Everything in it seems equally divine..." (90).

A passage such as that highlights the curious fact that while on the one hand both the style and content of *My First Summer* place Muir well in the background, on the other hand, the tone of the book brings him very clearly into focus. He expresses such an enthusiasm for all that he beholds that as he shares his reactions and appreciation of the Sierra, the reader becomes aware of a tone which is very much Muir's own.

When he tries to verbalize the impression made upon him by those wonderful months in the mountains, he declares that he can never adequately describe their impact. "It is easier," Muir says, "to feel than to realize, or in any way explain Yosemite grandeur" (175). "The whole body seems to feel beauty when exposed to it as it feels the camp-fire or sunshine, entering not by the eyes alone, but equally through all one's flesh like radiant heat" (175).

It is this conviction that the Sierra affects one's whole person and not simply the sense of sight or sound which prompts Muir, in my opinion, to work toward a prose style which will offer the reader a means of sharing with him the felt experience of the Sierra's grandeur. It is not surprising, therefore, to find that his diction appeals to the reader's senses through the use of concrete and particular words rather than ones which are abstract and generalized.

In *My First Summer in the Sierra* there are many passages in whch the imagery helps to re-create a scene or incident for the reader. Muir describes the Indians' way of walking, as "making themselves invisible like certain spiders I have been observing here" (71). When he spies some giant Sierra lilies, he remarks that some of their bells are "big enough for children's bonnets" (48). A bear is called a "broad rusty bundle of ungovernable wildness" (182). Occasionally his metaphors are mixed delightfully as in these two examples: "The dawn a glorious song of color" (317) and "The pines marshalled around the edge of the sky made a yet sweeter music to the eye" (29).

Although sight and sound imagery predominate in this book, there is also reference to the senses of touch and smell. In fact, throughout *My First Summer* the reader finds that all Muir's senses are engaged by the Sierra. He notices the varied sounds of nature, from a field humming with bees (112) to the "wind-tones in the great trees overhead" (118). He even likes to hear the "cheery tronk and crink" of the frogs (270). He often comments on the fragrance of the air (80, 116) and says after climbing a hemlock which was in full bloom, "How the touch of the flowers makes one's flesh tingle!" (203). When Muir tries to sum up the effect of the Sierra, he turns to images based on the sense of touch. "In the midst of such beauty, pierced with its rays, one's body is all one tingling palate" (206).

Some features of his style, however, are less memorable. Muir's adjectives, for example, are irritatingly trite. Phrases such as "nobly proportioned," "noblest view," "splashy brook" and "a worthy companion" are frequent and to us sound hollow. But Muir's similes are different. They often reflect his own unique way of perceiving and the reader can be engaged by the freshness of Muir's comparisons: "Saw a large black tailed deer, a buck with antlers like the upturned roots of a fallen pine" (273); "My fire squirmed and struggled as if ill at ease" (296); "A small brown partridge with a very long, slender, ornamental crest worn jauntily like a feather in a boy's cap" (234-5).

When Muir first ventured into the Sierra, he was a competent scientist. One might, therefore, expect his prose to be somewhat

factual and uninteresting to the general reader. However, that is
not the case. His scientific observations are couched in language
which reflects Muir's continuing enthusiasm and zest for living
amidst the mountains and which helps the reader experience the
grandeur of Yosemite. There seems to be little that escapes Muir's
attentive eye, and he is equally adept at describing both the small
and great in nature.

In the valley of Yosemite, for example, the sights and sounds
of the tremendous waterfalls are most impressive. How, one may
ask, can a writer distinguish one waterfall from another for the
reader? Here are passages from two scientists who attempt to do
just that. The first quotation is by J.D. Whitney, a California state
geologist, whom Muir knew:

The first fall reached in ascending the canon is the Vernal, a
perpendicular sheet of water with a descent varying greatly with the
season. Our measurements give all the way from 315 to 475 feet for the
vertical height of the fall, between the months of June and October. The
reason of these descrepencies [sic] seems to lie in the fact that the rock
near the bottom is steeply inclined, so that a precise definition of the
place where the perpendicular part ceases is very difficult amid the
blinding spray and foam. As the body of water increases, the force of the
fall is greater, and of course it is thrown farthest forward when the mass
of water is greatest.[6]

When Muir describes the same waterfall, his language is
much more specific, appealing to one's senses more directly than
that of the Whitney passage. Such stylistic choices reflect
accuracy and yet engage the reader more fully. Here is Muir's
verbal sketch:

The Vernal, four hundred feet high and about seventy-five or eighty
wide, drops smoothly over a round-lipped precipice and forms a superb
apron of embroidery, green and white, slighly folded and fluted,
maintaining this form nearly to the bottom, where it is suddenly veiled in
quick-flying billows of spray and mist, in which the afternoon sunbeams
play with ravishing beauty of rainbow colors (252).

It is not only such magnificent and grandiose features of

nature which attract Muir. He also has comments about nature's small creatures. In the following passage he combines precise observation with interesting description:

[The grasshopper] seemed brimful of glad hilarious energy, manifested by springing into the air to the height of twenty or thirty feet, then diving and springing up again and making a sharp musical rattle just as the lowest point in the descent was reached.... The curves he described in the air in diving and rattling resembled those made by cords hanging loosely and attached at the same height at the ends, the loops nearly covering each other.... How the sound is made I do not understand. When he was on the ground he made not the slightest noise, nor when he was simply flying from place to place, but only when diving in curves, the motion seeming to be required for the sound (185-7).

Here is another passage in which Muir vividly describes the bite of an ant:

I fancy that a bear or wolfbite is not to be compared with it. A quick electric flame of pain flashes along the outraged nerves, and you discover for the first time how great is the capacity for sensation you are possessed of. A shriek, a grab for the animal, and a bewildered stare follow this bite of bites as one comes back to consciousness from sudden eclipse (60-61).

In the foregoing selections the effectiveness of the imagery arises from its naturalness. The comparisons are apt and have a flavor all Muir's own. They arise from his experience and reveal a perceptive eye and keen imagination at work. The scenes and events encountered during those months exploring the Sierra have become transformed through Muir's prose style from personal autobiography to shared participation for the reader in a past event made present.

While Muir was in those mountains, he realized that the beauty and significance which he found in virtually everything surrounding him were not shared by everyone. He was appalled at the effects of careless mining in those mountains. "Wild streams dammed and tamed and turned out of their channels...like slaves...imprisoned in iron pipes to strike and wash away hills and miles of the skin of the mountain's face, riddling, stripping every gold gully and flat. These are the white man's marks" (73-4). Even Muir's companion during that first summer, Shepherd Billy, was unresponsive both to nature and to Muir himself. Once when the sheep were pastured within a mile of the Yosemite valley and the falls, he tried to persuade Billy to go off and have a look. Billy declined, "What," he said, "is Yosemite but a canon—a lot of rocks—a hole in the ground" (197). On another occasion Muir marvelled at a field where ferns more than seven feet tall were growing close together "overleaning and overlapping." When the shepherd was asked for his reaction, he merely replied, "Oh, they're only d[amne]d big brakes" (54-5).

It was a similar sort of obliviousness which Muir observed on other occasions when visitors came through Yosemite scarcely aware of their surroundings, "as if their eyes were bandaged and their ears stopped" (255). He has an amusing description of such visitors as they fished one day in Yosemite:

Yet respectable-looking, even wise-looking people were fixing bits of worms on bent pieces of wire to catch trout. Sport they called it. Should church-goers try to pass the time fishing in baptismal fonts while dull sermons are being preached, the so-called sport might not be bad; but to play in the Yosemite temple, seeking pleasure in the pain of fishes struggling for their lives, while God himself is preaching his sublimest water and stone sermons (255-6)!

Such early experiences with the indifference of others to the miracles which Muir himself constantly saw in nature were repeated throughout his lifetime. Later, when saving these unique natural areas from destruction and exploitation became urgent, he was able to write with people such as this in mind.

According to one recent author it is balanced tension in the account of any individual explorer, between the tendency to catalog or botanize, on the one hand, and the tendency to succumb to feeling or intuition on the other, which provides not only narrative characterization in the writing, but offers one means of distinguishing genuine literature of exploration from mere landscape description.[7] When such criteria are applied to *My First Summer,* it is clear that this book belongs among the volumes of authentic exploration literature. Clearly, Muir's work as an author flowed from his life as an explorer. And the pages of *My First Summer in the Sierra* not only describe the wonders of those mountains, but also disclose to the reader the mind of John Muir.

A glance at the years prior to 1869 shows Muir struggling to delineate his life's goals. It also shows a boyhood and adolescence filled with hardship and backbreaking labor. Perhaps that served to prepare him in some way for the rugged and solitary life of his adult years. The wonder is that he survived emotionally and physically, that his relationship with a stern father did not congeal the joy, curiosity and imagination which seem naturally to be part of him as a boy. It is known, for example, that on one occasion John's favorite horse died as a consequence of being ridden too hard by Muir senior as he dashed from one church meeting to another. Once John's father required the boy to dig a well ninety feet deep, eighty feet of which had to be chipped through limestone. Each day for weeks the elder Muir would lower John in a basket, haul him up for lunch at noon, then lower him into the hole where he chipped away at the rock until nightfall. One day the boy passed out from the noxious fumes, but after being brought to the surface, he was sent back down again by his father. This incident is recounted in *The Story of My Boyhood and Youth* with the comment, "constant dropping wears away stone. So does constant chipping, while at the same time wearing away the chipper. Father never spent an hour in that well."[8]

One can only guess the feeling of relief in adult years when John was away from the parental voice and no longer felt the threat of the rod. Yet he remained concerned about his father and family all his life, corresponded with them and saved enough money so that he could promise them that in an emergency he was ready to offer financial as well as personal assistance.

After such severity and grimness at home it is not surprising that Muir found a benevolence and joy in nature—though it need not have been so. In *My First Summer* he rarely comments about himself, but there seem to be unwritten volumes behind his entry written during his very first week in the Sierra: "We are now in the mountains and they are in us.... Our flesh-and-bone tabernacle seems transparent as glass to the beauty about us.... How glorious a conversion, so complete and wholesome it is, scarce memory enough of old bondage days left" (20-21).

The writing of John Muir, explorer, naturalist, humanist, deserves a revival. *My First Summer in the Sierra* is a good place to begin. In it, he speaks of gazing and sketching "without definite hope of every learning much, yet with the longing, unresting effort that lies at the door of hope... eager to offer self-denial and renunciation with eternal toil to learn any lesson in the divine manuscript" (175).

It seems clear that Muir succeeded in deciphering nature's hieroglyphics and in so doing revealed that his concern was not to flee from men into wilderness, but to seek to discover there the place of man in the world. A recent biographer offers this summary of Muir's significance: "It is his ability to convey a whole, living sense of wilderness—and to hold up the natural mirror to man—that mark his greatness."[9] This living sense of wilderness and keen understanding of man, Muir's gift to us, emerge clearly in *My First Summer in the Sierra.*

NOTES

[1]William Bade, ed. *The Sierra Club Edition of the Works of John Muir* (Boston: Houghton Mifflin Company, 1915-1924).

[2]Jerome H. Rosenberg, "Exploration Literature—A Distinguishable Genre," *Exploration,* III (December 1975), iv.

[3]John Muir, *My First Summer in the Sierra* (Boston & New York: Houghton Mifflin Company, 1911), pp. 28, 75, 343.

[4]Bade, II, 317.

[5]John Muir, "The Yosemite National Park," *Atlantic,* 84 (1899), 145-52.

[6]J.D. Whitney, *The Yellowstone Guide-Book* (Cambridge: University Press: Welch, Bigelow and Company, 1869), pp. 70-71.

[7]Charles D. Harrington, "Self-Definition in Literature of Exploration," *Exploration,* III (December 1975), 2.

[8]John Muir, *The Story of My Boyhood and Youth* (Boston: Houghton Mifflin Company, 1913), p. 186.

[9]Thomas Lyons, *John Muir* (Boise: Boise State College, Western Writers Series No 3, 1972), p. 15.

Originally published in *Exploration,* IV:2, July 1977. Reprinted with the permission of the editor and the author.

John Muir, Emerson, and the Book of Nature: The Explorer as Prophet

John Tallmadge

We are accustomed to thinking of John Muir primarily as a naturalist and to reading his works as inspirational tracts from the wilderness preservation movement he helped found.But he was also an explorer, a gifted mountaineer and a shrewd observer of both wild and human nature. Geographically, his explorations were not the kind to make history. He discovered no new lands. Yet, during the years he lived in Yosemite Valley he travelled more extensively in the little-known High Sierra than anyone else. And in his four subsequent voyages to Alaska he discovered and named many glaciers, most of them in and around the uncharted Glacier Bay. His explorations were, in a word, intensive: they raised no geographical landmarks. Yet Muir always considered himself an explorer and assumed that stance in his writings. My purpose here will be to examine Muir's stance, chiefly with reference to his *Travels in Alaska*. I wish to suggest a way to read and appreciate him both in the tradition of American wilderness writing and in the larger context of literature of exploration. For the former tradition we must begin with Emerson, for of all the early nineteenth century American nature writers, he was the most articulate and influential. And he was one of the first to proclaim that natural science, religion and the search for a national identity should be considered parts of a single enterprise.

I

Several commentators have discussed the transcendentalist strain in Muir's writings,[1] and Muir's cordial relationship with Emerson is well known. In 1871 Emerson visited Yosemite Valley during his grand tour of the west. Muir was living there at the time and he had been alerted to Emerson's arrival by a mutual friend. The two men spent many hours together, scrambling about the feet of the great cliffs and admiring the flora and the

113

views. Emerson's east coast companions were somewhat
alarmed, as they considered Muir rustic and uncouth. But
Emerson returned to Boston convinced he had found another
representative man, a type of the devout naturalist whose
scientific investigations were carried out in a spirit of worship.
This was the figure he had called for thirty years earlier when he
wrote in *Nature:*

But when a faithful thinker, resolute to detach every object from personal
relations and see it in the light of thought, shall, at the same time, kindle
science with the fire of the holiest affections, then will God go forth anew
into the creation.[2]

When Emerson returned to Concord, he wrote Muir urging
him to come east and meet Louis Agassiz, Asa Gray and other
eminent scientists of the day. Muir demurred, saying he had more
field work to do. [But at the same time he confided to a friend,
"Imagine me giving up God's big show for a mere profship!"[3]]
This refusal did not dampen Muir's enthusiasm for Emerson,
however. He continued to write long exuberant letters from
Yosemite. But when he finally did visit Concord, thirty years
later, it was to lay flowers on his friend's grave.

During his excursions into the High Sierra, Muir often
carried a copy of Emerson's essays. This remarkable book, well-
thumbed, scuffed, and stained with pine pitch and charcoal, now
resides in the Beinecke Library at Yale. Its markings reveal much
about Muir's intellectual relationship with Emerson. Reading it
along with Muir's books, one senses how easy it was for Muir to
consider himself a disciple of Emerson. Yet one also notices clear
lines of divergence in both the pattern and the substance of their
thinking.

The metaphor of the Book of Nature offers a good example.
This ancient literary trope is one of Muir's favorite rhetorical
devices, and Emerson gives it a central place in *Nature* as well.[4]
In his chapter entitled "Language" Emerson develops the
metaphor according to a doctrine of correspondences he distilled
from Swedenborg and the German Idealists. Words, he asserts,
are signs of natural facts. But natural facts themselves are signs

of spiritual realities. By extension, therefore, all nature becomes an expression of the human psyche and its perfected form in the Divine Mind. "The world is emblematic," Emerson writes. "Parts of speech are metaphors, because the whole of nature is a metaphor of the human mind. The laws of moral nature answer to those of matter as face to face in a glass.... The axioms of physics translate the laws of ethics."[5] This being the case, the study of nature can become a moral discipline. Science ceases to be merely the servant of commodity and becomes instead a tool of religion. It reveals the manner in which man participates in the creation, or rather, the true basis for any "original relation" which he may choose to establish with any part of the creation. The real aim of science, says Emerson, ought to be to bring man's vision into line with the "axes of things." "All things with which we deal preach to us," he concludes.[6] Man's difficulties arise because he cannot see things in their right relations, to each other, to himself and to God. The proper study of nature is an ethical one, teaching both reverence and self-reliance. It is therefore the true foundation of both culture and character.

Emerson's call for an "original relation to the universe," then, is really a call for moral and social revitalization. Nature is the new book of prophecy and enlightenment for Americans in search of an identity. Emerson's ideal scholar is one who can read this book in a spirit of devotion and humility, whose vision can pierce the veil between the material fact and the moral essence. In his chapter "Idealism," Emerson makes clear that nature, for all her charm, must be surpassed in order to reach true enlightenment. Though he may expand and live in the warm day like corn and melons, Emerson seems finally less interested in the natural facts themselves than in the spiritual realities they represent. "If the reason be stimulated to more earnest vision," he says, "outlines and surfaces become transparant, and are no longer seen; causes and spirits are seen through them."[7] Natural facts become stairs the mind mounts up in contemplation until at last it has no need of them and stands in the naked presence of God.

The euphoric optimism with which Emerson concludes might obscure this shift in his attitude toward nature were it not for the consistence of his central metaphor. The conception of the Book of Nature with its doctrine of correspondences allows him to rank his various uses of nature one above the other while at the same time viewing each use in terms of all the others. Thus poetry becomes a higher form of science, science becomes worship, vision becomes action and experience becomes revelation. Emerson's poet-scientist is the type of man seeing, the one whose vision is in line with the axes of things. He reads the Book of Nature and what he finds there are essentially moral lessons. Nature is to man "the present expositor of the divine mind."[8] It is therefore, from Emerson's point of view, fundamentally didactic.

Now Muir shared many of Emerson's concerns, but he did not embrace Emerson's Idealism. Like many another reader, he found Emerson highly quotable, but the markings in his copy of *Nature* show just how far he was willing to follow. For example, he scored several passages in "Language" where Emerson asserts the immanence of spirit in natural facts, but he left unmarked those passages where Emerson speaks of the moral aspect of physical laws. On the other hand, he marked almost every sentence describing the beauty of nature or the exhilaration produced by contemplation of landscapes, flowers, or the heavens. And in his own writings the metaphor of the Book of Nature appears in a manner significantly different from Emerson's. Here is a passage from one of his Sierra journals:

Glacial records. Nothing goes unrecorded. Every word of leaf and snowflake and particle of dew, shimmering, fluttering, falling, as well as earthquake and avalanche, is written down in Nature's book....

Glaciers, avalanches, and torrents are the pens with which Nature produces written characters most like our own, and every canyon of the Sierra displays examples of this writing.[9]

Clearly, Muir and Emerson do not mean the same thing when they speak of nature as a divine language. They share the metaphor but not the interpretation. Elsewhere, Muir speaks of a horizon of pine trees as "definite symbols, divine hieroglyphics written with sunbeams."[10] And in the same work he calls Yosemite Valley "a grand page of mountain manuscript that I would gladly give my life to be able to read."[11]

There is no doctrine of correspondences at work here. The "divine hieroglyphics" Muir writes of are glacial striae, morainal deposits and the channels of stream erosion. Rather than pointing beyond nature to spiritual essences, they point backward in time to pre-existent physical realities. They never transcend nature. They do not comprise a philosophical code or spiritual allegory, but rather a kind of sacred history.

When the Book of Nature appears as a figure in Muir, it is usually embedded in an enthusiastic landscape description. When all is said and done, Muir seems motivated more by a simple love of natural beauty than by an Emersonian zeal for visionary perfection. To Muir, the Book of Nature is worth reading because it was written by God, the true fount of all beauty. If there are morals to be drawn from such work, they are not complex ones. Muir studies nature and learns the language of praise. He discovers the delight of celebration, the exuberance of all beings participating in the creation. This feeling uplifts and rejuvenates, and therefore it seems reason enough for him to seek out the wilderness.

This aesthetic outlook distinguishes Muir's use of the Book of Nature from Emerson's. To Emerson, beauty was one of the more obvious and thus ultimately inferior uses of nature. But Muir, it seems, was unwilling to follow him beyond that point and into the rarefied atmospheres of "Idealism." In that chapter Muir underlined passages dealing with science and the joys of the nature lover, but he seems to have ignored the argument's key paragraphs. He apparently saw no need to render the world transparent. Rather than surpass nature, he wanted to fling himself into it. He sought his God in things themselves and searched out His inscriptions in the wildest regions, where they would not be obscured by the refuse of human enterprise. And it was this search, finally, which led him beyond the Yosemite to Alaska.

II

To understand the lure of Alaska in John Muir's mind, we

must remember that his wilderness conscience was formed by ten years of exploration in the High Sierra. It is difficult to conceive how deep an impression the stupendous glaciated landscapes of Yosemite made on him. Throughout his life glaciers and their effects remained his preeminent concerns, overshadowing even the love of botany which had originally brought him to California. So ardent was his passion for glaciers that it sometimes appears comical in the accounts. Linnie Marsh Wolfe, Muir's biographer, describes a typical incident during one of his botanical trips to the Mt. Shasta country:

> One day they were footing over a barren volcanic plain when Muir discovered glacial striae upon the lava. "Hurry, run, see this wonderful thing!" he yelled at them. Mrs. Bidwell, panting along in the rear, breathing red dust, gasped out: "I can't hurry any faster than I am. I'm spitting blood now." But Muir had no mercy. "Oh,never mind that. Hurry. This is worth dying to see!"[12]

Muir was dead serious about glaciers. To him they were the instruments God used to create sublime landscapes. The scriptures in the rocks revealed that God had been at work. Interpreting these scriptures was an act of appreciation, as one might learn to appreciate a work of sculpture as both craft and art. But since the artist was divine, the act of appreciation became an act of worship. Gazing upon the distant peaks of the High Sierra, Muir wrote: "Some one worthy will go, able for the Godful work, yet as far as I can I must drift about these love-monument mountains, glad to be a servant of servants in so holy a wilderness."[13]

But the Sierran landscapes were created long ago, and Muir finds that the glaciers which formed them have all but vanished. The tools of the Craftsman have been withdrawn. Thus, Muir finds the relation between man and the Creator mediated by the passage of time. The books of the rocks can reveal the power and grace of the Creator, but only when they have been interpreted. And this interpretation consists in reconstructing the ancestral landscape from the extant inscriptions. The work of the naturalist is a struggle to look back in time, to glimpse the origin of that sublimity in the landscape which so dazzles and uplifts the beholder. But suppose one could watch a Yosemite being born. Then one might stand directly in the presence of the Creator, with no need to see through or beyond the creation itself.

Muir's *Travels in Alaska* is full of references to Yosemite. In fact, it is his most common comparison and it occurs always in the superlative degree. For Muir, Yosemite was the archetypal sublimity. Describing one glacial fiord he entered while sailing up the coast from Ft. Wrangell, he exclaims:

No words can convey anything like an adequate conception of its sublime grandeur—the noble simplicity and fineness of the sculpture of the walls; their magnificent proportions....
...This is a Yosemite Valley in process of formation, the modelling and sculpture of the walls nearly completed...(79-81).[14]

Elsewhere he speaks of Sum Dum Bay as a "wild, unfinished Yosemite" (275). Along the valley of one of the Stickeen Glaciers he observes that "all the wall rocks...are more or less yosemitic in form and color" (127). That this is sacred ground to Muir becomes clear at once, for in his Sierran writings he has referred repeatedly to Yosemite as a temple. Now he calls the splendid fiord a "glorious temple" and the awe it inspires in him and his companions is "only the natural effect of appreciable manifestations of the presence of God" (80).

Muir seems drawn to Alaska for two primary reasons. On the one hand he seeks confirmation of his interpretations of the Book of Nature. After a few days of scrambling over the Big Stickeen Glacier, for example, he discovers a place where he can crawl down and watch the ice pouring over a hard granite rib. "A most telling lesson in earth-sculpture," he exults, "confirming many I had already learned in the glacier basins of the High Sierra of California " (139).

On the other hand, Muir seeks unobstructed vision. He wants to see God at work in the world. He longs to be caught up in joyful contemplation of that work. Thus, he travels farther and wider from the human world, seeking ever the regions more northerly and more wild. And at the point farthest out he has his vision. At the head of Glacier Bay, surrounded by the most spectacular glaciation he has ever seen, Muir watches the dawn come up on the distant Fairweather Range:

Instead of vanishing as suddenly as it had appeared, it spread and spread until the whole range down to the level of the glaciers was filled with the celestial fire.... Beneath the frosty shadows of the fiord we stood hushed and awe-stricken, gazing at the holy vision.... The white, rayless light of morning, seen when I was alone amid the peaks of the California Sierra, had always seemed to me the most telling of all the terrestrial manifestations of God. But here the mountains themselves were made divine and declared His glory in terms still more impressive. How long we gazed I never knew (186-87).

This passage lies at the visionary core of Muir's book. Its location in the plan of the voyage, at the point farthest from the "civilized" world, determines the cosmographic scheme of his account. For the journey is also a spiritual one. Muir proceeds from the profane landscapes of civilization to the sacred landscape of Glacier Bay, encountering every gradation in between.

Muir's references to civilization are generally deprecatory. Ft. Wrangell appears "at first sight the most inhospitable place I had ever seen" (22), though the "disorder and squalor" (33) belie the healthful climate and comfortable life of the Indians. In contrast, the surrounding wilderness is a veritable paradise, abundant with fish and wild fruits of all kinds (37-8). And this impression of lushness and fertility is not diminished the farther Muir goes from the settlements. On the moraine of one of the Stickeen glaciers he finds a botanist's dream-garden. "In the gardens and forests of this wonderful moraine one might spend a whole joyful life," he cries (137). And the country he paddles through on the way to Glacier Bay seems a "foodful, kindly wilderness" (153).

Needless to say, the people he meets are measured by the degree to which they participate in this spiritual geography. Thus the Indians, who depend so intimately upon the land, are described with glowing affection. At Glacier Bay Muir talks with his guides about the stars and recalls how "their eager, childlike attention was refreshing to see as compared with the deathlike apathy of weary town-dwellers, in whom natural curiosity has been quenched in toil and care and poor shallow comfort" (191). Elsewhere Muir praises the Indians for their woodcraft, their kindness as parents, their dignity, reverence and desire to learn. He attributes these high moral qualities to the influence of the land in which they live. In contrast, the influences of the white man's world (with the notable exception of the missionaries) are perverse and destructive. Time and again, Muir deplores the corrosive effects of whisky. He sees the gold rush as a plague and the miners as poor misguided souls who seek the wrong kind of riches: "Just struggling blindly for gold enough to make them indefinitely rich to spend their lives in aimless affluence, honor and ease" (107). As for himself, he finds the wilderness treasure enough, and returns from the Stickeen "happy and rich without a particle of obscuring gold-dust care" (107).

In fact, Muir finds in the Alaskan wilderness three traditional attributes of the earthly paradise: an innocent race, an abundance of nourishing life, and the tangible presence of God.[15] Needless to say, this view sets him apart from the mass of his contemporaries bred to civilization, who, for the most part, thought of the wilderness as a howling waste peopled by devil-worshipping savages. All of Muir's writing could be seen as an effort to correct that mistaken idea. In his own forthright and exuberant manner, he is always trying to bring our own vision into line with the axis of things. This sense of duty combines with the spiritualized geography of his Alaskan voyages to determine his narrative stance: he is a prophet who goes to the wilderness in search of a vision.[16] He loves the wilderness, for that is where his vision abides. It is where he sees God. But the truth of the vision is always directed toward the human world and thus, for all his ascetic yearnings and love of the wilderness, the prophet is bound to return. It is his role to bear witness, so that the world may be changed.

Muir comments often enough on his own enterprise to make it clear that he takes the prophetic role seriously (though he is not above jesting about it from time to time). He feels as if he has literally been called by the mountains. For example, as he gazes at the Big Glacier of the Stickeen, he can exult, "So grand an invitation displayed in characters so telling was of course irresistible" (128). And when he answers the call, we find him depending to an almost superstitious extent on his own instincts and good luck. When Mr. Choquette, the keeper of Buck Station on the Stickeen, warns him about the dangers of the Big Glacier, adding that many have been killed on it, Muir replies breezily, "Never mind me. I am used to caring for myself" (130). And near the entrance to Glacier Bay, when the Indians are dismayed by the foul weather and dangerous ice conditions, Muir confidently assures them "that for ten years I had wandered alone among mountains and storms, and good luck had always followed me: that with me, therefore, they need fear nothing" (179). This is big talk for a man on his first visit to Alaska, yet it proves true. Nothing, it seems, can shake Muir's enthusiasm. Despite narrow escapes from clashing icebergs, labyrinthine crevasse fields or storms at sea, despite miserable nights in a leaky tent, hours of bashing through hideous Devil's Club thickets or dreary, bone-chilling days in an open canoe, he still writes with all the fervor of a true believer.

Both the lineaments and message of Muir's vision are easily grasped. He says: "The care-laden commercial lives we lead close our eyes to the operations of God as a workman, though openly carried on that all who will look may see" (282). Our lives in the human world seem impoverished to him. He means to restore them by rectifying our attitudes. First, we must learn to see the Creator manifested in His creation, to see that creation going on all around us. "One learns," Muir writes, "that the world, though made, is yet being made; that this is still the morning of creation; that mountains long conceived are now being born..." (85). This awareness comes about through the discipline of voyaging itself, whereby "you may be truly independent and enter into partnership with Nature; to be carried with the winds and currents, accept the noble invitations offered all along your way..." (252). The result of this vision-cleansing will be a return to joy. "How delightful it is," Muir exclaims, "to get back into the reviving northland wilderness! How truly wild it is, and how joyously one's heart responds to the welcome it gives!.." (251).

Rejuvenation lies at our fingertips. In a sense, it is almost as though we had never left Paradise at all, but merely ceased to acknowledge its presence.

III

As a wilderness writer, Muir set out to answer Emerson's call for an original relation to the universe. He stands near the head of a tradition which includes Thoreau, Robert Marshall, Robinson Jeffers, Aldo Leopold, Theodore Roethke and Edward Abbey. As a voice crying out for wilderness he has few rivals, and few writers have had more impact on the nation's land-use policies. He embraced Emerson's desire to make the study of natural history a tool of religion, but beyond that his thinking diverged. His attention was always directed outward, toward the creatures and things of this world. He remained a passionate celebrant, concerned not to achieve union with God in the purest mystical sense, but always to behold Him at work in His creation. Thus, he did not choose to follow Emerson beyond nature. And he did not attempt in his writings to measure the mind of man, nor to account for the vicissitudes and turbidities of his own consciousness, as Emerson did, through the medium of a universal philosophy.

As an explorer, Muir belongs in that class for whom the expedition was always a solitary enterprise, undertaken for personal and largely private reasons. In this respect he resembles men like Thoreau, Joshua Slocum and Bertram Thomas. These explorers were all in a certain sense exiles. Estranged by circumstance or temperament from their native societies, they made their spiritual homelands elsewhere. In their writings, they lean heavily toward the confessional mode. If they succeed, it is because, while attempting to justify their ways to men, they present such a compelling alternative that our lives are enriched. They change our angle of vision.

Muir's enthusiasm is endearing and often infectious, though at times the reader may sympathize with Mrs. Bidwell running across the lava after him. Despite its extremism, his love for the wilderness is absolutely sincere, and this is finally what makes him such an engaging writer. Nowhere in Muir's scientific discussions is there any hint that he means to astound the academies. He seeks no breakthrough, only to improve his own knowledge. He lacks the self-conscious professionalism of a Darwin or a Whitney. And his descriptions of remarkable mountaineering feats, such as the rescue of Rev. Young on Glenora Peak or the terrible crossing of the Taylor Bay Glacier with the dog Stickeen, are all told in the frankest and least melodramatic fashion. Obviously, Muir took physical vigor, endurance and courage for granted. One does not find in his writings the athletic posturing of a Clarence King, nor the grim determination and rock-jawed nationalistic pride of a Shackleton or a Burton.

Perhaps Muir's most inspiring contribution, though, is the example he sets for exploration as a way of life. His Alaska travels are finally not so important to the geographer as they are to the literate adventurer. With him, the literature of exploration takes one more step away from geographic chronicle in the direction of self-conscious, universalized autobiography. He answered Emerson's call by establishing his own relation and then writing about it, exactly as Thoreau had done a generation before. With splendid sincerity, he tests the stance himself, and Thoreau, who had travelled much in Concord and read copiously in the literature of voyages, would certainly have approved.

NOTES

[1]See, for example, Herbert F. Smith, *John Muir,* N.Y. (Twayne Series), 1965; Thomas J. Lyon, *John Muir,* Boise, Idaho, 1972; Roderick Nash, *Wilderness and the American Mind,* New Haven, p.125-29.

[2]Emerson, *Nature,* in S.E. Whicher (ed.) *Selections from Ralph Waldo Emerson,* Boston, 1957, p.55.

[3]William Frederic Bade, *Life and Letters of John Muir,* Boston, 1923, vol. 2, p. 292.

[4]See, for example, E.R. Curtius, *European Literature and the Latin Middle Ages,* Princeton, 1953, pp. 319-26; also the discussion in Arthur O. Lovejoy, *The Great Chain of Being,* Cambridge, 1964, pp. 67-73; for an example of medieval

attempt to "read" the Book of Nature, see Pierre Bersuire, (1290-1362), *Morale Reductorium super Totam Bibliam,* Lyons, 1520. Emerson's use of the metaphor is actually closer to the medieval sense, which assumes that species are fixed and have been since the Creation. Emerson does not take the historical view of natural history which is so important to Muir. To Emerson, nature is more a museum than a process.

[5]Emerson, *Nature* (ed. cit.), p. 35.

[6]*Ibid.,* p. 39.

[7]*Ibid.,* p. 43.

[8]*Ibid.,* p. 50.

[9]*John of the Mountains: the Unpublished Journals of John Muir,* ed. Linnie Marshe Wolfe, Boston, 1938, p. 171.

[10]John Muir, *My First Summer in the Sierra,* Boston, 1911, p. 29.

[11]*Ibid., p. 135.*

[12]Linnie Marsh Wolfe, *Son of the Wilderness: The Life of John Muir,* New York, 1945, p. 195.

[13]*My First Summer in the Sierra,* p. 22.

[14]John Muir, *Travels in Alaska,* Boston, 1915. Page numbers in parentheses refer to this edition.

[15]For a summary of literary topoi associated with the earthly paradise, see A.B. Giamatti, *The Earthly Paradise and the Renaissance Epic,* Princeton, 1966, chapter 1.

[16]The scenario of the prophet's visionary sojourn in the wilderness is a commonplace in the Judeo-Christian tradition. For biblical examples, see Exodus 3:1-2, 18 (Moses), 1 Kings 19:4-15 (Elijah), Matthew 3:1-4 (John the Baptist), Luke 4: 1-15 (Jesus). See also the discussion and references in Nash, *op. cit.,* pp. 13-17.

Originally published in *Exploration,* IV:2, July 1977. Reprinted with the permission of the editor and the author.

Travel & Exploration
as a Theme
In American Literature

Hawthorne's "Foot-prints on the Sea-Shore" and the Literature of Walking

Roberta F. Weldon

Much of the American literature of the nineteenth century is a "literature of movement."[1] As in the English and German Romantic tradition, the central figure of the major novels is often a wanderer[2] who is in quest of himself and of some redemptive knowledge. Some of these questers, like Ishmael or Huck Finn, journey, with great explicitness, to some goal, while others, like Natty Bumppo, are driven to escape some inexorable force—call it progress or civilization. The strength of the fictional literature of travel in America is rightfully undisputed, but its unquestioned dominance has unfortunately tended to cast into the background another vital aspect of the literary tradition of this century—the non-fictional travel narrative.[3] This form shares many of the characteristics of the fictional literature of travel. At its best the essay will also use the metaphor of travel to provide the shape for an internal journey. Oftentimes, the movement of the journey will involve something more significant than a review of the landscape, for it traces the progress and growth in perceptive awareness of a sensitive persona as he encounters the world outself the self.

The characteristic American journey tends to be imagined in at least two common ways. The first, of course, is that the American journey moves westward, and the second, that the mode of conveyance which the traveler chooses probably depends upon how quickly it can bring him to the destination. The American mind is fascinated by speed—perhaps ever since some of the earliest explorers in seeking a faster passage to India happened upon this land. And yet, the most significant form of the travel essay in nineteenth century America is the essay which focuses on walking.

It is perhaps especially ironic that the generation that built the railroads and first gave shape to many of our ideas about the power of speed should also produce some of the finest writers in the tradition of the American literature of walking. It is ironic, but

127

not inexplicable, for lying behind what a writer like Thoreau or Hawthorne says about walking as an imaginative and redemptive process is the spectre of "the steam fiend." In *Walden*, Thoreau sets the sounds of nature against the whistle of the locomotive. For him, the railroad with its velocity and direction is a symbol of the "restless world" which threatens to disrupt and eventually destroy the pastoral life. In Hawthorne's sketch "The Celestial Rail-road," the railroad symbolizes the too easy philosophy of Mr. Smooth-it-away that hinders a pilgrim's progress to the Celestial City. It becomes an almost diabolical presence in whose "horrible scream" is distinguishable "every kind of wailing woe, and bitter fierceness of wrath, all mixed up with the wild laughter of a devil or a madman." For both these romantic writers, the railroad not only cannot permit reflective progress but stands in opposition to closeness with nature or a true encounter with reality that walking encourages.

Admittedly, though, the essay on walking is not a new form that first appeared in the nineteenth century in response to the phenomenon of the railroad. To make this assertion would be, at best, to oversimplify and to overlook an entire British and American tradition of walking literature. Even during the seventeenth and eighteenth century works were published that describe walking excursions in this country. Most of these were written simply to acquaint the reader with locales inaccessible to him or to describe local history and points of interest. These works served a purpose by broadening the reader's knowledge of his new land and offering an access to experiences he often could not have hoped to enjoy. Still, the nineteenth century did perfect this form as imaginative art.

Washington Irving was among the first to extend the possibilities of the walking tour form in America. In *The Sketch Book* he adopts the stance of the gentleman or cultivated observer describing his surroundings both to enrich his own and his reader's experience and to provide a vehicle for his reflections on society, its manners and customs. Significantly, Irving chooses the British, not the American countryside for his walks because, as he says, he is not "merely a lover of fine scenery" but is more concerned with "the charms of storied and poetical associations."

When moving through the landscape Irving does not journey into the future of America's "youthful promise" but steps back into Europe's "shadowy grandeurs" of the past, reviewing the history of the landmarks he visits. Irving's walking tour essays, then, while among the first in the American creative essay tradition, are still close in their style and form to the British tradition of Addison and Steele. Irving's persona makes an excursion not to discover himself to achieve a greater understanding of human nature. Thus, he is concerned less with the intensity of his experiences than with "the range of his observations," accepting that the more he can experience and the more human types he can encounter, the more accurate will be his conclusions about the human condition.

In this respect he is very unlike Thoreau, who readily asserts that he has only "traveled widely in Concord." Thoreau's excursions are intense journeys of self discovery. When he describes himself as a saunterer in "Walking" he acquaints the reader with the etymology of the word, as if he were consciously attempting to distinguish his type of sauntering from Irving's in "An Author's Account of Himself." Thoreau's walking is an excursion to a holy land ("sainte terre"), a blessed region of introspection and oneness with nature, and bears little resemblance to Irving's rambling and poking about in the "nooks and corners and byplaces" of European society. While Irving journeys to the east, choosing to walk on trodden land retracing the progress of past ages, Thoreau walks westward to the future to embrace its wildness and newness.[4] Thus, Thoreau's walking seems to be a reflection of a more uniquely American experience.

Perhaps because Thoreau's position in the American essay tradition is so central, and his essays on walking so well known it is natural to assume that he was the first American romantic writer to develop the literature of walking. And yet, Hawthorne's essay "Foot-prints on the Sea-shore," which shares much of Thoreau's philosophy of walking, antedates by five years Thoreau's first published excursion, "A Winter Walk," written in 1843. This essay is so important because it reveals a matrix of ideas out of which developed much of the conception of walking common to the essay and even to fictional literature of travel.

Like so much of the literature of travel, "Foot-prints on the Sea-shore" is structured as a sensitive observer's account of an excursion through a landscape. It is impossible to read the sketch without recognizing that the author is attempting to structure a description of both an outward and inward journey. Its symbolic overtones are certainly as intense as any of Thoreau's early excursion essays, and the metaphor of self exploration at its core makes it clear that this essay belongs in the company of the romantic tradition of literature of the journey. Yet, unlike Thoreau, the narrator of the essay rejects the journey westward. Hawthorne tells the reader, almost apologetically, that, although the forest beckons him "I must wander many a mile, ere I could stand beneath the shadow of even one primeval tree."[5] Still, he does not choose to journey eastward, as Irving does, to the haunts of the past. He walks instead to the shore and makes his progress along the coast. In this way, he skirts the antipodal regions of Irving and Thoreau to stake his claim instead in a borderland world, that many American writers also choose, bridging the old and the new, Europe and America.

Hawthorne sounds uncommonly like the British neo-classical writers and their poetry of retirement when he admits at the beginning of "Foot-prints on the Sea-shore" that when his "health and vigor" (451) need to be restored he walks from town to exchange "the sultry sunshine of the world" for "the cool bath of solitude" (451). On the most immediate level, Hawthorne seems to understand his walk as little more than a ramble which affords the opportunity to retreat from the heat and dust of the arena of daily life. But it is soon apparent that the narrator's impressions and feelings about his solitary walk run much deeper and are more complex. When we explore the internal region of his walk, we find that it could stand in the company of some of the finest descriptions of travel in romantic literature. Like the "water gazers" in *Moby Dick,* Hawthorne is inevitably drawn to the sea by its primitive power. Walking along the coast almost necessitates introspection, for Hawthorne would agree with Melville's assertion that "Meditation and water are wedded for ever." Nevertheless, it is not simply the meditative aspect of the walk which signifies that this essay has more in common with a romantic, rather than a neo-classical, sensibility. What distinguishes Hawthorne's reflections on walking from those of a British essayist, like Addison and Steele, or any American writer like Irving is that the literal walk comes to objectify the quest for self-awareness and for some knowledge of life's meaning. In this respect, it seems especially significant that after Hawthorne walks down the coast he chooses to return and to retrace his steps. By describing his walk in this way, he presents a recognizable version of the circular journey, a journey in which the traveler ultimately returns to the place where he began but with a different and usually deeper awareness that is the result of the intervening period. Further, retracing his steps here anticipates a larger structural pattern which is realized at the conclusion of the sketch.

The design, then, of Hawthorne's internalized quest also points to his romantic vision. The action of retracing his steps allows him to step aside and reflect on experience. He can now contemplate his "mood" while in a sense distancing himself from his feelings about his seaside walk so that he is better able to understand it:

When we have paced the length of the beach, it is pleasant, and not unprofitable, to retrace our steps, and recall the whole mood and occupation of the mind during the former passage. (453-4)

The recollection of emotion in tranquillity helps him to reorder his experience, perhaps to shape it into the raw material of his art. But whether or not reflection is directed toward the creative act it is still important because "to track our own nature in its wayward course" will always "make us wiser" (454).

This personal wisdom is gained for Hawthorne, as it often is for the American romantic writer, by a movement into nature. Hawthorne chooses to take his walk along the shore, not in the city, because for him the self educative journey involves a wedding with nature. In the sketch, the meeting between the solitary walker and the ocean is described as "mutual"—his "homage" is repaid by the sea's "sweet breath" of blessing. What the narrator experiences is a transcendence of the self, or in

Emersonian terms, a merging or union of the me and the not-me. The walk frees his spirit to "leap forth and suddenly enlarge its sense of being to the full extent of the broad, blue, sunny deep" (452). The act of walking provides the immediacy or the concreteness, the Emersonian experience described in "Nature" of "standing on the bare ground," which can bring with it the uplift "into infinite space."

Hawthorne values this experience because it allows him to escape from himself, while paradoxically moving most deeply into himself. As a result, he is awakened to hear "the sea's unchanging voice" and lets "the infinite idea of eternity pervade his soul" (460). His walk into nature provides him with a way outside of life; he journeys to the only place where he can get in touch with the "unchanging" and the "idea of eternity." Consequently, on the solitary walks the artist is not upset that the ocean washes away his verses. The idea of his own death and the impermanence of his art no longer frightens him, for by his union with nature he is able to approach a knowledge of a constant in the flux. In an important episode in "Foot-prints on the Sea-shore," Hawthorne celebrates this new covenant with nature in "a recess in a line of cliffs, walled round by a rough, high precipice, which almost encircles and shuts in a little space of sand" (458). Within this circle of solitude the progress ends in an almost sacred or ritualistic way. Here he sups on a communion feast of biscuits and water and consecrates the day with a prayer of thanks to God.

Thus, Hawthorne's day ends with his lost integrity restored and with a renewed sense of what he must be and do. His walk circles back at the conclusion to the place from which it originated. But the circular pattern does not reflect an absurdist view of reality, as it will in *Ethan Brand*, where the journeyer travels a never ending circle and returns to the same spot exhausted and embittered. Instead, the shape defines the harmony and wholeness that the circularity of the walk brings to the traveler. Hawthorne reinforces the impression of unity, as Thoreau does in many of his walking essays, by consciously using the time interval of a single day's walk as an analogy for the whole of one's life. Hawthorne's ramble begins in the morning; he progresses through the zenith of the day and concludes his journey "as the sun sinks over the western wave" (461). In this way the cycle of renewal appears never ending, for there is always the implicit promise of a new day. The religious imagery—the walk is described as a pilgrimage; the traveler as a "holy hermit" consecrated with "vows"; the union with nature as a "soul's communion" (451)—supports his day's walk as a holy quest for a personal redemption. The circular walk becomes the way of the soul in quest of wholeness.

"Foot-prints on the Sea-shore" concludes with the narrator's reunion with society. The marriage of his mind with a reality outside the self prepared him for a reintegration with society. Putting aside his private meditations he joins with a group of people on the shore and seals a new covenant with society which brings to fulfillment his earlier covenant with nature. In a scene that neatly parallels the solitary communion repast, he now sups on fried fish and chowder with his new friends and acknowledges that "after all my solitary joys, that this is the sweetest moment of the Day by the Sea-Shore" (462). Thus, the literal walk reaches its fulfillment in return. As in the fictional journey of Ishmael and Thoreau's journeys to the woods in *Walden* and the excursion essays, the process involves departure *and* return.

Perhaps, though, the pattern implicit in "Foot-prints on the Sea-shore" is most fully realized in Hawthorne's major work, *The Scarlet Letter*. Hester considers but rejects the journey west, and, although she chooses to make the journey east to Europe, she eventually returns to live in the borderland world near the sea. The circular pattern of the romance operates against the play of these polarities, with the scafford scenes providing the continuity and unity. And still, related to the opposition between east and west are other contraries which sustain this pattern. These implicit polarities are also developed as journeys—for example, Hester's walk from the prison to the scaffold; Hester and Dimmesdale's journey to the woods; and Dimmesdale's progress from the Election Day pulpit to the scaffold. Thus in *The Scarlet Letter*, as in "Foot-prints on the Sea-shore," the organizing figure of the journey works on more than one level. The literal journey modulates into the symbolic journey. In addition, the departures and returns, which can be thought to exist on a linear plane, are eventually assimilated or resolved into the circular pattern.

Perhaps because of the implicit tension between the movement of departure and return and the circular pattern, the dynamic element in Hawthorne's walk is not lost. Instead, it operates to impress the reader that the restored unity that the narrator achieves at the conclusion of his walk is not the same as the original state of the departure but represents an advance. The journey pattern of "Foot-prints on the Sea-shore" as well as *The Scarlet Letter* and *The Marble Faun,* can be represented most accurately not by the circle but by a dominant romantic symbol, the ascending spiral,[6] for the journeyer has aspired toward a higher harmony and wholeness and has achieved it. He returns, like Wordsworth in *The Prelude* and the Ancient Mariner in Coleridge's poem, with a renewed sense of individuality. Still, in Hawthorne's account of the walk, the integrity of mind he achieves is justified not in itself but by what this mind can now contribute to society. Without the renewed sense of "individuality unviolated" (461), Hawthorne would be incapable of "affection" and "sympathy":

And when at noontide, I tread the crowded streets, the influence of this day will still be felt; so that I shall walk among men kindly and as a brother, with affection and sympathy....(461)

Wordsworth may state that "love of nature" leads to "love of man" but there is not a sense in this work, as there is in Hawthorne's, that individuality may somehow be a threat if it is not directed toward the good of the social whole. The emphasis on the return to the social order is simply more dominant in Hawthorne's journey than in that of the British romantic writer.

Undoubtedly, then, in structuring "Foot-prints on the Sea-shore," Hawthorne has created a remarkably developed work with a complex and detailed unity. Certainly, the pattern of the walk shares much with that of voyages in the British romantic tradition. Still, in subtle, yet important ways it becomes clear that Hawthorne is describing an American walk—one that looks ahead to Thoreau's excursion more than it does back to Irving's rambles; and one that has at its core a metaphor of travel which anticipates the romance accounts of the journey. The description of walking in "Foot-prints on the Sea-shore" is one example, and a strong one, indeed, of Hawthorne's ability to assimilate the traditions of past literature while breaking new ground for the American artist.

Notes

[1] Novalis, *Briefe und Werke* (3 vols.; Berlin, 1943); III, 173-4. As quoted in M.H. Abrams, *Natural Supernaturalism* (New York, 1971), p.186.

[2] Abrams, p.186.

[3] Two kinds of non-fictional travel narratives were popular during the nineteenth century. The first group includes descriptions by American writers of journeys in their native land. Within this group certain narratives concentrate on historical descriptions and record factual data; for example, Daniel Drake, *Natural and Statistical View, or Picture of Cincinnati and the Miami Country* in *Physician to the West* (1815; rpt. Lexington, 1970), pp. 66-125, and Amos Stoddard, *Sketches, Historical and Descriptive, of Louisiana* (1812). I am more interested in the travel narrative which, while it may primarily be an observer's record, may also give some evidence that the writer tried to create a more consciously artistic work; for example, the narrative may be architecturally shaped, or may include landscape descriptions that reveal some poetical as well as pictorial power. Some examples of this type are: John Bradbury, *Travels in the Interior of America* (1817; rpt. Ann Arbor, 1966); Timothy Flint, *Recollections of the Last Ten Years in the Valley of the Mississippi* (1826; rpt. New York, 1968); N. Parker Willis, *A L'Abri or The Tent Pitch'd*, 1839; Henry David Thoreau, "A Winter's Walk," 1843 and *A Week on the Prairie*, 1835; Margaret Fuller Ossoli, "Summer on the Lakes," 1844. A second group of travel narratives describe the excursions of Americans abroad. This genre was an extremely popular form in the middle of the nineteenth century and includes such well-known narratives as: Washington Irving, *The Sketch Book*, 1819-20 and *Bracebridge Hall*, 1820; N.P. Willis, *Pencillings By the Way*, 1835; Margaret Fuller Ossoli, "Things and Thoughts in Europe," in *At Home and Abroad* (1856; rpt. New York, 1971); James Russell Lowell, "Leaves of My Journal," 1854; Nathaniel Hawthorne, *Our Old Home*, 1863.

[4] Frederick Garber, "Unity and Diversity in 'Walking',"*Emerson Society Quarterly*, 56 (1969), 36.

[5] *Twice-told Tales*, ed William Charvat, et al. (Columbus, 1974), IX, 451. Citations in my text to "Foot-prints on the Sea-shore" are to this edition.

[6] Abrams, p. 184.

Expatriation and Exploration:
The Exiled Artists of the 1920s

Marjorie Smelstor

Expatriation is often a form of exploration, an exploration for new values, new insights, new experiences. This was especially true for many of the expatriated artists of the 1920s, for they left America, transplanted themselves on the Continent—usually in Paris—and appeared to have withdrawn in order to escape from the American way. Disillusioned by the War and discontented with the post-war atmosphere in the United States, these artists apparently were abandoning the nation in the hopes of finding a place more conducive to their artistic and personal drives. This typical interpretation of expatriation, however, is simplistic and reductionist. Expatriation was more complex than mere escape because it was, for the most part, withdrawal for the sake of clearer vision, better articulation, freer expression. The expatriates did not sever themselves from their origins, but rather altered their relationship with that source. They left America for negative reasons, and only temporarily, as one exile explained:

If we were sometimes called 'expatriates' the appellation had only a partial truth. We were really removing ourselves for a while from our business civilization, and from our middle-class families that counted fondly on our making our career in an advertising office or a bank.[1]

Paradoxically, they returned to America for positive reasons because they experienced, not an embittered cynicism, but a new sense of loyalty to their homeland, a loyalty which was characterized by a reflective, analytical and critical posture. In this respect, many expatriates were cultural nationalists of a special type, sharing the same concerns as the earlier, pre-War nationalists, such as Randolph Bourne and Van Wyck Brooks, as well as the post-War natioinalists who remained at home, and yet manifesting these concerns in new ways and from different geographical perspectives. These Americans who uprooted themselves from the United States remained faithful to their

136

homeland, and their critical stance was the manifestation of their fidelity to and hope for their nation.

One of the best summaries of this expatriate criticism with its nationalistic basis is given by Warren Susman, who suggests that six concepts informed it: a concern with the aesthetic task; a rejection of current tools for cultural analysis that were prominent in America at the time; an awareness of the major problems connected with modern industrial capitalism, as well as an insight into the consequences of the machine; an understanding of the confusion left by the War and newer philosophical concepts; a desire to create a new and non-imitative American culture; and a belief in the American cult of optimism.[2] These concepts indicate that the expatriates, even at a distance from their nation, were concerned with the two questions that America as a whole was grappling with: What was the new America? What was American culture? Furthermore, these concepts suggest that the expatriates were not abandoning their country, but rather declaring their belief in it and in its future.

Gertrude Stein, one of the most vocal in the discussions of expatriation, offered several explanations for this physical withdrawal from America. For her, America was the "most important country in the world—but a parent's place is never the place to work in."[3] Furthermore, it was a good thing for a writer looking at his own civilization "to have the contrast of another culture before him."[4] Thus distance from the "parent" country and internationalism were two motivations for expatriation, which, in turn, led to a strengthened belief in America:

Paradoxically, one of the most important results of exile was a new faith in America and a desire to rediscover it. . . . The rediscovery of America was not, for these intellectuals, merely the assertion of values long since discarded; it was the beginning of a belief in the present and future potentialities of American culture and a belief that these possibilities could be realized by ending middle-class dominance of culture. The trip to Europe also revealed how profoundly American culture had influenced Europe, how important advertising, jazz, and the skyscraper had become to the avant-garde artists of the Continent.[5]

Furthermore, for most of the self-exiled artists, the process of expatriation revealed the mythic pattern of alienation and reintegration, of departure and return.[6] In this respect, their homecoming reminds one of Eliot's description:

> We shall not cease from exploration
> And the end of all our exploring
> Will be to arrive where we started
> And know the place for the first time.[7]

One way to examine this expatriate-as-explorer idea is to study three exiles who edited *Broom,* a little magazine of the 20s. Harold Loeb, Matthew Josephson and Malcolm Cowley—explorers who searched for new ways to express America's cultural identity after the War—published *Broom* from 1921-1924 in Rome, in Berlin, and then in New York City. *Broom's* history is an interesting one, with its colorful and often eccentric editors, its censorship problems, its difficulties with finances and editorial policies, its printing of significant works by artists like Ernest Hemingway, Gertrude Stein, e.e. cummings, Marianne Moore, Paul Strand and others, and its movement from the Continent to the United States.[8] *Broom* itself was an exploration, a search for the ways in which a little magazine could be an effective vehicle for artistic and national expression. More specifically, however, the major editors of *Broom*—Loeb, Josephson and Cowley—were explorers who deserve our attention, for these expatriates were leaders in the effort to see America from a new perspective and to praise the country which they were seeing in this new light. By examining each of these editors' views of America, views expressed both in their *Broom* articles published during the expatriate period and in their memoirs published after the exile experience, we can see that their expatriation was not simple alienation, but rather more complex exploration.

Harold Loeb's memoirs, *The Way It Was,* published in 1959, describe Loeb's motivation for both his expatriation and his founding of *Broom.* The son of a father who was a Wall Street broker and a mother who was a member of the famous Guggenheim family, Loeb enjoyed a privilege of the wealthy, the opportunity to test out all sorts of occupations.[9] For young Loeb, this included being a Princeton student, a day laborer, a building contractor and a purchasing agent. Probably his most important job was a partnership in the Sunwise Turn bookshop in New York City, for this position plunged him into the artistic world of the 1920s, the world of literature, literati and aesthetic movements. Because of his exposure to this milieu, Loeb developed definite literary convictions, and in 1921 he decided to found a new literary magazine, one that would be experimental and innovative. He decided to publish his magazine in Italy. In addition to the financial advantages and the good printing and paper available there, this location would give the magazine an international dimension since it would be an opportunity to communicate American culture to Europe. "As far as I knew," Loeb recounted, "no one had ever published America's young writers in old Europe, where it was supposed in certain circles that American literature had stopped with Edgar Allan Poe" (*Way*, p. 6).

Loeb needed editorial assistance for his publication, and he found it in Alfred Kreymborg, a writer who had edited his own little magazine, *Others*. When Loeb met Kreymborg during a poetry evening at the Sunwise Turn, Loeb realized that the two men were attracted to each other "by a congruity of tastes. Both of us prized the new, the different, and the experimental, and tended to underrate traditional expressions...we both deplored the obeisance to Europe prevalent among Americans who aspired to culture" (*Way*, pp. 7-8). These words suggest the way in which Loeb and Kreymborg reflected the combination of expatriation and American cultural nationalism which would permeate *Broom*. Loeb specifically justified his expatriation in cultural nationalist terms: "I was convinced that whatever priority Europe may have had in the past, the new world was taking shape in these United States. And I believed I could recognize America's significant aspects more easily by living abroad for a while and observing them from a distance" (*Way*, p.8).

In his memoirs, Loeb remembered how *Broom* began, how this exploring, American publication took its first steps:

...I continued to welcome the visitors who came singly and in groups with bulging briefcases and large portfolios. As much as the conventional and the steadfast, they constituted America's strength, breaking ground when the old ways faltered: men and women with hopes, faiths, and doubts, smiling and scowling, agreeing, sometimes snarling: riffs and raffs from farm and city, the maladjusted and the visionary, those with fixed ideas and those with no ideas but nonconformism; marginal America, roles for which their conditioning should have prepared them, individuals who preferred to ask questions and to seek more congenial solutions.

To this task, in the field of values, *Broom* was dedicated (*Way*, p. 15).

Loeb's various articles in *Broom* were tributes to this American strength and to these American values. For example, in the February number, he contributed an editorial comment which emphasized the importance of a non-imitative, indigenous culture for the new American popular culture: "The Kid" by Charlie Chaplin, popular novels, *Saturday Evening Post,* the American newspaper, American architecture, street planning and the football stadium. These aspects of American life were of the utmost value in Loeb's view, for they were both enjoyed by and representative of the majority of the nation's populace.[10] As his contemporary, Gilbert Seldes, would later write: "...entertainment of a high order existed in places not usually associated with Art."[11] Loeb concluded that this new American Art was especially significant, for it was a national experience which should help its audience to recognize the "intrinsic value" and "originality" of their culture (pp.378-379).

In "Foreign Exchange," published in May, 1922, Loeb considered the same subject by describing the effect Europe was having upon the exiled American writers. Originally, these American expatriates, these "artistic pioneers," had withdrawn for two reasons: first, faced with a choice between deadening hack work or flight, they chose the latter; and second, confronted with democracy's negative results—the curtailment of individual liberty such as the adoption of Prohibition—they opted for exile. Paradoxically, these expatriates, in Loeb's view, were coming to a new vision of technological America, however, because of the admiration of the French artists for industrialism. In addition, the French writers were exposing the young American artists to a meticulous attention to form. In Loeb's opinion, this was a most desirable combination, for it merged art and cultural nationalism, a nationalism which revered technological culture and communicated it to the rest of the world. This nationalism, unlike the version of critics like Waldo Frank and Van Wyck Brooks, was not skeptical about the machine's effects upon modern America; on the contrary, it championed this technological progress and its influence upon the cultural life of the United States.[12]

In the September, 1922 issue, Loeb's article entitled "The Mysticism of Money" also expressed this nationalistic bent. (In 1941, Loeb said that "The Mysticism of Money" was badly written;[13] thus readers should be prepared for the article's stylistic inadequacies.) Analyzing modern "religion" and its effects upon the new America, Loeb called this religion the "mysticism of money":

Money, because that which was originally but a medium of exchange and valuable metal, has become the measuring staff of all values and the goal and reward of all efforts conventionally accepted as proper.

Mystic because the validity of the money standard and the intrinsic merit of money making are accepted on faith, extra-intellectually....Reasons are superfluous when a belief is obviously true.[14]

Using this definition of American religion, Loeb explored the relationship between the new technological art and its "religious" motivation:

The art of forming objects in the round or in relief by chiselling, carving, modelling, casting, etc. has reached greater proportions to-day than possible ever in the past. Engines, forges, hearths, furnaces, turbines, kettles, motors, generators, dynamoes, automobiles, ships aeroplanes—the list has no end. The purpose of all these is the efficient performance of specific tasks, which tasks are required by the industrial organization brought into existence and urged ever onward by the Mysticism of Money. These forms are not static but, like the older art forms, continually evolve through the introductions of small variations, in the direction of greater efficiency. The result is simplification, elimination of inessentials, balanced beauty. As perfection is approached the designer becomes more and more conscious of the aesthetic possibilities so that in well developed forms, such as the automobile body, new variations are primarily justified aesthetically. Other things being equal, the more beautiful form has a higher selling value. Thus in the end the technical intent of the designer is aesthetic (p. 120).

In addition to its influence upon technology, the mysticism of money, in Loeb's view, had a direct effect upon American writing. Specifically, three areas were transformed by the new religon. First, a new language was evolving: "Vigorous, crude, expressive, alive with metaphors, Rabelaisian, resembling Elizabethan rather than Victorian English. Conceived on sidewalks and born over bars, it can be found comparatively anywhere on the sporting sheets of newspapers, on the funny pages, occasionally on advertisements and on the stage, quite frequently in short stories" (p.125). Secondly, a new narrative technique had emerged, a technique best seen in the Nick Carter stories. With speed as their essential ingredient, these stories eliminated the data which usually accounted for logical continuity and produced, instead, stories characterized by their shock value, emotional intensity and sensationalism. Finally, new human types were being created by the mysticism of money. Strong man, chaste young girl, villain—these were all formed by some aspect of money, that "measuring staff of all values and the goal and reward of all efforts conventionally accepted as proper" (pp. 126-27). This last seems to have been more of an innovation to Loeb than to other literary critics, but Loeb nevertheless saw it, without any apparent irony, as a curiously contemporary development.

In addition to his praise for Nick Carter, Loeb also championed other examples of American art which are now identified as popular culture: the high place of Charlie Chaplin in the artistic world; the influence of American advertising upon Marinetti, Wyndham Lewis' *Blast,* and the dadaists; the difference between jazz as a universal ("Its melodies come from everywhere, stolen, bought and invented...") and Negro spirituals as true American folk music. Of particular significance, however, was Loeb's description of Spenglerian-like stages of civilization. America, according to Loeb, was still in the youthful stage—the "formative-creative art epoch"—and it was still searching for ways to express itself culturally and artistically. This process meant that America and the mysticism of money had not yet arrived at maturity, but were still coming of age. As they came of age, moreover, one idea, according to Loeb, should remain paramount: "America must not imitate Europe" (p.115).

Thus Harold Loeb, founder and editor of *Broom*, was clearly a nationalistic explorer. He believed in his country even as he exiled himself from it, and he especially believed in America's newness, superiority and originality.

Matthew Josephson was another proponent of these same ideas. He joined *Broom*'s staff as assistant editor in 1922, and, like Loeb, his nationalistic interests motivated him as exile and as artist. Born in Brooklyn in 1899 and graduating from Columbia University's College of Liberal Arts in 1919, Josephson was an outspoken critic of the pre-War Victorian culture and an enthusiastic supporter of modernism, literary experimentation and artistic excellence. During his college years, he became acquainted with others who shared his views, "iconoclasts" like Malcolm Cowley, Kenneth Burke and William Slater Brown. Later, Josephson lived in Greenwich Village and continued to be involved in the avant-garde world of artist, newness and challenge which Loeb and Kreymborg had also enjoyed. As Josephson would later write of himself:

My curse has been extreme versatility; I began as a poet and belle-lettriste, have written one novel; numerous biographies; short stories that were precieux; essays on political questions; journalism on the same; and for some years I have been a kind of historian, according to my own unacademic ideas...[15]

After the War, Josephson joined the expatriate movement and lived in Paris, the place he called his "second country," from 1921-1923. He described this experience in his autobiography, *Life*

Among the Surrealists, published in 1962.[16] During this time, he collaborated with Gorham Munson to found and edit the little magazine *Secession.* The two men, however, had quite different views about the purpose and policy of their publication, for Munson preferred writers like Theodore Dreiser and Waldo Frank, while Josephson believed that *Secession* should be "publishing and championing the adventurous experimenters of America, translating the work of the avant-garde in France and Germany, and vigorously assailing the Mrs. Grundies of literature" (*Life,* p. 154). Unable to accomplish this in the pages of *Secession,* Josephson turned to *Broom.*

Because Josephson was, at different points, a champion of many European art movements—dadaism, surrealism, symbolism, imagism, constructivism—*Broom*'s German issues reveal the impact of these avant-garde "isms." It is important to note, however, that Josephson saw these European developments, particularly dadaism, as influenced by American materials and American popular art. In his autobiography, Josephson best formulated what he had been arguing as early as 1922 when he announced that many Continental art forms were "derived in great part from American source materials" (*Life,* p. 190). As one example of this, he commented that the American cinema greatly influenced French poetry, especially the works of Guillaume Apollinaire, Blaise Centrars, and Phillips Soupault. He quoted Soupault as one illustration of this influence:

'Those darkened halls...became the living theatre of our laughter, our anger, our pride. In those miraculous crimes and farewells our eyes read the poetry of our age. We were living with passion through a most beautiful period of which the U.S. cinema was the brightest ornament' (*Life,* pp. 123-24).

Similarly, Josephson observed how Marcel Duchamp had abandoned Cubist painting and had gone to live in America, thus ultimately affecting the direction of the European art movements.

He collected bits of rubbish, absurd machines, dummies, clothing racks, and other such disjected membra of America's 'ready-mades,' offered them as artifacts selected and signed by himself. The troubling humor with which this great mystificator attacked the art of the past—a humor inspired largely by the American environment favoring such activity—made a profound impression upon the Dada and Surealist cults in Europe (*Life*, p. 124).

Furthermore, Josephson pointed to a young France that was "passionately concerned with the civilization of the U.S.A., and stood in a fair way to being *Americanized*" (*Life*, p. 125). This realization prompted him to read Apollinaire as a visionary, a man whose ideas "were nothing if not Whitmanesque and American in tone": "Is there nothing new under the sun? For the sun perhaps so—but for man everything!... The poet is to stop at nothing in his quest for novelty of form and material; he is to take advantage of all the infinite new combinations afforded by the mechanism of everyday life" (*Life*, p. 125).

Because Josephson believed that European art was influenced by American art, *Broom*'s associate editor was convinced of the magazine's need to be more American in its contents, contributors, and attitudes. He felt that *Broom*'s literary tendency "was all too catholic," and he intended to "bring it [*Broom*] home to the U.S.A" (*Life*, p. 188). This, in fact, he would accomplish, for *Broom*'s German issues were succeeded by a series of American numbers published in New York City.

Josephson's contributions to *Broom* focused upon his belief in America's cultural superiority. For example, to the June, 1922 issue he contributed an article entitled "Made in America" which emphasized the technological aspects of American culture. For Josephson, the machine was "our magnificent slave, our fraternal genius, and because it was indigenous to America and reflective of the nation's emerging identity, it was worthy of both praise and celebration.[17] This technological wonder was "made in America," and therefore it was alive, it was valuable, and, most important, it was superior to any other culture's products or symbols.

Similarly, in the November, 1922 issue, he published "The Great American Billposter," an evaluation of this indigenous

American art. He suggested that the advertisements which surrounded the American people were, in fact, the "folklore" of modern times, and as such composed "a faithful record of the national tastes, the changing philosophy, the hopes and fears of a people."[18] He cited several examples to illustrate this position.

The American is emotional and generous, but at the same time he is thrifty:
USURY.
Six per cent is considered a fair rate of interest; too high a rate of interest is condemned as usury. Yet there are several thousand American homes in which an IDEAL TYPE A HEAT MACHINE is paying back 33 per cent on its cost—so great is the proportion of fuel saved and so little does it depreciate in comparison with cheaper heating plants (p. 308).

Similarly, the American is "far more amenable to suggestion, to hypnosis rather than to logic":

ASK DAD HE KNOWS
ASK THE MAN WHO OWNS ONE

or better this:

DAY BY DAY IN EVERY WAY
I AM GETTING BETTER AND BETTER (p. 308).

Furthermore, the American possesses an "uproarious self-assertion":

ZIEGFELD FOLLIES
GLORIFIES THE AMERICAN GIRL (p. 309).

This billposter phenomenon, according to Josephson, was definitely "art":

The art of people is a two-edged sword: it spring [sic] from the moods and virtues of that people. But we have learned recently to extend the meaning of 'art' inasmuch as modern man expressed himself in a far greater variety of manners than did prehistoric or classical man. An ethnological study of a group such as the Americans (of the United States of America) could no longer restrict itself to its politics, sculpture, and mythology; for, thanks to the aggressive application of the arts to new inventions, we find that the automobile is on the road to becoming a thing of beauty and that the advertisements contain the fables of this people. We would, thus, be obliged to observe the motion picture, the sports, the machinery, and many other aspects of the group's behaviour in order to really know its culture (p. 304).

This rationale provided the basis for Josephson's approach to popular culture, for his belief in what Loeb had called "the intrinsic value" and "originality" of American culture. It gave Josephson a framework in which he could evaluate the style of the popular artist and thus appraise him as a new kind of poet:

The particular restrictions of this medium [advertising] make for extraordinary ingenuity in the 'copy writer'; the call for vigor of conviction and interest, are probably more stimulating by far toward creating beautiful conceptions than an intensive course in Victorian poetry at Harvard University. The terse vivid slang of the people has been swiftly transmitted to this class of writers, along with a willingness to depart from syntax, to venture sentence forms and word constructions which are at times breathtaking, if anything, and in all cases far more arresting and provocative than 99 per cent of the stuff that passes for poetry in our specialized magazines (p. 309).

Josephson, then, like Loeb, was not an embittered exile; on the contrary, he was an American who believed in his country and who tried to identify the new symbols of a new nation. He was indeed an explorer whose nationalism provided a kind of map for his travels.

Malcolm Cowley was another nationalist who joined *Broom*'s staff at Josephson's urging. A Harvard graduate, he was part of the expatriate generation in Paris from 1921-1923, an experience he later described in his book *Exile's Return*.[19] Like the other editors of *Broom*, Cowley was interested in many current ideas and involved in numerous literary endeavors, including poetry, prose, magazine work, and editing projects. Especially important for this study, however, is Cowley's nationalism, a critical yet loyal belief in America's cultural superiority which he shared with other *Broom* editors. As he commented in a recent letter to this writer asking for his attitude toward this nationalistic posture: "In general it was that of a critical patriot— it's a hell of a country, I seemed to be saying, but it's mine."[20] Furthermore, Cowley demonstrated his nationalistic belief in a manner which was similar to Josephson's. Where Josephson pointed to America's influence upon and consequent superiority over European art, Cowley began with the opposite assertion but arrived at the same conclusion: European art influenced American art because Americans built upon Continental developments to produce their own superior cultural forms. Writing to Waldo Frank in response to Frank's article, "Seriousness and Dada," Cowley explained this building process:

You have been to Paris and have brought back the gossips of Monsieur X the poet and Monsieur Y the novelist. I have been to Paris and met Messieurs X and Y. Other American writers have been to Paris. Some of them meet Paul Fort and write polyphonic prose in his manner, some meet Paul Valery and become classicists, some meet Soupault, Aragon or Tzara and write a Yankee Dada, some meet Jules Romains and his serious little groups, study his treatises on Unanimism, adopt his more solemn thoughts and some of his virtues and are proud to be called the Unanimists of America. There are also Americans who go to Paris, meet many people of many schools, take the best of each, and retain the conviction to write about their own surroundings in their own manner....[21]

Cowley announced that he was a leader in this process of merging international and national tendencies:

In this day of advertising slogans one must have a little ticket which admits one to the Sunset Limited or the Oriental Express, blue or yellow, a slip of cardboard printed with the name....I, Mr. Frank, am...the clever but not corruscant smart or swift young man who clutters our serious magazines, the American Dada.[22]

Like Loeb and Josephson, this "American Dada" contributed articles to *Broom* which revealed his interest in post-War

American values. An interesting contribution was "Young Mr. Elkins," a satire of those people who did not appreciate the inherent values of the nation's popular culture. Appearing in the December, 1922 issue, this article presented a portrait of "an American intellectual," a man who belonged "to the professionally young," who, at sixty, would retain "the discouraged deep scepticism of adolescence."[23] Young Mr.Elkins, disturbed by what he saw emerging in post-War America, by "the new feeling" engulfing the nation, tried to quell the movement of the New American culture and to channel the American energies into creating a culture that was imitative of the Continental experience.

The new feeling that is in America...it inspired young Mr. Elkins to thunder against billboards, Billy Sunday and Methodism, proportional representation, Comstock, elevated railroads. One year with a special fulgurance he thundered against the commercial ugliness of cities. American civilization listened and moved uneasily like a sleeping volcano. Stung finally to action by his criticism it spewed forth city planning commissions, commissions specially trained at the Beaux Arts and specially delegated to make Paris, Okla. the replica of Paris, France, in miniature. (p. 54).

In his efforts to reform the new America, Mr. Elkins acted from a simple principle:

Puritanism is bad; America is puritan; therefore America is bad. (Or, to state his syllogism in its more usual form: America is bad; America is puritan, therefore puritanism is bad). (Or: badness is puritan; badness is American; America is therefore badly puritan). He has never tried to define puritanism or America (pp. 54-55).

Cowley's portrait ended with a supreme touch of irony, for young Mr. Elkins, anti-American Mr. Elkins, wrote his reactionary sentiments "on a typewriter which is the most finished product of a mechanical civilization," a civilization which "howls outside his window":

...An elevated express rumbles up Ninth Avenue and an elevated local rumbles down Ninth Avenue. Precisely under Mr. Elkins' room four subway trains crash past each other. One of them is bound for the 273rd Street hugest Tabernacle, where Mr. Sunday preaches that afternoon to an audience of over fifteen thousand....Thirty stories below an automobile skids into a shop window, killing two and a wax dummy....A cable snaps on Brooklyn Bridge; fire spreads to the oil tanks; on the docks a carload of dynamite explodes....

Young Mr. Elkins, annoyed by the racket, rose nervously and closed his window (p. 56).

The America which was despised by Mr. Elkins was praised in another aricle by Cowley, "Pascin's America." This piece is significant more for its comments on the new American culture than for its description of the style of the Bulgarian artist who became an American citizen in 1914. Pointing to Pascin's ability to paint the American people and capture the American spirit, Cowley expressed what he believed to be the continual newness of the American nation:

Before Walt Whitman America hardly existed; to him we owe the pioneers, the open spaces, in general the poetry of square miles. Bret Harte created California and Twain the Mississippi. Woodrow Wilson, Chaplin, the James brothers; each created a separate America, an America which frightened pleasantly or amused us, a God-righteous America for which we fortunately did not die. America is a conception which must be renewed each morning with the papers. It is not one conception but a million which change daily, which melt daily into one another.[24]

This comment is especially applicable to *Broom*'s editors, the expatriate explorers Loeb, Josephson and Cowley. Trying to renew America, they separated themselves from the land of their roots and searched for new ways to see, to create, to express themselves. Their vehicle was the little magazine; their attitude, nationalism; their posture, loyalty. They were not like Bill Gorton's description in *The Sun Also Rises*: "You're an expatriate. You've lost touch with the soil. You get precious. Fake European standards have ruined you. You drink yourself to death. You become obsessed by sex. You spend all your time talking, not working. You are an expatriate, see? You hang around cafes."[25] Rather, they were explorers who carried within them the country they were trying to renew.

Notes

[1]Matthew Josephson, *Infidel in the Temple* (New York: Knopf, 1967), p. 4.

[2]Warren Susman, "American Cultural Criticism," (Thesis University of Wisconsin 1950), pp. 176-79.

[3]Quoted in Hugh Ford, *The Left Bank Revisited* (University Park: Pennsylvania State University Press, 1972), p. xxi.

[4]Quoted in Ford, p. xxi.

[5]James Gilbert, *Writers and Partisans: A History of Literary Radicalism in America* (John Wiley & Sons, Inc., 1968), pp. vi-viii.

[6]Malcolm Cowley, *Exile's Return* (1934; rpt. New York: The Viking Press, 1969), p. 289.

In his discussion of the expatriates, Cowley also offers the reasons for calling this generation "lost," reasons which help to illuminate the withdrawal patterns of the exiled artists:

> It was lost, first of all, because it was uprooted, schooled away and almost wrenched away from its attachment to any region or tradition. It was lost because its training had prepared it for another world than existed after the war (and because the war prepared it only for travel and excitement). It was lost because it tried to live in exile. It was lost because it had formed a false picture of society and the writers's place in it (p. 9).

[7]T.S. Eliot, *Four Quartets* in *The Complete Poems and Plays* (New York: Harcourt, Brace and World, Inc., 1952),p. 145.

[8]*The Little Magazine: A History and Bibliography* (Frederick J. Hoffman, Charles Allen, Carolyn F. Ulrich [Princeton: Princeton University Press, 1946]) is an excellent study of *Broom* and many other little magazines.

[9]Biographical information on Harold Loeb primarily taken from *The Way It Was,* Harold Loeb (New York: Criterian Books, 1959). Specific references to this book, unless otherwise noted, will be indicated by a parenthetical insertion in the following way: (*Way*, p.   ). The reader might be interested to know that Harold Loeb was Hemingway's model for Robert Cohn in *The Sun Also Rises.*

[10]Harold Loeb, "Comment," *Broom,* I (February 1922), pp. 377-379.

[11]Gilbert Seldes, *The Seven Lively Arts* (New York: A.S. Barnes and Company, Inc., 1924), p. 3.

Although Seldes did not contribute any articles to *Broom,* he did influence the magazine's position on popular arts. In Loeb's memoirs, the Broom editor recalled a luncheon with Seldes during which Seldes discussed the importance of American popular art, reinforced Loeb's ideas on the subject, and suggested some new avenues for Loeb to pursue (*Way*, p. 109).Seldes was even more influential, however, because of the general impact of his ideas upon the cultural milieu of the twenties. His numerous magazine articles and his 1924 book proclaimed the excellence of the American popular arts—comic strips, motion pictures, musical comedy, vaudeville, radio, popular music, and the dance—and his ideas had a definite impact upon the critics and artists of the decade. e.e. cummings, for example, was probably influenced by Seldes' theories when he attempted to merge high-brow and low-brow art in his play *him*, first produced in 1927. (see author's article, " 'Damn Everything but the Circus': Popular Art in the Twenties and *him*," *Modern Drama*, [March, 1974], pp. 43-55).

[12]Harold Loeb, "Foreign Exchange," *Broom*, 2 (May 1922), pp. 176-181.

[13]Harold Loeb to Charles Allen: August 25, 1941. Collection of American Literature, the Beinecke Rare Book and Manuscript Library, Yale University.

[14]Harold Loeb, "The Mysticism of Money," *Broom*, 2 (September 1922), p. 117.

[15]Matthew Josephson to Professor Fred Millet: April 26, 1937, Matthew Josephson Papers, Yale, quoted in Paula Fass, *Matthew Josephson—A Biography* (Collection of American Literature, The Beinecke Rare Book and Manuscript Library, Yale University, 1966), p. 1.

[16]Matthew Josephson, *Life Among the Surrealists* (New York: Holt, Rinehart and Winston, 1962), p. 79. Specific references to this book, unless otherwise noted, will be indicated by a parenthetical insertion in the following way: (*Life*, p.   ).

[17]*Broom*, 2 (June 1922), pp. 266-270.

[18]Matthew Josephson, "The Great American Billposter," *Broom*, 3 (November 1922), p. 309.

[19]This book is an extremely useful and interesting study of both expatriation and the reintegration of the expatriates; because of this two-faceted approach, Cowley's study is a particularly enlightening cultural document of the 1920s.

[20]Malcolm Cowley to author: August 21, 1974.

[21]Malcolm Cowley to Waldo Frank: November 23, 1924, Malcolm Cowley's papers, The Newberry Library.

[22]Malcolm Cowley to Waldo Frank.

[23]Malcolm Cowley, "Young Mr. Elkins,"*Broom*, 4 (December 1922), p. 53.

[24]Malcolm Cowley, "Pascin's America,"*Broom*, 4 (January 1922), pp. 136-7.

[25]Ernest Hemingway, *The Sun Also Rises* (New York: 1926; rpt. Charles Scribner's Sons, 1970), p. 115.

The Family Journey to the West

Paul T. Bryant

Traditionally, one of the more dramatic aspects of the settlement of the American West is the journey westward of the pioneer family in quest of a homestead and a new life. This westering suggests a standard picture of covered wagons drawn by oxen plodding slowly across treeless plains and over towering mountain ranges. The stalwart father walks alongside the ox team with a goad in his hand, while the courageous mother sits on the wagon box and assorted children peer anxiously from under the edges of the canvas wagon cover. Perhaps a milk cow shambles along tied to the tail gate.

At night the wagons stop in a circle for protection from marauding Indians. Meals are cooked over fires fueled, on the plains, by dried buffalo chips. The men take turns standing guard, and sometimes Indian raids actually occur. At dawn everyone turns out for another plodding day, until finally the promised land—Oregon or California or wherever—is reached. There the train disbands and each family finds its own piece of land, builds its sod hut or log cabin, tills the soil, and the story ends.

Like many cliches, this picture is essentially accurate for many pioneer families, but it has perhaps caused us to overlook other significant aspects of this basic pattern and to neglect both their cultural and literary importance in the settlement of the American frontier. Historians give us the broad historical patterns while understandably neglecting individual family experiences. Writers of fiction—one thinks, for example, of A.B. Guthrie's *The Way West*—draw upon the tradition and clothe it with dramatic reality, or some may attempt to de-romanticize it by emphasizing the ignorance, squalor, and plain wrong-headedness that were sometimes features of the western migration. Here one might cite some of the short stories and sketches of H.L. Davis, for example. Even with the negative presentation, seldom does the picture vary much from the standard pattern we have come to expect.

153

One window to a more varied and detailed view of the pioneer family in its epic journey to the West is the family history. This is a form of folk literature which has received some attention as sources for local and regional history, but no notice from literary scholars. Yet these histories form a distinctive literary genre of which there are hundreds, perhaps thousands, of examples deposited in museums, libraries and archives all across this country.

Perhaps we should begin a consideration of the pioneer family history with a general definition of the genre. Such a definition cannot be absolute in its boundaries, but it can suggest the general parameters of those features, most of which can be found in any given work designated a pioneer family history.

First, of course, it is a history through more than one generation of a family that has pioneered on the western American frontier. As such, it is more than a diary, journal, or autobiography of one individual. Although it usually focuses on the generation or generations directly involved in the move to the West and the early settlement there, the history of earlier generations will be at least summarized as a necessary background to understanding the pioneers, and the experience of later generations down at least to that of the author will be included. Although the biography of one pioneer may be central to the work, the true family history will go beyond the life of an individual to give a sense of the continuing history of the family.

It must have been prepared in written form as contrasted with taped oral histories. This means that it must have been intended as a formal written document.

Many, perhaps the majority, of these histories were written by a member of the family from a later generation using as sources memoirs, letters, journals, family traditions, and the personal reminiscences of surviving members of earlier generations. Rarely, but occasionally, they will be by members of the actual pioneering generations, and sometimes they will be by local history enthusiasts acquainted with the family. A high percentage of the authors are women, the daughters or granddaughters of the pioneers. Seldom is the author a professional writer or scholar, a characteristic that may reduce the average level of literary polish but clearly adds to the "folk" quality of such works. The language may be awkward, repetitious, even ungrammatical, but it generally represents the vision and mode of expression of its author's generation and social context in the West.

The authors' reasons for writing these histories seem most often to rise from one central impulse: to record what earlier generations endured and accomplished, so that such a record might serve as an inspiration to similar achievement.

For a very numerous and significant subdivision of this genre, the Mormon family history, these temporal reasons are supplemented by doctrinal concerns regarding the immortal souls of ancestors not already in that church, and by a desire to record the blessings of God on the church and its members, and the strength and achievement possible through faith. David King Udall, for example, when he was assisting his daughter in preparing his biography, which became a family history, wrote, "I have no ambition to tell the world of our experiences—such would be vanity indeed. But deep in my heart, I do desire to bear record to my kindred and to my posterity of the goodness of God unto us, as shown in the unfolding of our family life."[1]

Such rationales, of course, are part of a common American tradition traceable back to the earliest journals and histories of Massachusetts Bay and Plymouth. Both the democratic impulse and Protestant theology have suggested to even the earliest European settlers in America that the affairs of the common people, as well as of kings and generals, are of interest and significance to later generations. At the same time, the achievements of one's own people can serve both as a guide and as a challenge to make the present measure up to the past.

These family histories are usually privately printed in small quantities for limited distribution, mostly to members of the family. Some have been printed by local history groups for somewhat wider local circulation, and some are still only in typescript or manuscript in local history collections. The works are often of book length, but not always, sometimes appearing in local history collections of "old timers' tales" and memoirs. For the most part they are difficult to locate or even to identify by bibliographic means, and copies are rare and not easy to obtain for study.

As a group, these histories form a folk literature recording family traditions and giving an insight into the experiences and attitudes of individual pioneer settlers of the West. Many present individual adventures, and of course there is a great temptation merely to relate some of the best of these for their own sake. But as a genre these family histories fall into certain patterns that illuminate the American pioneer experience in the westward journey and at the same time help define traditional patterns in a folk literature.

Two types of patterns emerge from an examination of numbers of pioneer family histories. One type is cultural, arising from the experiences of the pioneers, and from their responses to those experiences, and coming also from the cultural perceptions and assumptions which the individual family brought to its pioneering adventures. The other type of pattern is literary, arising from the techniques of narration, description, and interpretation imposed on the material by the writer. It is not always clear when the written presentation only reflects the attitudes and understanding of the pioneers themselves, and when it is the interpretation of the writer, viewing the events from a later generation, but some few patterns emerge that suggest a developed literary tradition imposed upon the original material. Examples of these two types of patterns should serve to illustrate.

Cultural Patterns

Among the cultural patterns that emerge frequently is that of continual movement on the part of the pioneer families. Modern literary treatment of the pioneer trek westward generally presents it as a single journey accomplished in one continuous effort and aimed at a specific goal, such as the Willamette Valley. Again Guthrie's *The Way West* provides an excellent example in a contemporary novel. Certainly this was often the case, as illustrated in the Powell family history of a wagon train to Oregon.[2] The prime movers of this wagon train were Illinois farmers, apparently reasonably prosperous and settled, but:

Our people had been reading of the Oregon country for a number of years, and had also received direct information from a man who had visited the Willamette Valley. In 1850 they decided to sell their farms in Illinois and seek the advantages of a milder climate and the fertile land offered by the government. When they arrived in the valley in September, 1851, and viewed the beautiful mountain scenery, the wonderful evergreens, and the valley covered with native grass waisthigh, unfenced and largely unclaimed, they felt that they had really reached the promised land....[3]

But this somewhat static impression of settled families uprooting themselves for one grand pioneering move westward, followed by permanent settlement, is quite misleading if it is taken as a totally representative pattern. Many families made the journey across the plains as only one part of a lifetime, or even generations, of footloose wandering that did not end until the close of the frontier, if then.[4] The move westward was not a single venture, but rather a part of a lifelong search for something that many families never found. Perhaps what the families said they were seeking will shed some light on their continuous movement.

One of the most commonly expressed reasons for going West, of course, was a search for greater economic opportunity. Some hoped for land, for farms that were larger and more fertile than they could hope for back east, or for ranches that had not been overgrazed and exhausted. Some hoped for business opportunities as merchants or freighters or innkeepers. And some sought El Dorado's quick wealth in the western gold and silver mines.

Better health was another benefit sought in the West by many pioneer families. Malaria, tuberculosis, asthma and dozens of other, less clearly identified ills were to be left behind in the higher, drier, clearer air of the West. The Promised Land, after all, would surely have not only fertile soil but also health-giving air and sunshine, as escape from the fever-ridden South and Midwest.

The traditional frontier search for "more room" provided a third though less distinct motivation for continuous westering, a drive that was automatically self-defeating as more and more people followed it into the "new" country. The benefits of "more room" were never spelled out, particularly when the seekers were often moving from country that was only partially settled and certainly not crowded. Most commonly those who gave this reason for westering appear to have been strong minded, self reliant individualists who perhaps were seeking freedom from social restraint. Many of these demonstrated that they were men willing to shoot first and ask questions later.

The large number of families for whom the journey westward ended only with the closing of the frontier suggests that the western dreams of Eden, of El Dorado, the search for land and health and wealth and freedom, did not come true. Social and economic pressures, human depravity and their own mortality followed them wherever they went, but the persistence of the dream itself is demonstrated over and over by the fact that they kept on moving in search of its realization. In these terms the journey westward became for many families an unending search for something more than this world can provide. It thus became the stuff of which myths are made.

These central motives, of course, were those of the male "head" of the family. Family histories repeatedly reveal that the father of the family was the one who made the decision to move West. If the opinion of the mother of the family is mentioned at all, she is likely to have been, at the least reluctant, if not downright opposed to the move, and understandably so in most cases. At the beginning of the family's westering, the father and mother were usually young. There were usually young children and more often than not the mother was pregnant—if not when the move began, at least before it was completed. Miscarriages were not uncommon and the mortality rate among young children and their mothers was high. Yet pregnancy did not appear to be a deterrent to any move the father might decide to make. It seems to have been accepted as a standard condition of life and part of the burden women must bear as they followed their husbands' search for the Promised Land.[5]

Of course, those women who successfully resisted their husbands' urge to move west would not be likely to appear in a study of pioneer family histories, but some did manage to resist.

One case in point was the wife of John Jacob Miller (the first names of many of these women are not given in the histories). John Miller was a frontiersman and hunter and spent much of his time in the West, but his wife steadfastly refused to leave their farm in Illinois. On one of his visits home (and he must have made several—the family had nine children), John secretly made arrangements to sell the farm, presumably as a way to force his wife to go west with him. Unfortunately for his plans, she learned of his arrangements and "put a stop to them" before he could carry them through. Mrs. Miller never went west.[6]

This is not to say that all women went west unwillingly. Many were willing to face the hardships and dangers if they could gain something worth the risk and effort.

Another standard assumption about the pioneer family's journey to the West is that the entire trip was accomplished in a single season. In many cases this was true, but in a significant number of instances the journey was interrupted by extended stays along the route, and sometimes the original objective was never reached.

When the Julius Sanders family set out for California in 1861, they stopped near Denver to raise a crop of corn on Wild Plum Creek. They sold the corn for travelling expenses and continued on to California the following year. Even then they did not settle. In 1863 two of the sons went to Arizona, found gold, returned to California for the rest of the family, and arrived in Arizona in 1864.[7]

Substantial delays might be caused by anticipated Indian trouble. Military posts along the trails would sometimes stop emigrant parties until they could be better equipped, or until several smaller parties could be gathered to make up a single, stronger group. Often this might mean only a few days' delay, but on occasion it might hold up a group until the following spring.

Clearly the westward journey of the pioneer family was not purely a success or disaster, "California or Bust" type of undertaking. Most of these people were resilient and resourceful, able to adapt to changing circumstances even of the most extreme kind. If California was not possible, they would settle for Colorado or Kansas or Nebraska or Iowa. If they could not complete the journey the same year they started, they would winter as best they might and continue the following year. The journey westward for these families was not an interruption in their lives, but an integral and sometimes extended part of it.

Tradition presents the mode of travel of the pioneer family as the covered wagon, drawn by horses, mules or oxen, and the tradition is largely accurate.[8] However, there were significant variations. For example, migrants westward from Texas often had large herds of cattle, or more rarely large flocks of sheep, to drive with them. Instead of wagon trains such as were standard on the Oregon and California Trails, the herd would be the main element of the group, accompanied by horsemen and a few supply wagons, in which might be riding the women and children. As the railroads penetrated the Southwest, a portion of the journey even for the livestock might be made by train. To keep the herds healthy and intact, the journey might be made through two or more seasons with planned stops for grazing the stock for extended periods of time.

In the years after the completion of the transcontinental railroad, families might use it to make a major part of their westward journey, sometimes going all the way to the West Coast and then coming back eastward into Arizona or southern Nevada by ship around Baja California to the mouth of the Colorado and then up that river by steamer for as far as it was navigable, or overland eastward across the southern deserts. By rail, of course, travel was quicker, the hazards were fewer, and the introduction to the West more directly concentrated in the arrival rather than being spread through weeks or months of slow travel and nightly camping.

The travellers' attitudes toward the Indians also varied perhaps more than is generally supposed. They range along a spectrum from sheer hatred and terror through suspicion and paternalistic condescension to respect and sympathy for their plight, although such sympathy was apparently rare, and seldom acted on.

Families venturing into the West for the first time were naturally fearful of Indian attacks. They had heard many stories of Indian raids on wagon trains and isolated settlements and ranches, and these stories coupled with the element of a danger outside their previous experience often led them to expect the worst. Settlers who had lost friends or loved ones in Indian raids might have been expected to have an implacable hatred for Indians, but even here there is often a surprising dispassion in the relation of such losses. At times in such accounts, losses to Indian hostilities seem to be accepted in much the same spirit as losses to floods or droughts or other natural disasters, as if the Indians were a natural force that unavoidably went with the western landscape.

At the same time, there were whites who believed the Indian version of such events as the Skull Valley massacre in Arizona,[9] and who saw the injustice of the Kern River massacre in California.[10] Certainly even the inexperienced travellers made distinctions among the various tribes and did not regard all Indians as the same.

In Colorado a train of 60 wagons captained by Joseph Ehle, in about 1864, met an unexpected instance of fraternal cooperation from the Indians. Ehle, a Mason, was told by an old trapper that he could get through a dangerous stretch of Indian country to the south because someone had made the chief in area a Mason. Accordingly, Ehle painted the Masonic emblem on the lead wagons of the train. True to his fraternal obligations, the chief sent a group of young warriors to escort the train through his territory safely and to hunt for them. They stayed with the train for twenty days.[11]

In short, white settlers and Indians are presented in these family histories as more often enemies than as friends, but the white attitudes toward the Indians seldom match some of the more extreme present day stereotypes of white racist attitudes in the West.

Literary Patterns
    In addition to these cultural patterns common to many of the family histories' accounts of the journey westward, a few conventions emerge that might be called literary patterns common in family histories. It is these more than the cultural patterns that might justify calling pioneer family histories a

genre of folk literature.

One of the most striking and common of these is the idea that the urge and the aptitude for pioneering are at least a cultural if not a biological heritage. The fact that so many family histories present a continuing movement westward through several generations makes such an interpretation understandable, but it appears in these histories so frequently and in such similar terms that it becomes conventional. Albert Banta wrote, of his family, "For generations the Bantas have been pioneers.... My parents, being pioneers by heredity, migrated to the Territory of Wisconsin in 1846."[12] With more emphasis on environment than heredity, another family historian writes, "Mr. Shivers was a lifelong pioneer of the West, as even his ancestors before him were pioneers of Tennessee....Mr. Shivers was fit by precept and education for the trials and difficulties of a life such as always confronts the pioneer of a new country."[13] Again, Alfred Hight went West from Delaware because he "had pioneer blood in his veins!"[14] Thus the westering of these families came to be regarded, in retrospect at least, as something like the individual equivalent of the nation's Manifest Destiny. This helps to explain the frequent interest in genealogy, and the interest of each author in writing the family's history, particularly when the author is a member of that family. The reader may be reminded here of the intricate genealogies of heroes in the sagas of northern Europe.

As might be expected in folk histories of this type, the tone is almost uniformly laudatory. Any cruelty, meanness, or questionable practices are glossed over or justified, sometimes elaborately. John Slaughter may have had a habit of ending a trail drive through cattle country with two or three times as many cattle as he had had when he started, but that was merely a "common" practice of the time. A tendency on the part of some pioneers to shoot Indians without apparent provocation was rationalized into an "understandable precaution" in the face of the supposed perfidiousness of the red man. And of course the occupation, by force if necessary, of land already held by Indians was justified as nothing more than wresting the land from the wilderness and elevating it to a higher use. Thus these family histories can not be expected to be either objective or highly analytical, but they probably reflect the justification the pioneers would have presented for themselves. Certainly these histories were written from a distinct viewpoint that is very similar from one to the next.

Pioneer family histories often draw upon the written memoirs of the actual participants in events, and from historical documents of various types, but they also draw to a considerable extent upon an oral tradition within the family, what Mody Boatright has called the "family saga."[15] This is sometimes acknowledged directly by the family historian: "This volume is part of the living tradition of a family. My brother and I heard this story, and particularly the highlighted episodes, many times during our childhood, and our children have heard them in their turn. Expressions have flowed from these experiences into the family vocabulary and have contributed to those intimate ties by which a family group develops its own characteristic patterns."[16] This same work exhibits some characteristics one might expect from such an oral tradition, distilled from memories of actual events over the years. For example, the author reports having personally observed, as a child in a wagon train along the Platte, "a prairie dog and an owl or two sitting on the rim of a hole with a rattlesnake coiled alongside." This, the author says, was "a common sight."[17] The same author reports in impressive detail a meeting between her father and Buffalo Bill in the town of North Platte in 1873. Cody's clothing, down to the silk thread embroidery of his cowboy boots, is described. Cody introduces himself as a government scout and gives a detailed warning about a Sioux village the wagon train will soon encounter on the trail to Denver. Yet not only is a government scout unlikely to have been dressed as Cody is said to have been (except in a Wild West show), but also Cody left government service in 1872 for show business. Apparently an indistinctly recollected encounter with a government scout has become embellished in the family saga with the trappings of the later show business hero and has then been set down in the family history. Similar discrepancies in the story (the 54 mile journey from Greeley to Denver, by wagon, is telescoped into a single day with arrival in the early afternoon, for example) also suggest the tendency of the oral tradition to discard the duller aspects of the story and make it more interesting and direct, a tendency common also in folklore and the folk ballad.

Similar phrases occurring in different accounts of the same events also suggest the oral tradition that often lies behind the written family history. An example of this may be found in the Powell family history, in which the narrative of the journey to Oregon written by S. Hamilton, and that written by L. Jane Powell, conclude almost identically with the observation that they arrived at their destination September 3, "having been five months to a day from our starting point in Illinois" (Hamilton) or "five months to a day since we left Illinois" (Powell). Both of these sources seem to have heard the same narrative of the family saga of the train to Oregon enough times to have absorbed the standard phrasing.

Perhaps most significant to our present consideration of the journey westward is that in most cases the family history does not focus on the journey westward either as the climactic or the central episode of the family's story. Most often the pioneering after arrival, pioneering that frequently includes a series of further moves, forms the center of the narrative. Unlike Steinbeck's "The Leader of the People," most of the actors in these family histories seem to have found challenges at the end of the journey at least equal to the challenges of the journey itself.

NOTES

[1]David King Udall, *Arizona Pioneer Mormon, David King Udall,* written in collaboration with his daughter, Pearl Udall Nelson (Tucson: Arizona Silhouettes, 1959), p. 2.

[2]James Madison Powell, *Powell History: An Account of the Powell Ancestors of 1851—John A., Noah and Alfred—Their Ancestors, Descendants and Other Relatives* (privately printed, 1922). I am indebted to Professor Gilbert Powell Findlay for giving me access to this volume.

[3]Powell, p. 27.

[4]Examples of this continued wandering are myriad. For example: Albert F. Banta,*Albert Franklin Banta, Arizona Pioneer,* ed. Frank D. Reeves, Historical Society of New Mexico Publications in History, Vol. XIV (September, 1953), p. 4; Fannie Wingfield Stephens, "A Pioneer of the Verde Valley," *Echoes of the Past: Tales of Old Yavapai,* 3rd ed. (Prescott, Arizona: The Yavapai Cow Belles, 1972),

pp. 129-135; Allen A. Erwin, *The Southwest of John H. Slaughter, 1841-1922,* Western Frontiersmen Series X (Glendale, California: The Arthur H. Clark Company, 1945); Robert H.Forbes, *The Penningtons, Pioneers of Early Arizona* (Tucson: Arizoa Archeological and Historical Society, 1919).

[5]Three instances of death from childbirth on the trail occur in a single family history: Marcia Rittenhouse Wynn, *Pioneer Family of Whiskey Flat* (privately printed,1945), pp. 6-15, 28. A copy is deposited in the library of the Arizona Historical Society in Tucson. I am grateful to the Society for permission to consult this and other material in their collection.

[6]Rachel Redden Koontz, "The Miller Story," *Echoes of the Past,* Vol. 2, ed. Robert C. Stevens (Prescott, Arizona: The Yavaplai Cowbells, Inc., 1964), pp. 11-40.

[7]Koontz, "The Miller Story," p. 26.

[8]A classic description of a traditional wagon train, giving details of equipment, food, routines, and hazards on the trail may be found in Jennie Atcheson, Wriston, *A Pioneer's Odyssey* (privately printed, 1943), pp. 24-69. A copy is deposited in the collection of the Arizona Historical Society in Tucson.

[9]Pat Savage, *One Last Frontier* (New York: Exposition Press, 1964), pp. 78-79.

[10]Wynn, *Whiskey Flat,* pp. 109-111.

[11]Mrs. Charles Herbert Bowers, "Joseph Ehle and Margaret Williams Ehle and Descendants," typescript in the Sharlot Hall Museum, Prescott, Arizona. I am grateful to the Sharlot Hall Museum for permitting me to consult this and other materials in their collection.

[12]Banta, p. 4.

[13]Learah Cooper Morgan, "Casa Del Rio: The Home of Hannah Shivers Postle Rees," *Echoes of the Past,* p. 3.

[14]Wynn, *Whiskey Flat,* p.3.

[15]Mody Boatright, "The Family Saga as a Form of Folklore," *The Family Saga and Other Phases of American Folklore* (Urbana: University of Illinois Press, 195), pp. 1-19.

[16]Wriston, *A Pioneer's Odyssey,* p. vii.

[17]Wriston, p. 43.

The Incorporative Consciousness:
Levertov's Journey From Discretion to Unity

Victoria Harris

A constantly self-evaluating, non-static poet, Denise Levertov has developed markedly since her first book, *The Double Image* (1946). That book, as Stephen Stepanchev notes, was influenced greatly by remembered English "metrical and stanzaic patterns and rhyme schemes."[1] Bothered by the dishonesty and irrelevance of such "importations," Levertov began a concentrated effort to wean herself from poetic models, and to achieve not merely a poetic voice of her own but a relationship to reality that is uniquely hers and that informs as it makes possible her own poetic voice. This struggle, while evident in *Here and Now* (1957) and *The Jacob's Ladder* (1961), is perhaps best represented in her fourth volume, *O Taste and See*.[2]

In this volume, Levertov approaches and at times achieves that reciprocal relationship with reality made possible by what may be called the incorporative consciousness. This type of poetic consciousness encompasses both internal and external reality, integrating self, others, and nature into an organic whole. The centripetal motion which brings in the sensory landscape, its taste and sight, is met by centrifugal forces issuing from the poet herself. Organically incorporating her world, the poet's psychic awareness expands. This growth transforms the interior landscape, expanding her creative potential. The incorporative consciousness continues to grow, like a tree organically enlarging its boundaries. Her vision increasingly expanded from bringing in the world, Levertov balances these incoming energies with centrifugal energies. From the deep—and deepening—interior landscape, Levertov reaches outward, crystallizing this reciprocal motion with the gift of her perception, the verbal equivalent to that perception: the poem itself.

The necessary first step toward balancing interior and exterior landscapes involves the discovery and total integration of one's self. Such self-actualization does not involve separation from the natural world, however. To the contrary, the self must include an organic integration of all the energies and influences centripetally brought in. The poet must somehow incorporate that influx of material from outside into her private consciousness. Part of this process involves learning to distinguish addition and reflection from incorporation and creation. One must not copy the world, but energize it with dynamic involvement and inspired creations. Profound intuition, not additive memory, becomes the mode. Levertov's astonishingly honest and painful struggle to attain the "incorporative consciousness" forms an important part of *O Taste and See,* the first lines of its title poem hinting at the necessarily intense involvement with the surrounding universe: "The world is/not with us enough/O taste and see."

The journey toward poetic self-actualization recorded in *O Taste and See* involves several "matters" or concerns, some of which become stages in the poet's growth. The first is the poet's attempt to overcome dualism. This attempt often fails, a failure underscored by Levertov's use of language. Fragments and run-on sentences are employed, as though the very vehicle of creation is inadequate to convey the creator's impulse toward harmony. Of course, once Levertov discovers a language that overcomes dualism, dualism for her will have ceased to exist. Dualism and the search for a language that overcomes it, then, are two important concerns of *O Taste and See.* A third concern is the need for that authentic perception that allows the reciprocal interchange of inner and outer energies necessary if dualism is to be transcended. But such perception becomes possible only after the poet has come to terms with her own interior spaces, a fourth major concern in this volume and one which receives its fullest treatment in "To the Muse" and "Into the Interior." The fifth and perhaps most important concern in *O Taste and See* involves the poet's emergence as the fully developed "I-as-poet," an emergence signified by Levertov's discarding of poet-personae and her consequent shift to the first-person "I."

"The Ache of Marriage," the third poem in this volume, represents a good example of the first concern mentioned above, the need—in this case a frustrated need—to overcome a world of distinctions.

The ache of marriage:

thigh and tongue, beloved,
are heavy with it,
it throbs in the teeth.

We look for communion
and are turned away, beloved,
each and each.

It is leviathan and we
in its belly
looking for joy, some joy
not to be known outside it

two by two in the ark of
the ache of it.

Rooted in a field of distinctions, the poet stands bereft of the "joy" she seeks, for her marriage is marked by division rather than unity. Senses become heavy with the ache of unfulfillment; "thigh and tongue, beloved,/are heavy with it,/it throbs in the teeth." The very fact that this house of marriage is characterized by a leviathan image housing separate entities, and that the body is characterized as holding distinct senses, seemingly separate, routinely must lead to division rather than to organic joining. Quite explicitly, Levertov admits the lack of fulfillment: "We look for communion/ and are turned away, beloved." Obviously the problem is an unfulfilled expectation of harmony. The very motion toward harmony, however, may be the cause of disharmony; the fulfillment of harmony, that is, is sought through a *decentralizing* energy. The speaker and her spouse are divided "each and each," but centrifugally seeking communion. The gesture overcomes itself: harmony can not be the culmination of otherness, attained through closures big or small, be they houses, marriages, or bodies in which quantifiable distinctions are put together. Outsideness is admittedly the wrong path to the joy of harmony: "looking for joy, some joy/not to be known outside it." The "it" seems to have a double referent: the joy will be found within the leviathan's belly, but also within itself. The direction of the search must be changed, centripetally drawing the distinctions—be they different senses, or different people—into the hub, else "two by two," a mathematical compounding of one individual plus another, will additively fill up the ark with more and more pairs of distinctions, eluding the joy, continuing "the ache of it," the notion with which Levertov is left.

"The Message" continues the additive process, leading again to a failure of expectations, whereby maps, additions, and memories cannot comprise the mode to the "great Spirit." In a dream the persona receives a letter from "cross country" in which a Bard claims "seeds of the forget-me-not." The residual notion of the past comes to the speaker from "out of the sea fog," a hazy reminder from "a Bard" of a different country, apparently Levertov's native England. The message seems to be to take the seeds from this other country and plant them here on this land where they will grow. In other words, the past is come here to haunt the speaker, making not only the seeds but the speaker herself an importation. The motive is to produce a hybrid forget-me-not, thereby making a stronger variety. Explicitly, the speaker is asked to plant the seeds on this soil, then send the new seeds back to her old land, "Not flowers but/their seeds." The Bard of the other land gives the seeds, and the "Spirit of Poetry" asks for the new seeds back. The power of the image—here the generative seeds—overcomes the flatness of the message to remember. Moreover, the message comes horizontally from across the sea. The seeds come across also, but to fulfill their potential, they also need vertical space. They must penetrate beneath surfaces to transform potential into growth.

In the next stanza, the transplanted flora are metaphorically represented as a map, "The varied blue/in small compass." In multitude the distinctions among the individual herbs become blurred from "a cloud of blue, a river/beside the brown river." But the transplantation remains one of going from one spot to another, and the hazy collection of flowers is described by "compass," or "Multitude," "Beside" the real thing to which it is compared, a field gotten by a collecting and transferring process. In metaphoric relation to the seed stands the poet who is also transplanted—a hybrid—and reminded by her ancestor soil to "Remember [her] nature." Thus, her sense of poetry, she is advised, should be gotten through memory—ignoring her landscape, perception, intuition, and imagination. Then the speaker relates that this Bard-become-Spirit from across the sea speaks of her *nature* as a power; "And he bids me/remember my nature, speaking of it/ as of a power." Thus, the advice reminds the speaker of a component of herself brought across the sea. This importation becomes an integral part of her makeup and is elevated into the eminent position of a power. A somewhat paradoxical notion resides in the advice to call the inheritance from a former home, something to be remembered, a power—the former seeming fixed, the latter generative. One seems an inert part of formation; the other seems the formulator itself. Although the advice connotes collecting, the power connotes something more essentially integrative than addition. The speaker relates the further advice which itself speaks of the additive nature of the advisor: "And gather/the flowers, and the flowers/ of 'labor.'" In other words, cultivate the seeds and pick the blossoms, those of labor, through your hybrid nature in order to gain results. The flowers of labor—the poems—become the mode of fusion: "(pink in the dream,/ a bright centaury with more petals./ Or the form changes to a seapink)." But the perception is parenthetical.

The italicized lines in the next stanza—"*Ripple of blue in which are/distinct blues. Bold/ centaur—seahorse—salt—carnation/ flower of work and transition*"—comment on the distinction of the many parts, urging this dichotomized vision on the speaker, who is but blurred when leaving the dream state: "Out of the sea fog, from a hermitage,/ at break of day./" Finally, she is left only questioning whether or not she can find the "flower of work and transition": "Shall I find them then—/here on my land, recalled/ to my nature?" Surely the question proposes, at most, lack of confidence. The pun on the word "Recall" shows the poet taking the wrong path to find her own nature on her own land. Transference goes linearly back and forth, and the resulting hybrid would be an additive of memory and parts, a wrong way to the power she seeks, a power wrongly attributed to seeds of memory from past lands. Her final search shows her looking in the wrong direction, collecting (or importing) foreign seeds and seeking outwardly for the power, "O, great spirit," as if it were something "out there" and functionally separate from the "I" and "nature" of her question.

So, importations of remembrances are not the answer, leaving a distinct problem for a hybrid such as Levertov—especially with regard to language and the problems of incorporating and expanding the past, instead of merely "recalling" it. One important aspect of this poem may be that the poet is operating intuitively. Although cognitively unaware of the force which would drive the poem, the impetus for the poem itself comes from a dream. This forms the optimism undergirding the poem. Although the speaker has not yet organically assumed the role of poet, she begins to collect herself with a drive from intuition, "out of sea fog." It will be shown that she increasingly realizes herself as poet, with concomitantly increasing involvement in her poems. Indeed, she will come to swallow that "seed." She begins the poem "The Breathing" with calm resolve. "An absolute/patience" like Eastern passivity characterizes the tree with which she is in reverie. The next sentence, "Trees stand/up to their knees in/fog," envisions this splendid tree engulfed in a creeping fog—one which moves upward, and one which blurs the base or the roots, a conventional portrayal of beginnings or past. The blurring continues as the fog proceeds uphill: "The fog/slowly flows/uphill."

Not only is the persona standing apart from the creeping fog, but she doesn't have the "absolute patience" needed to wait for the change from addition to mergence. The next stanza goes from one very distinct image to the next. Still above or outside the creeping fog, the poet details "White/cobwebs, the grass/leaning where deer/have looked for apples." The distinct images are presented in a sentence fragment, thus formally showing the tension between the holistic vision and, if not the incomplete vision, then at least the inability of language to portray the insight in any but a fragmentary way. This comprises an important failure to Levertov who does not view the poet as one who first has a vision, then tries to find the words to express it. Quoting William Wordsworth, Levertov asserts that "Language is not the dress but the incarnation of thoughts."[3] It should be emphasized, then, that to Levertov, when a gap exists between feelings and the words to express them, "that is language used as dress." Poems written in such language "are not musical, though they may sometimes be superficially so. The *music* of the poetry comes into being when thought and feeling remain unexpressed until they become Word, become Flesh (i.e., there is no prior paraphrase)."[4]

Contextually emphasizing this point, the poet shows her perception of the deer, an objective correlative of the poet, looking for apples, an objective correlative of the poem, and not finding them, thus also not fulfilling their search. The lines, "The woods/from brook to where/the top of the hill looks/over the fog, send up/not one bird," suggest that the area of foggy outlines is not the place for atomistic scrutiny of distinctive images. The narrator lessens the gap between herself and those foggy places by the end of the poem, when she approaches something beyond the senses; "a breathing/too quiet to hear" concludes the poem with the sense of life rhythms which cannot be sensorially perceived. But whatever this life force may be, it remains something *outside* the narrator's consciousness. She remains outside the space from which she derives the perception; maintaining the subject-object dichotomy, the perceiver seems somehow removed from the perception of the "so absolute, it." The scene of "happiness itself," then, is finally physically separate from the viewer describing it. Yet once again Levertov approaches her intuition, the "sea fog," thereby not yet organic with, but approaching, her existence as intuitive poet.

The paradox between happiness residing in a silence, wherein even its breathing is too quiet to hear, and the very act of writing poetry continues throughout this volume. In the very next poem, "September 1961," the poet elucidates the painful process of shedding layers of memory, be they derived from either influences or words themselves. But the poem ends with the failure to fulfill the hope, leaving memory and thought to conclude the poem, excluding the narrator from her space of perception.

The beginning of the poem shows initiation of the speaker in a new territory without her previous guides, left "alone on the road." "This is the year" signals a new way. Although more than the speaker must depart from the old direction, this departure must not be clustered into a group, for the many who leave the old way still go their own. The old school will "leave us alone," thus the several leaving are going in individual "obsecure directions." This obscurity carries a double existence for the poet. Surely, she has not yet "seen" her direction. But, more positively, she moves forward without the constricting parameters of a clearly delineated path. Obscurity, then, not only suggests hiding meanings through defective expression, but also allows freedom to move in undefined directions. The inheritance to be veered away from is not only shed because it is old, but because it is passe. This inherited thought was only previously considered "great." Consider, for example, the different connotation between "great old ones" and, as the narrator calls them, "the old great ones." Anyway, one finds increasing evidence within the poem that not only are old tutors no longer adequate, but so are all referential systems through which reality must be distilled by some external criterion, such as words. Referential systems are done with, as the initiate travels with the words in her pockets. Although seemingly tucked away, these words are brought along. Old structures no longer work; those modes "have taken away the light of their presence." Words stored in pockets become lights over a hill, seen "moving away over a hill/off to one side." The "old ones," which gather more than one metaphoric attachment within the space of the poem, "...are not dying." Finally, the pocket-storing and peripheral sighting of these old ones relocate: "They are withdrawn/into a painful privacy." The impetus changes. Although the speaker initially takes the road away from them, she finally brings the words. The insistent retention of these linguistic artifacts imbues the subject with pain. But the motion, foreshadowing organicism, bears attention. Instead of additively toting the words, the speaker begins to incorporate them; she centripetally draws them in. The digestion will allow the consciousness to expand whereas the mere carryovers would challenge only the memory.

Articulating the cause of this pain, the subject begins the next stanza with the end of the sentence, "learning to live without words." When consciousness itself may be defined as language, the repercussions of its denial are indeed traumatic. "E.P.," presumably Pound, declares that "It looks like dying." William Carlos Williams declares that he "can't/describe to you what has been/happening to me." H.D. is "unable to speak." There is a double significance to the inclusion of these poets' reactions. First, they must be included in the "us" who are leaving the old ones. Each must go alone, and though their individual reactions seem similar, the privately found answers cannot transfer. To the eye of E.P., it is death. Williams is unable to deliver the message to the listener's ear. His statement pointedly negates a linear message code between speaker and listener. H.D. is not yet capable of the utterance apart from the old ones. Though disclaiming referential articulation and passive reception, the speaker's imaginative voice and conscious ear have not as yet developed.

The second significance to the inclusion of the poets is that not only are they of "us" relevance to the poet, but they are also themselves "old ones." If any of their conclusions were adopted by the speaker, such conclusions too would be referential to reality, would come between the poet and her perception, and thereby call forth passive reception of another's views instead of active individual intuition. Retention itself is the act of memory; retention of another's solutions are to this poet lies. Cognitive transferences do not allow the poet to perceive the universe unfolding around her. This simply does not do; Levertov will not accept importations, and finds herself "alone on the road, not following the direction 'old words' can give," and not led by the "light of their presence" (old words and old tutors). She is moving, but not yet arrived, as finally the speaker seems surrounded by an energetic darkness: "The darkness/twists itself in the wind." The only light remaining is that of the stars which are far and small, and of the city which is "confused urban light-haze." The poet sheds her old guides—words and mentors—but still gropes in darkness.

On her road, although she recalls the message, she ends in silence. They have laid a map for her to follow, somehow—a method of approach objectively attainable by the subject: "They have told us/the road leads to the sea." Along with the reified experience comes the inherited gift: "and given/the language into our hands." This handing down of words for shaping makes the communication a matter of manual dexterity. This notion is anathema to Denise Levertov. The poet's task is to hold in trust the knowledge that language, as Robert Duncan has declared, is not a set of counters to be manipulated, but a Power. And only in this knowledge does he arrive at music, at that quality of song within speech which is not the result of manipulations of euphonious parts, but of an attention, at once to the organic relations of experienced phenomena and to the latent harmony and counterpart of language itself as it is identified with those phenomena.[5]

The atomistic parcelling out of space, here language, seems inadequate to the speaker. This may be related by the sensory additions in the next sentence which lead to silence. We "'hear'/our footsteps each time a truck/has dazzled past us and gone." Thus, there seems to be something in the image allowing the subject to approach a despatialized time, whereby she transforms a reified map made by her footsteps into an I-in-the-world perception. The footsteps seem to remain past the time when a passing truck has gone, thus perhaps extending the subjective moment. But, unable to cope with this intuition, the poet is left in "new silence," not yet "in touch" with the organicism. Subjective involvement is implied here by the description of the silence being new; but nonetheless muteness remains.

Levertov changes the collective "us" and "we" to the singular (although abstract) "one" when she reaches her insight of negation. This road is not the fruitful path; "one can't reach/the sea on this endless/road to the sea unless/one turns aside at the end, it seems,/follows/ the owl that silently glides above it/ aslant, back and forth." Her unidirectional path becomes an unending labyrinth, which has no end. But the image augurs the reciprocal energizing movement in the later *Footprints* (1972).

Levertov tentatively suggests that "it seems" that a person alone (one) must go off the path, one prescribed and apart from the individual. Levertov pointedly advocates departure from linear modes, of both language and inheritance, at the end of this insight. First she advises, go "aslant, back and forth," at least mixing directions, skewing the unidirectional linear mode; then the poem climaxes with the one-line stanza, "and away into deep woods." Here the reciprocal motion gathers energy to create deep landscape, as back and forth transforms to "deep wood" and "across" changes to "into." Thus, Levertov presents an image for a place both internal and external, confusing the separation and the clear delineation of the road. The woods contain a more profound depth than the flat directions strung out on a linear plane even when moving back and forth. But the functional thematic anticlimax is foreshadowed by the mention of following "the owl that silenty/glides above it." Though surely the owl is seer in the night, and copes with the new silence, following from a distance precludes intuition and forebodes a negative result. One should remember the previous intention not to follow anything apart from one's own preceptions.

Thus, although singular, "one" is abstract and other; this leads to the additive motion allowing "one" to become "us" in the concluding stanza. Levertov again portrays an atomistic composite collecting on the maplike road. Levertov reinforces this additive propensity by portraying the speaker counting the words; "But for us the road/unfurls itself, we count the/words in our pockets." Even the road seems to appear apart from the poet's interaction with or choice of it as she passively notes that the road unfurled itself. The speaker is left with a nagging intuition of something beneath logical ordering. Levertov even semantically points to its logical inadequacy by concluding in a run-on and yet unfinished thought: "we wonder/how it will be without them, we don't stop walking, we know/there is far to go, sometimes/we think the night wind carries/a smell of the sea. . . ." Thus the linear path can only lead the speaker to atomistic accumulation, utilizing already given modes (the words in the pocket); although one may add and add onto the string, it remains incomplete. And the pain inside remains "sometimes." "Sometimes" is given a tension appearing first on the line with "there is far to go, sometimes," then syntactically a part of "sometimes/we think the night wind carries/a smell of the sea..." On the horizontal road there are times when she perceives a distant place, but ends on the other times when her linguistically arranged "thinking" notes sensory impressions. The speaker never relates that there is something beyond sensory perception. Moreover, she ends twice removed from an "I-enveloped-in-the-world" perception. The potential depth of the image seems constrained by the thought. The sensory perception of the smell of the sea is not perceived by the person in the world, but conceived by the thinker—apart from it—using memory. She moves closer but still is far from the sea if she perceives its smell through thought and pursues the wrong road.

Levertov moves closer to the authentic perception hinted at in "September 1961" in "The Ripple." The poem begins with a description of a tau cross lying on a piece of white linen, that white linen retaining its traditional suggestion of purity. The tau symbol aptly applies to Levertov herself. First of all, it is the Greek symbol, and Levertov admittedly has much debt to the Greeks, claiming that she may be closer to them than to her own English ancestors. Also, the symbol is derived from the Semitic letter, the Hebrew Taw, therefore applying to the poet who herself is of Jewish descent. It becomes a single symbol representing a mergence of distinct parts, itself casting shadows on the white linen. A glass jug and tumblers rise from their own shadow. The tau cross seemingly bears witness to the image of water throwing back, not a gray shadow, but a luminous one: "and luminous/in each/overcast of/cylindrical shade." The road to the river seems not so remote when the narrator now perceives an "image/of water, a brightness." This brightness begins to seem like the kind of light only suspected in the previous poem. Here the suspicion becomes more and more a perception, the anticipation of which begins to bring with it an hysteria. The light is not the luminous familiar kind, "not gold, not silver," therefore not attributable to the shiny stuff we know. Rather, a strange luminosity appears from such an unsuspected source as a shadow. The lights can be seen playing on the moving water, which is finally perceived "rippling/as if with laughter." The energy derived from what is initially a description of a shadow, seems incredible; not only are perceiver and image involved and with motion, but the motion seems to become an effervescent spilling out and around of joy.

Here may be the beginning of a new mode of perception for Levertov, when the importations seem centripetally drawn into the single image of the tau cross. From this image, the poem opens up as the motion seems to pour outward with the "jug and tumblers' rise." Then the cylindrical shades are perceived by the luminosity shining through the overcast, or shining out. This luminosity finally breaks the bounds of its physicality—beyond the shininess of even the previous metals we know, until it, itself, seems alive when its waves are rippling outward. The motion goes inward and outward, gaining energy with each turn. Tentatively, but finally, it is seen moving "as if with laughter." Thus, the mixture, which presented transplanting problems, unites appropriately in the tau cross image; this distinct image of a shadow's becoming the source of a shimmering luminescence, rising above itself, getting power from the center out, and vibrating, shows Levertov overcoming not only the shadow of the past, but the very physical structures in the present.

The light-from-darkness imagery, along with the difference from linear, that of inheritance and transference, to deep moments, that of consuming energies from sources simultaneously outward and inward, continues in the very next poem in *O Taste and See*, in which luminous glistenings of "The Ripple" become "Sparks." The poem deals with the notion of messages and incorporation of "importations," portraying a speaker who receives a poem which incorporated a carpe diem message from Ecclesiastes. Solomon prescribes, "Whatsoever thy hand/findeth to do, do it with/thy might:/for there is no work,/nor device,/nor knowledge/nor wisdom,/in the grave, whither thou goest." A first consideration may be the linear inheritance implicit here, where part of the substance of the poem itself is derived. Though from the wise man himself, and put in a new context, the message remains one of memory, and one that, like the previously cited example of a perfectly rewritten Shakespearean sonnet, has everything but the fresh perception and new intuition; thus, this message seems quite similar to the transplanted forget-me-not seeds. The speaker's reaction to a letter enclosed with the poem reveals her feelings regarding the value of receiving and storing messages. Once again, Levertov notes the problem of language. Borrowing Solomon's words is not the answer, for horizons broaden in other ways. The lines, "A letter with it/discloses, in its words and between them," suggest that the wisdom which may possibly be incorporated does not come from replanting a message. The true worth lies in the space between the lines.

The comment upon the poet's poem is inherent in the mode of perceiving the poet's words. When entering this space between the lines, one can see the self unfolding in a reciprocal kind of self-regenerative activity that counteracts the enervating experience of memorized inheritance. Non-linear, "a life opening" becomes more than logical cause-to-effect assertions. The non-linear involvement is clarified further in the next two descriptions, "fearful, fearless," then "thousand-eyed." First, the male letter writer encompasses two emotions which would objectively cancel one another out. Second, the "thousand-eyed—image suggests an infusion-diffusion type of perception from the very pores of perception, instead of an eye-to-object, one-to-one relationship. The man seems protean, now different from the poet who passes down "old great ones" in his poetry. Levertov again describes the metamorphosis with a living luminosity emerging through darkness—here "a field/of sparks that move swiftly/in darkness." And the motion, again not a hand-me-down deliverance of used materials, consists rather of a regenerative reciprocation from outward and inward energy sources: "to and from a center." The speaker's method of receiving the message itself portrays the concept with which she is dealing. First of all, one cannot derive truths from old messages. This is seen throughout this volume of poetry; so the incorporation of Solomon's message in the man's poem cannot possibly afford the best way to form a poem. Secondly, the reader cannot proceed linearly through words already laid out for his passive reception. The more active reader—the speaker here—grasps a thought through the "words and between them." Finally, not only is the thought to be grasped someone else's thought, but the very gleaning process itself inherently includes enervation. This active reader concludes, "He is beginning/to live." Thus, something living in the space involved the reader, who actively, personally, reacts with her own energy and her own insight; this perception is not derivative, but regenerative.

Furthermore, whatever she sees between the words of the letter of her correspondent, leading him to new life, is not to be adopted by her. His message of imminent doom is explicitly disclaimed: "The threat/of the world's end is the old threat." Her message, from the "Book of Delight," seems a double one, suggesting that *now* you prepare for the future world, and day by day you prepare for this world. In other words, go through your own individuation, a process through which you encompass the here and now and the other world, and a process through which time itself is subjectified. The tension implicit here is one requiring immense energy, and the energy of "sparks" is the imperative metaphor dominating this poem. No easy "passing down of" or "putting away for" will result in these "sparks." A self-emanating and self-enclosing reciprocation is the action necessary for "beginning to live."

It may be seen, then, that Levertov senses something new beginning. What is old, characterized by message, tutors, transference, inheritance, and even language, must be overcome in a continual struggle. Many of the above-mentioned poems carry with them the residual effect of a loss of spontaneous energy and original intuition. Levertov struggles with beginnings and with the necessary energy and freshness such beginnings require. The failures are many, thus the book is embroidered with run-ons and fragment. But even when the inability to express wins, an underground movement pushes its forces upward like the fog pushing up the tree in "The Breathing."

As we have seen, Levertov works strenuously in *O Taste and See* with the problems of memory and distinction, focusing on considerations ranging from a past inheritance to a reference system such as language itself. Sometimes the eschewal of scientistic referential modes seems impossible, leaving unresolved confrontations resulting in fragment or silence. The crucial necessity seems to be the incorporation of an integrated being as poet. Levertov's strides and successes are achieved through her scrupulous honesty, impelling a growing awareness and poetic revelation of herself. Levertov's gathering up of herself involves incorporating the muse in her body-house. I suggest preparation, not completion. Only when her own harmonious energy system is achieved can it mingle with the energies in the universe. Only then can she poetically participate with and reflect the energy system that is the world.

The direction and the mode of this self-realization become apparent in Levertov's poem "Into the Interior.":

> Mountain, mountain, mountain,
> marking time. Each
> nameless, wall beyond wall, wavering
> redefinition of
> horizon.
>
> And through the months. The arrivals
> at dusk in towns one must leave at daybreak
>
> —were they
> taken to heart, to be seen
> always again,
> or let go, those faces,
>
> a door half-open, moss
> by matchlight on an inscribed stone?
>
> And by day
> through the hours that
> rustle about one dryly,
> tall grass of the savannah
>
> up to the eyes.
> No alternative to the
> one-man path.

The journey of life takes the traveler across the scene. "Mountain,

mountain, mountain" begins the poem, placing the landscape monotonously and horizontally across the line. Indeed, on the next line, time seems spatialized, showing the speaker "marking time." But Levertov relieves the apprehension of a flat map world with detemporalized space and despatialized time in her conclusion of the stanza. First of all, Levertov portrays each "wall beyond wall" as "nameless," perhaps indicating no intellectual predilection about the world, which would undercut the acquaintance with it. This stanza pointedly undermines all static notions; the least resilient notion, of "definitions," here becomes "redefinitions." And such an abstract characterization as a definition of space and time relents before contactual involvement with the unfolding universe. Levertov counteracts the static characteristic of definition itself, transforming inertia into fluctuation. Here, we not only witness definition give way to "redefinitions (which would be just one step further, exchanging one inert phase of abstraction for another), but the word "redefinition" joined to "wavering" connotes a quality of awareness, rather than capitulation. The constant quality, then, is the ongoing awareness; the changing quality is the perception. Levertov reaffirms this central notion of being involved/with one's universe at the end of this stanza. The traveler's movement through space unfolds the world with each step taken. The undergirding notion dominating the participation of the subject with her world asserts that reality is process. Indeed, reality is the very awareness of one's world as she moves through it. Thus, definitions such as "mountains" re-form with each step toward and away from the peak. Levertov undercuts the predisposition of the world-as-other with her "wavering/redefinition of/horizon." The very perception of the landscape, then, forms the reality. This reality fluctuates with each movement of the world traveler.

In "Into the Interior," Levertov depicts the direction of this involvement. It is, as this first stanza portrays, the movement through the world, whereby awareness remains constant but the articulation of this reality always changes. Levertov balances the motion of looking out with the centripetal motion of drawing in. Thus the time "through the months" and the time and space— "The arrivals/at dusk in towns one must leave at daybreak"—

must be pulled into the speaker in order to reach the internal resident: the poetic muse. The poet therefore must question, "were they/taken to heart?" Only then could the interior eye relish the passing universe, allowing it "to be seen/always again." This drawing-in-process preserves that fluctuation. Here the poet foreshadows an image predominant in the later *Footprints*—she herself becomes the passageway, the very spot where the motions of incoming and outgoing meet. She is Denise, Daleth, doorway—"a door half-open." The option is to bring the fluctuating world "to heart" or to "let it go." The choice is clear, and the procedure of centrifugal awareness and centripetal incorporation adumbrates the energy condition dominating *Footprints*. The poet, then, affirms her commitment as a poet, by showing how the world becomes, and what to do with it. Indeed, she must bring it "Into the Interior," as the title suggests. This will be shown as signifying the growing assurance of herself as a poet, whose muse resides internally—indeed perhaps existing as "the heart" of the being. Moreover, the walk through life is always a singular commitment: the consciousness cannot forsake its very growth by *attaching to definitions*— poetic schools, modes of vision. The odyssey is arduous and wonderful, and singular: there are "no alternatives to the/one-man path." Thus, in "Into the Interior," Levertov depicts the world, space and time, as process; the motion as centripetal and centifugal; and the commitment as unrelenting awareness along the deep singular path. This is the starting point for the odyssey—literal, symbolic, and poetic where that "half-open door" will open onto a wonderful luminescence imbuing the literal horizon with a light from the internal, spiritual muse of poetry.

Levertov designates that inner region as the residence of the muse. In an earlier poem in this volume, "To the Muse," the speaker alerts the reader in the first stanza to her suspicion that the muse is not a transient visitor—"not one who comes and goes." Instead, Levertov portrays the muse as a permanent resident of the chosen body-house—one who travels through the "garden for air and delights/of weather and seasons." The interior landscape, then, is a changeable place too, in which the muse reacts to those changes. The body-house becomes an elaborate work which must make room for the muse. Only then can the internal landscape become this reservoir of poetic insight. So, Levertov says, "Who builds/a good fire in his hearth/shall find you at it/with shining eyes and a ready tongue." That this heart-hearth must be well-lit implies that those images taken "to heart" from "Into the Interior" must be brought to a well-cared-for place. The warmth of the hearth prepares an inviting home, an apt receiver for the muse. Levertov indicates the imperative "O taste and see" of the book by the image of muse with "shining eyes and a ready tongue." The important motion is apparently the preparing for and opening up to the guest. Even if the house may seem paltry, the effort of sharing one's humblest offerings bespeaks the dignity such as that witnessed in the humble host in *Electra*. Indeed, the sharing of the humble repast brings "joy." Levertov declares that no enclosure should exclude the guest; not even should one "lock the door of the marriage/against you." Thus, the involvement with the guest becomes total. In fact, reforming the interior landscape allows the spiritual light provided by the muse to radiate. This light is hinted at at the end of the fourth stanza with the "shining eyes" and reinforced in the seventh stanza with the description of the muse's being "as/the light of the moon on flesh and hair." Thus, the human quality will gain a radiance, but one really more organic than the simile conveys, since it is an internal irradiation.

In Levertov's delightful tour through her internal corridors, she depicts an intricate system whose hidden places at times elude the host, yet become known to the muse. So, often when the host believes the muse is gone, the muse is actually hiding in places "unknown to the host." The reason for the evasion is the erection of a barrier excluding the guest. It is always the responsibility of the poet as receiver to prepare the house for the muse as guest. It must be stressed that Levertov is getting herself together as the house of the muse. Either the hearth or the table, the heart or source of nourishment, has somehow neglected the guest. Or the doors, that now apparent motif, have not "been unlocked," thereby closing off the passageway. If Levertov is to realize herself as I-as-poet, this matter must be straightened out.[6]

Her lack of preparation for the muse, as well as the lack of appropriate position afforded her, reflect a closing motion diametrically opposed to the reciprocal energizing motion. Instead of receiving, the speaker "forgets" to do so, then frantically searches elsewhere for the muse. The false direction joins emotional falsity as the joy and light beginning the poem change to accusations of faithlessness and a tone of "demanding," and finally a situation which "is intolerable." Not only does the unfulfilled poet-house become a "great barracks," but those internal garden places of "air and delight" in the human house transform into an enclosure as stifling as Plath's "bell jar." Indeed the house becomes a prison, and its intricate corridors become meaningless in themselves when the only significant feature becomes enclosing walls. Thus, "it is too big, it is too small, the walls/menace him." At last the frantic energy of reaching elsewhere snuffs out the inviting heart-hearth fire. The blaze of light, life, and spirituality burns out in the stifling image where "the fire smokes/and gives off no heat." Here, the opposite of the spiritual image, that incandescent glow, results from the poet's not meeting her joyful and continual responsibility as host to the muse. Frantically rushing elsewhere for the answer closes off those interior spaces which must be the reservoir of inspiration.

Finally, the ridiculous question of this outward seeker, "But to what address/can he mail the letters," is answered with the calm, "And all the while/you are indwelling." The discovery of the interior reservoir opens up all the wonderful qualities that the negligent host closed. First of all, the spiritual golden illumination becomes assuredly a part of the internal landscape. Twice Levertov declares "a gold ring lost in the house"; then she affirms that the glimmer of gold is indeed the muse's presence by transforming the "gold ring," subject of the previous two sentences, to "you," subject in the next. In fact, the spiritual glow emanates from the place where the muse hides, "glowing with red, with green,/with black light." The poet approaches the muse with this very intuition of her. Levertov follows the "glowing" line, with the assertion that the "gold ring/waits" in the "crack in the floor." The stifling bell-jar type image transforms into a place where a crack can open a place for the air of intuition.

Finally, the other-directed poet completely changes in motion. She exchanges frantic seeking for calm recipience, once again revealing the dignity of the humble host. With "a calm face" the poet makes ready for the muse. Importantly, not even the wise man can relate how to prepare. This is the "one-main path" previously articulated, and the speaker moves in the correct direction—internal. Once again, the body-home becomes an inviting scene with table laid, fire trimmed, and even flowers, from those garden spaces, sought. The inward direction matches the resurrection of the dominant mode of awareness. The speaker alerts herself to "be ready with quick sight." Then the spirituality can issue; then the speaker can "catch a gleam between the floorboards/there, where he had looked/a thousand times and seen nothing." Thus, the "Light of the house" is a spiritual one, kindled by the calm receiving nature of the inner-directed poet. The spiritual light joins the symbolic door at the end of the poem, setting the scene appropriately invitational. The dutiful host now has the intuition that "someone had passed through the room a moment ago," and the poem culminates with the image of spiritual radiance in the sight of the "ring back on its finger."

The spiritual glow illuminates the internal landscape only when the poet becomes increasingly aware that the muse resides internally, indeed only after the epiphany: "You are in the house!" A preparedness of the house joins the internal direction as landscape, while calm vigilance of the host comprises the mode for finding the muse. Levertov, then, has gotten her house together. She is on her way, changing the search for the internal muse to the effects of it. This reflects the increasing dimensions of her poetic consciousness.

"In Mind," significantly written in the first-person, further reveals Levertov's identification with the internal muse, and shows that this identification is not always delightful. The poem depicts two internal beings.

> There's in my mind a woman
> of innocence, unadorned but
>
> fair-featured, and smelling of apples or grass. She wears

a utopian smock or shift, her hair
a light brown and smooth, and she

is kind and very clean without
ostentation—
                but she has
no imagination.
                And there's a
turbulent moon-ridden girl

or old woman, or both,
dressed in opals and rags, feathers

and torn taffeta
who knows strange songs—

but she is not kind.

Significantly, the first more quiescent person "in my mind" is fresh, and fair, and a woman. Though "kind and very clean," she "has no imagination." The second, darker being, though introduced as a picture in the mind, somehow has dominance over the mind. Indeed the speaker cannot even distinguish whether she is a "girl/or old woman, or both." What is clear, however, is that this being differs markedly from the easily characterized innocent fair creature. Indeed, Levertov portrays her as a "turbulent moon-ridden girl" in gypsy disarray of "opals and rags, feather/and torn taffeta," suggesting perhaps the highs and lows, wealth and poverty, endemic to the poetic consciousness. Levertov reveals the most significant feature of all, however, that she "knows strange songs" in the most casual way. In this way, the fact of being a poet is shown as well incorporated into the poet's self-awareness. The question is not whether or not she metaphorically houses the poet; this seems conclusive. Here the poem ends on the effects of this internal dark lady. Indeed, Levertov states that "she is not kind." Thus, the spiritual resident is no handpatting lady, but a resident who demands, strains, and is "not kind" to her host. The commitment, then, to be the being "who knows strange songs" must be strong; the "I" reveals the poet's mature acceptance of herself as poet— dark singer of songs.

This commitment becomes clearer in the poem "The Prayer." In this poem the speaker prays for continuation of her poetic powers. Again Levertov calls upon the image of light to indicate the spirituality igniting the poem. And again this spirituality emanates from within the first-person speaker: "I prayed...that he maintain in me/the flame of the poem."

The flame remains inside the poet: "since then, though it flickers or/shrinks to a/blue head on the wick,/there's that in me that/burns and chills." With the combination of burning and chilling, Levertov repeats the kind of image seen in "The Elves," "unless a woman has that cold fire in her/called poet." This time, however, the speaker becomes first person. Levertov assumes her position as ark of the resident muse, though often this internal resident, dark and moody, causes pain. Not only does the flame burn and chill, but the speaker finds it often "blackening my heart with soot," or "flaring into laughter," or "stinging/my feet into dance." Indeed, this blackening, flaring, and stinging suggests no quiescent guest. Yet the act of prayer bespeaks commitment. There are structural similarities here to the poem "In Mind," which almost offhandedly assumes the fact of being a poet within the poem and then ends on a different note. Almost paralleling the kind of thought concluding "In Mind," that the one "who knows strange songs" "is not kind," here Levertov also assumes that "the flame of the poem" resides internally, then ends by saying that perhaps the gift does not come from the youthful, light, healing Apollo. The admission of a dual nature seems a frank self-evaluation. It becomes increasingly evident in Levertov's poems that she does not exclude herself from her scrupulously honest evaluations. Linda Wagner asserts that "One of the most noticeable expansions has been in the poet's depiction of herself...."[7] But pride is mixed with revelation of those aspects not usually admitted. Here, Levertov passes the real test of honesty with her awareness and first-person portrayal of the darker parts of herself.

A tirade against hypocrisy, odious to the woman, dominates

her poem "Hypocrite Women." Here, Levertov rails against women who pare their dreams like toenails, "clipped...like ends of/split hair." The whole feminine zeitgeist seems overcast with whorish "psychopomp" whereby roles overcome feelings. When, for example, "a dark humming fills us, a/coldness towards life," we cannot face ourselves. "We are too much women to/own to such unwomanliness." Thus, Levertov taps those coverings of role, or predisposition, hurling womankind into honest, and painful, self-discovery. Her tirade against hypocrisy is a personal one as well. Thus, she admits that the very spirituality for which she prays "is not kind," but rather is a "blackening," "flaring," and "stinging thing."

But Levertov reveals the honest evaluation of a poet who does not go through her world with the easier shell of "psychopomp." The point is that Levertov's demands for honesty extend to herself, to the incorporative consciousness housing pleasing and not-so-pleasing aspects. Perhaps this is why in her first-person poems, the "I," which includes Levertov as *poet*, openly unfolds her darker sides. Levertov very consciously uses the "I," as she suggests in her interview with David Ossman: "I think that a poet has to be skilled and experienced before he begins using 'I.' He can come to it eventually; and I'm really beginning to let myself say 'I' because I feel that now I can do it without the kind of crudity with which some people who have just begun to write poetry write about their own feelings."[8] Here, Levertov makes the prose statement similar to the poetic statements that affirm assurance of herself as a poet. The inclusion of "I," then, is organic. This inclusion in the poem foreshadows Levertov's inclusion of herself in her poems in *Footprints*. In this next volume, Levertov sparingly, but with marked effectiveness, walks into the space of her poems. The insertion of the word "I," then, looks forward to the spatial opening whereby the poet honestly confronts her universe.

The change in technique signifies an alteration in focus. *O Taste and See* shows Levertov as poet, as woman, increasingly coming to grips with herself. The "I" becomes more and more filled up; the poet increasingly realizes her space. In *Footprints* this space becomes an energy force to interact with the energies of the world. The evolving consciousness expands into its own constellation—as indicated by the many-corridored house image. Levertov imperatively asserts that the "house is no cottage, it seems,/it has stairways, corridors, cellars,/a tower perhaps,/unknown to the host." But this unknown aspect increasingly diminishes, causing a concurrent shift in focus. Now, while the consciousness never stops expanding, at least some aspects become realized—such as the I-as-poet aspect. Once realized, the poet must yet continue her life as honest endeavor. Therefore, she uses her space as poet, to confront her perceptions as a poet. This much at least is already realized. Thus this space will enter the poetry, and the walk through *Footprints* reveals the collected impressions of *O Taste and See* consumed in the consciousness of I-as-poet. I do not speak of conclusions, then, but rather indicate starting points.

NOTES

[1]Stephen Stepanchev, *American Poetry Since 1945* (New York: Harper Colophon, 1965), p.157.

[2]Denise Levertov, *O Taste and See* (Norfolk, Conn.: New Directions, 1964). All poems will be taken from this volume.

[3]Denise Levertov, *The Poet in the World* (New York: New Directions, 1973), p.16.

[4]Levertov, *Poet in the World,* p.17.

[5]Levertov, *Poet in the World,* p.54.

[6]In my discussion here and elsewhere of house imagery, I am indebted to Gaston Bachelard, *The Poetics of Space* (Boston: Beacon, 1969).

[7]Linda Wagner, *Denise Levertov* (New York: Twayne Publishers, Inc., 1967), p.56.

[8]David Ossman, *The Sullen Art* (New York: Corinth Books, 1963), p.75.

Originally published in *Exploration,* IV:1, December 1976. Reprinted with the permission of the editor and the author.

"No Time for Fainting"
The Frontier Woman in Some Early American Novels

Edna L. Steeves

Before I had read very far in the subject of this paper, I discovered that the image of the frontier woman reflected in the works of James Fenimore Cooper, William Gilmore Simms, and Charles Seasfield was very unlike that which our history books have led us to expect. In fact, the heroines of these three novelists strike the reader at first acquaintance as even more Victorian than the typical Victorian female. Of course that feminine stereotype is, perhaps, to be expected, since all three authors lived and wrote in the mid-nineteenth century. Yet the image of the frontier woman is so firmly fixed in the mind's eye that I found myself in the position of the redoubtable Sherlock Holmes who, in one of his who-dun-its, found the clue to the crime in the dog who did *not* bark in the night. After a close look at some of these heroines, one wonders how they could have survived the hazards of the American frontier.

Lowell once complained about the insipidity of Cooper's females; and Bret Harte wrote a story about a fainting Ginevra who, attacked in the forest by five wild beasts at once, was saved in the nick of time by a shot from Natty Bumppo's rifle—one shot from Killdeer killed all five beasts, naturally. Nevertheless, the women portrayed by these early writers on frontier life do manage to survive the hardships of their rugged environment.

For the purposes of this paper I have confined myself to Cooper's Leatherstocking series; to Simms' best-known novel, *The Yemassee,* and to two of his novels in the Revolutionary War series; and to three of Sealsfield's works: *Tokeah, or the White Rose,* his first novel; *Nathan the Squatter-Regulator,* a narrative of the Southwest frontier; and *The United States of North America As They Are,* a pseudo-literary, sociological document which is in effect a travelogue.[1]

Cooper's five Leatherstocking novels appeared between 1823 and 1841. Their settings vary from Lake Otsego in upstate New York in the 1740s, when Deerslayer is a youth of twenty or thereabout, to the western prairies beyond the Mississippi at the turn of the century, when Natty is an old man of four-score. However one defines the frontier, it always meant beyond the settlements, which were, originally of course, along the Atlantic seaboard. So the frontier is always in a western direction, and the term *West* to an American has a long and respected mythology connected with it. In the early nineteenth century, the terms *frontier* and *West* are practically interchangeable. As Edwin Fussell has pointed out: "The American West is almost by definition indefinite and indefinable."[2] But about the conditions of the frontier there was no question: they were wild and woolly. And the man and woman who braved them needed the strength of ten. Resourcefulness, endurance, daring, courage, skill in marksmanship and woodcraft, adeptness in handling Indians, willingness to eat-it-up, wear-it-out, make-it-do, the sheer ability to survive—these were the traits needed for life on the frontier. Cooper's Leatherstocking has all of them: he is a kind of Davy Crockett, Dan'l Boone, Kit Carson, and Jedediah Smith rolled into one. He is an idealized frontiersman. Natty does not swear, drink, or spit tobacco juice. Considering these highly desirable qualities, we marvel that Natty manages to stay a bachelor all his life. But unmarried to the end he remains, despite the fact that at least two young ladies nearly succeed in getting him into their clutches, and despite his highly romantic view of "the gentle ones"—one of his favorite phrases for the various young women who from time to time wander in and out of his orbit.

Since these are novels wound around a dominating male character, our image of the frontier woman in Cooper's Leatherstocking novels comes through the eyes of this male hero. There is little reason to think that that image differs much from Cooper's own view of woman, for Cooper was a Victorian gentleman who himself never knew frontier life.

The general ladylikeness of Cooper's heroines has often been remarked. They faint dead away on occasions when females were supposed to faint. They are, with a few exceptions, the angel-in-the-house type, or, more precisely, the angel-in-the-log-cabin. They are the moral inspiration of their men—the figurative light in the clearing. For all their distinctively feminine attributes, they do not lack courage or resourcefulness. In *The Deerslayer* (1841) Judith Hutter is a good example of the kind of frontier woman who enters into the life of Natty Bumppo. (She is, incidentally, one of the would-be Mrs. Natty's.) Judith and her sister Hetty set off alone by canoe to reconnoiter an Indian camp in order to aid the captured Natty. Because Hetty is feeble-minded, she has nothing to fear, Indians supposedly respecting the dim-witted as wards of the Great Spirit. But Judith, fair game for any Indian, decks herself out in a really fancy ballgown and boldly enters the savage camp, posing as a queen bearing a reprieve for the prisoner. The ruse does not work. On another occasion, when Indians attack the Hutter houseboat, Judith dashes out amid flying bullets and pushes the Indian about to clamber aboard into the lake. When Judith finds her scalped and dying father, she does not faint (one might excuse a lady for fainting at sight of a scalped head), but dresses his wounds and tries to make his last hours comfortable. In the course of the narrative, Judith loses her father, sister, and home, and is rejected by the man she loves, all within a few days. Yet she does not die of a broken heart, but marches off alone through the forest following a contingent of troops to the nearest fort. Since rumor had it that Judith was once interested in these same soldiers, we might read her action as more than a little ironic. But Cooper does not mean us to do so. She is, for him, a brave and tragic heroine.

There is a fainting female in *The Last of the Mohicans* (1826). Alice Munro faints after an Indian massacre in which her friends have been scalped before her very eyes. One might say it was a cutting experience. She has been separated from her father and her lover, and, with her half-sister Cora, is being carried off by Indians. Alice and Cora, tied to trees and threatened with torments, stoutly refuse to buy their lives in exchange for becoming the house-mates (wigwam-mates) of their savage captors. It's the old spirit of "I'd rather die than say yes."

In *The Pathfinder* (1840), the heroine, Mabel Dunham, shows courage and nimble-mindedness in her defense of the blockhouse against Indian ambush. With enormous daring, she dashes out of the blockhouse to seek the wounded body of her father and bring him aid or a proper burial. Mabel is no Antigone, but she is brave and resourceful—and she captured Natty's heart. In fact, Natty has a very near miss with matrimony in the person of Mabel Dunham. Unfortunately for him Mabel loves faithfully—from first sight, of course—a bonny young sailor. Mabel has many characteristics of the typical Victorian heroine, but then so has Dorothea Brooke. It is simply that one does not expect typical Victorian heroines to stand up so well to frontier conditions.

In *The Pioneers* (1823), the heroine, Elizabeth Temple, has been, like many of Cooper's heroines, educated in a finishing school in the East. Yet frontier hardships do not finish off this young lady. When Elizabeth and her friend Louisa Grant, the minister's daughter, take a walk in the forest, Louisa is attacked by a panther, whereupon she faints, not unexpectedly. Elizabeth refuses to leave her, and manages to stave off the panther (presumably by saying "Go Away, naughty Kitty!") until Natty rescues the girls with a bull's-eye to the panther's forehead. Elizabeth also is trapped in a forest fire. Naturally she is rescued, but the reader wonders how long skirts, lacy collars and cuffs, and little straw bonnets can emerge unscorched from a raging inferno.

In *The Prairie* (1927), the heroine, Ellen Wade, is a more liberated female than the typical Victorian maiden. Ellen sneaks out of the Ishmael Bush camp at night under a prairie moon to rendezvous with her lover. Unlike the creole beauty Inez, a noblewoman and heiress who has been captured by the Bush family, Ellen Wade is a believable frontier woman—her conduct, her speech, her dress do credit to a young person in her situation. Like all of Cooper's heroines, she has courage, devotion, faith in God and in her man. Perhaps Esther Bush, the squatter's wife, is as close as Cooper ever comes to drawing the frontier woman whom the history books depict. Esther and her daughters are a bunch of Amazons, always taking the long chance. With a little education and social position, Esther might have been another Dolly Madison, who, when the White House burned, tucked up her skirts and dashed out at the last moment with the Declaration of Independence in one hand and in the other Gilbert Stuart's portrait of George Washington.

Cooper's heroines, then, always ladylike and generally

clinging vines, astonish us by managing to survive frontier conditions, where Indian attacks were a daily ritual and physical hardship a part of life. Cooper's heroines are not his major achievement. That achievement, rather, lies in the fact that he is our first major novelist to deal with the American experience. The problems he portrays are part of our national history: questions of liberty vs. law; of the role of public opinion in a democracy; and of the place in society of the extraordinary man—and the extraordinary woman who shacked up with such a man.

If Cooper obviously did not know the realities of frontier life in America in the early nineteenth century, Charles Sealsfield, the Austrian monk who fled to America to escape the Metternich repression, certainly did know at first hand the American "Wild West" of the 1820s and 1830s. As mirrors of frontier life and character, Sealsfield's works and Cooper's present interesting similarities, and even more interesting differences, in points of view at almost the same historical moment and upon the same facet of the American experience, the frontier. Simms' descriptions of the Southern frontier (the settings of his novels are the colonial and Revolutionary periods) broaden the territory, but do not materially alter the details.

As the leading literary figure of the ante-bellum South, William Gilmore Simms published more than eighty volumes, including some twenty novels. He was in his day the South's most representative man of letters. Because he wrote in the tradition of the historical romance, his characters shape themselves to that tradition—a tradition dominated by Scott and Cooper. In all three novelists the background of their stories is the conflict between two cultures, the new and the old, in the course of which the old goes to the wall. The basic conflict in *The Yemassee* (1835) is between settler and Indian played out against the backdrop of the Revolutionary War.

In his extended travels as a young man visiting his father in the Southwest (Alabama, Georgia, Mississippi, and Louisiana) Simms picked up a first-hand acquaintance with Indian character. His portrait of the Indian is a very faithful one, far more realistic than Cooper's. His knowledge of frontier life and of the Indian-white conflict enabled him to draw an uncommonly true-to-life picture of Indian life in *The Yemassee*. In his depiction of the Indian chief Sanutee, his wife Matiwan, and their son Occonestoga, Simms provides an insight into Indian domestic life not to be found in the typical American romance of the period. The noble, courageous, and devoted Matiwan is as worthy a heroine as the nominal romantic heroine, Bess Mathews. Bess is a model Victorian heroine, fainting at every possible occasion. She faints when a rattlesnake attacks her, when Indians storm her father's house, when the pirate Chorley abducts her, when the pirate's boat overturns, and when her lover, Gabriel Harrison, rescues her from drowning. In fact, much of her time seems to be spent in graceful unconsciousness in some man's arms. In contrast to Bess's helplessness, Matiwan's definitive action in crisis is in strong contrast. The climax of the novel occurs when Matiwan kills her beloved son to save his honor and the honor of the family and the tribe.

The wife of the Indian trader Granger is likewise a contrast to Bess Mathews. Mrs. Granger, like most of the "low" characters in Simms' romances, is scarcely marked as a heroine. Yet she manifests grim courage and resoluteness and a capacity for self-sacrifice. But like all women in romances, she knows her place. When the blockhouse is in imminent danger of falling to Indian attack, she suggests to Wat Grayson practical means of defense. "This she did with so much unobtrusive modesty," Simms assures the reader, "that the worthy woodsman took it for granted, all the while, that the ideas were properly his own."[3] It is Mrs. Granger who saves the blockhouse by fending off the Indian gaining entry through an upper window. In almost sickeningly realistic detail, Simms describes how Mrs. Granger breaks the Indian's arm across the sill, how the Indian faints and falls to the ground, and how thereupon Mrs. Granger faints as the help no longer needed belatedly arrives. But Mrs. Granger is allowed the escape hatch of lady-like fainting only once in the course of this novel.

Simms' other heroines in his seven Revolutionary War romances conform to the general pattern which the Victorians deemed proper for a young lady hoping for a husband. Let us look first at the heroine of one of Simms' most popular novels,

Katharine Walton (1851); and secondly at the two attractive widows over whom Captain Porgy nearly comes a cropper in *Woodcraft* (1852).

Katharine faints constantly and consistently on those occasions when custom demands that she sink into graceful unconsciousness. The villain Balfour, the British commandant in charge of the garrison city of Charleston, bargains for her hand with a promise to save her father from execution. What could the proper kind of heroine do except resist to the last moment, and then sacrifice her "all" as the noose was about to descend on Papa's neck. Of course she must not be permitted to sacrifice her virgin body to this deep-dyed villain. Obviously a *deus ex machina* is needed in a hurry, and help arrives in the form of a determined young schemer, a rival for Balfour's heart, whose interference succeeds in getting Walton hanged, thus freeing Katharine from giving her hand without her heart. Since the Walton plantation is on the outskirts of Charleston, and the amenities of one of the cultural capitals of the South are part of Katharine's life, it is not to be expected that this heroine should manifest characteristics useful to frontier life. Katharine was not bred to cope with Indians or to live in a ramshackle cabin in a lonely clearing.

In *Woodcraft* (1852), the last chronologically in the seven-volume series of the Revolutionary War romances, Simms replied to the emotional anti-slavery sentiment stirred up by Harriet Beecher Stowe's *Uncle Tom's Cabin*, published earlier in the same year. Simms handles his characters in this novel always with sympathy for the South's view of its most tragic problem, slavery. As his protagonist, Simms chooses a true son of the Old South, Captain Porgy, owner of a backlands plantation to which he is coming home after the end of the War. His homecoming presents a dismal scene of rape and devastation resulting from the warring forces of British, loyalists, and partisans.

The two ladies in the life of Captain Porgy are his near-neighbors, the Widow Eveleigh and the Widow Griffin. Both ladies are notable portraitures, and both are suitable enough objects of attention from a gentleman who is himself no longer a spring chicken, though something of a gallant.

The Widow Eveleigh is the strongest character in the book—highly intelligent, refined, product of an old established Southern family of means, liberal-handed, demanding responsibility of her slaves, yet extremely solicitous of their welfare. In this respect, she is Simms' answer to the ineffectual wives of Mrs. Stowe's plantation owners, just as Porgy's black cook Tom (Simms chose the name with Uncle Tom in mind) is limned in strong contrast to the northerner's Uncle Tom. Simms' southern readers felt that he had replied effectively to Mrs. Stowe's propaganda.

The Widow Eveleigh has all the attributes commonly dubbed masculine: she is a competent manager of her plantation, possessed of fortitude and presence of mind in crisis, active in promoting her own affairs, a leader among her neighbors. As a foil to her, the Widow Griffin is dependent upon men to manage her affairs for her. Even the physical contrast between the two women is emphasized—Mrs. Eveleigh being robust, mannish, and bold; Mrs. Griffin feminine, languishing, and modest. Porgy courts them both, but succeeds with neither. Mrs. Eveleigh rejects Porgy's offer of marriage because she recognizes it for what it is: a convenience rather than true love. And when Porgy then directs his interest to Mrs. Griffin, he discovers that she has already engaged herself to another man.

Simms' purpose in this novel—to defend the South's "peculiar institution"—forced him to treat his theme with grace and humor, and the roly-poly Captain Porgy, one of Simms' most accomplished character portrayals, cannot therefore be the kind of matinee idol who inhabits the typical American romance. The two women in his life share the same ambience of humor and irony which surrounds the Captain. A single quotation from this novel (which, interestingly enough, was originally entitled *The Sword and the Distaff*) gives the clue to Simms' characteristic distinction between male and female. Porgy's old crony, Sergeant Millhouse, is advising him how to court the Widow Eveleigh:

This courtin' of woman is just the sawt of business that calls for fast usage.....And a woman of ixperance [*i.e.*, a widow] likes a man the better if he gives her no time for long thinking. Courtin' is like storming an inimy's batteries. Women expects naterally to be taken by storm. They likes a good ixcuse for surrenderin'. You must go at it with a rush, sword in hand, looking mighty fierce, and ready to smite and tear everything to splinters; and jist then she drops into your arms and stops the massacree by an honest givin' in....Put on your biggest thunder, cappin, and go to the attack with a shout and a rush, and dang my peepers ef she don't surrender at the first summons.[4]

Sealsfield first arrived in America in the summer of 1823, landing in New Orleans. For close to a year he traveled around the Louisiana Territory, then spent some time in the Mexican-held Texas territory, returning to the Continent for a few months in 1826 and again in 1827 to see about the publication of the books he had been writing. For the better part of six years, 1823 to 1829, he traveled around America, up and down the Mississippi, the Missouri, and the Ohio River, residing for a long period in Kittanning, Pennsylvania, and on a plantation which he had bought on the Red River in Louisiana. His first published work, entitled *The United States of North America As They Are,* was written in 1826 and published in London in June, 1827. This book was quickly followed by *Austria As It Is,* written while Sealsfield was on the Continent between January and June, 1827, and published in December of that year after he had returned to America. A third book, entitled *The Americans As They Are,* was published in London in March, 1828. All appeared anonymously, all sold well, establishing a reputation for the "unknown author," and the first and third demonstrated that author's substantial knowledge of frontier America.

Some of Sealsfield's comments on domestic life in America throw light upon the frontier woman. "The American," he writes,

treats wife and children with the same formality as he treats his neighbor. He is reserved and unimpassioned. His fireside exhibits great decency of conduct. Due to his being much in the public eye, American life is open and everybody knows what everybody else does. The wealthier families live in style, especially in New York. The women act like British peeresses, forgetting that something more is required than a Cashmere shawl, a bonnet trimmed with Brussels lace, and a London watch with a gold chain. Their forenoon is employed in dressing, playing on the pianoforte, and other trifling occupations, with visits from female friends accompanied by a dandy. They talk much scandal. Then they make the rounds of the fashionable shops until three, when they dine. After dinner they ride. Then they attend the Italian opera or the theatre. After that, supper, and a ball in the evening. The ladies are attractive, especially when a foreigner appears sporting a diamond, which brings out the fortune-hunter in them. American ladies have a certain assurance, perhaps because there are not ranks in society; they think themselves the center of a man's attention, and will even claim it as their right.[5]

In a country where so much attention is paid to the fair sex, it is to be expected that proper attention is paid to their education. The female wholly destitute of learning is seldom to be met with in the United States.... The wealthy families usually send their daughters to boarding schools [in the East]. The price of the first class is from $400 to $600 a year, for board and lodging, independent of tuition, which amounts to $200 or more. The instruction comprehends writing, reading, mathematics, drawing, painting, geography, astronomy, history, French and Italian, singing, pianoforte, and harp. The prevailing custom of introducing the pupils once or twice a week into the society of good families essentially contributes to the improvement of their manners.[6]

The foregoing comments, of course, pertain to the education offered in the Eastern settlements, but the settlements were rapidly spreading westward, and many a young woman with parents of means living in Cincinnati, St. Louis, and New Orleans, towns which were in the early nineteenth century on the virtual edge of the frontier, was sent East for her schooling. Cooper's heroines Elizabeth Temple and Mabel Dunham are simply two examples among many of young women who, after completing their education in an Eastern boarding school, return to their home on the frontier and to their future there.

Sealsfield's first novel, *Tokeah, or the White Rose* (1829), is a story of Indian natives and white settlers in Louisiana just before Jackson became president. The White Rose when an infant was saved from a scalping party by the Indian chief Tokeah and raised as his daughter. Her parentage is a mystery. This forest maiden at age twenty is thus described: "Soft black eye, rolling languidly, under long silken lashes...light heaving of a delicate bosom, cheek suffused with a rosy tint, the form tender, yet elastic, seeming to breathe love, exquisitely molded forehead, ruby lips delicately formed, over all an air of mild dignity and sweetness, more the air of an ethereal than a human being. Jet black hair fell in long curls round a neck of almost transparent whiteness, a dark green silk dress, closed with a girdle, veiled her form and reached down to a pair of the smallest feet, covered with scarlet moccasins. Round her neck she wore a white silk handkerchief....In her hand she carried a straw bonnet."[7] This young lady is decidedly fruitcake.

When the young English nobleman, Arthur Graham, wounded and in need of soft feminine attention, stumbles into Tokeah's camp, she falls in love with him at first sight. Her influence upon him is described thus: "It seemed as if the delicate being looked up to him with awe, but still with a dignity, a nobleness, which inspired him with sentiment not unlike that with which a pious Catholic regards his favorite saint. It was the visible power which pure, uncontaminated innocence exercises....'Arthur,' repeated she, musing; it was as if his name had brought him still nearer to her heart. She drew nigher to him—her hand trembled in his; its soft palpitation thrilled like electricity through his veins. The moon shed her silvery light faintly through the window....'My sweet beautiful Rosa!' exclaimed the youth, overpowered, clasping her to his bosom. She suffered the embrace with yielding tenderness; his lips sought hers—they touched—their breath mingled—it was a delicious moment."[8]

Rather surprisingly, considering the fact that he is an aristocrat and that her parentage is unknown, he marries this flower of the wilderness, to discover, conveniently enough, that she is the long-lost daughter of a Creole nobleman, Don Juan D'Aranzo, who, nineteen years before, had lost his wife and baby in an Indian raid. So although living for the first twenty years of her life with a Creek Indian tribe, the White Rose now takes her place with complete propriety in the aristocratic society of the British West Indies, where Sir Arthur owns a plantation. By some marvelous process she has learned the use of forks and bathtubs.

With both Cooper and Sealsfield, one wonders how intimately they knew Indians—or even women. But after all, this is fiction, and life on the American frontier could be stranger than fiction.

In Sealsfield's narrative, *Nathan the Squatter-Regulator, or the First American in Texas* (1838), Nathan Strong tells the story of his squatter neighbor Asa Nollins and his wife Rachel who, with four others, withstood an attack on their blockhouse by a Spanish military unit brought in by Asa's Creole neighbors who wanted his land. The attackers numbered eighty-eight to Asa's six. In the fracas, Asa was killed, but he took thirty-one of the enemy with him. As Asa prepared for battle, his wife suggested that they take time from priming the rifles to pray. Asa replied: "Ain't no time for praying, woman! I sure like praying with you, but not now. Put down the Good Book, Rachel Nollins. It's *doing* time now."[9] It was Nathan who, with his wife, his sons, and his two daughters, had squatted on a parcel of land on the Red River in the Louisiana Territory, cleared it, built a home, and successfully managed a small plantation. When France sold the Territory to the United States, surveyors came around and told Nathan to move "one house farther along." Nathan, rugged individualist that he was, picked up bag and baggage and moved to the Mexican-owned territory of Texas. There on the wide-open frontier he staked out another homestead, secure from the invasions of the land office, the land sharks, and the sheriff. Nathan always held the notion that land should be as free as air and water. As he put it: "A good rifle and a good woman by your side, and you can tell the devil to go to hell."[10] There is much in Nathan's narrative that has the smack of the real frontier about it. And Rachel Strong is a real frontier type—no moon-June-spoon notions about her.

My last quotation, from *The United States of North America,* gives a fascinating glimpse into the life of the average American farm family on the frontier.

The whole family are in motion from morning til evening. Children from six to eight years of age have their allotted tasks. As soon as school has ended, about mid-February, the sugar-boiling engages their time... The labors of the field follow; while the lads are plowing or sowing, the daughters are breaking flax, or spinning, or weaving.... The boys until sixteen and the girls until fourteen are sent to school during the three winter months. Thereafter, the parents generally let them work and thus provide for themselves. When a lad has worked from two to four years and acquired a sum sufficient for his establishment (rarely over $100), he thinks of marriage. The object of his affections he knows from church meetings or corn huskings. He repairs to her house before supper, which being ended, he approaches his beloved with his hat on. The preliminaries are short. 'Do you like my company?' If the reply is no, the matrimonial candidate moves off with a 'very well.' If the reply be 'I don't know' or 'perhaps,' that is taken as half-consent. If 'Yes, I do,' that is decisive. In the latter case, they sit up during the night by the kitchen fire entertaining each other as best they. can.... The following day the clergyman is summoned, or a justice of the peace, and the couple are joined. If the parents are wealthy, a dinner provided; if not, then whisky must suffice. The long and tedious courtships of towns and cities are here [on the frontier] unknown; if the youth be of age, and the girl likewise, they marry without asking leave of anyone, and if not, they frequently do the same.... The portion of the farmer's son is a horse, a plow, and some seeds. The girl's dowry is her bedding, a cow, a few pots and pans, and, if her parents are rich, a bureau, table, and six chairs. With these, and $60 or $70, to which the wife adds $15 to $20 from her savings, the couple begin their husbandry by purchasing 100 acres of woodland at one dollar per acre. With the help of neighbors, they build a cabin and a barn, and in the course of two years they are free from debt, as they are both accustomed to work hard and lead a plain life. Their pastimes are corn-huskings, cabin and barn-raisings, and such frolics.[11]

boys until sixteen and the girls until fourteen are sent to school during the three winter months. Thereafter, the parents generally let them work and thus provide for themselves. When a lad has worked from two to four years and acquired a sum sufficient for his establishment (rarely over $100), he thinks of marriage. The object of his affections he knows from church meetings or corn huskings. He repairs to her house before supper, which being ended, he approaches his beloved with his hat on. The preliminaries are short. 'Do you like my company?' If the reply is no, the matrimonial candidate moves off with a 'very well.' If the reply be 'I don't know' or 'perhaps,' that is taken as half-consent. If 'Yes, I do,' that is decisive. In the latter case, they sit up during the night by the kitchen fire entertaining each other as best they can....The following day the clergyman is summoned, or a justice of the peace, and the couple are joined. If the parents are wealthy, a dinner is provided; if not, then whisky must suffice. The long and tedious courtships of towns and cities are here [on the frontier] unknown; if the youth be of age, and the girl likewise, they marry without asking leave of anyone, and if not, they frequently do the same....The portion of the farmer's son is a horse, a plow, and some seeds. The girl's dowry is her bedding, a cow, a few pots and pans, and, if her parents are rich, a bureau, table, and six chairs. With these, and $60 or $70, to which the wife adds $15 to $20 from her savings, the couple begin their husbandry by purchasing 100 acres of woodland at one dollar per acre.With the help of neighbors, they build a cabin and a barn, and in the course of two years they are free from debt, as they are both accustomed to work hard and lead a plain life. Their pastimes are corn-huskings, cabin and barn-raisings, and such frolics."[11]

This could well be a representative picture of the life of a frontier woman, especially if she had married a man with an itching foot. Young or old, well-born or of lowly birth, amply dowried or poor as a church mouse, she went west beside her man when the settlements became crowded and land prices soared. At the age of eighty, you will remember, Natty Bumppo had traveled from the eastern seaboard across the Mississippi to the western prairies because he could not tolerate in his ears all day the sound of the axes in the clearings. If that seems more fiction than fact, we should call to mind that Daniel Boone at the age of ninety-two emigrated to a spot 300 miles west of the Mississippi River because he felt that his home state of Kentucky, with a population then of ten people to the square mile, had become too crowded. For the frontier woman, the hardest thing to bear must have been the solitude, the fearful loneliness. She did indeed need courage, resourcefulness, and endurance—not to mention faith, hope, and love.

NOTES

[1]Quotations from Cooper. James Fenimore Cooper, *Cooper's Novels*, 32

volumes, the Darley-Townsend edition, 1859-61. Quotations from Simms. William Gilmore Simms, *The Yemassee: A Romance of Carolina* (edited by C. Hugh Holman), Houghton Mifflin Co., 1961; *Katharine Walton* and *Woodcraft* (new and revised edition from the 1854 Redfield printing), A. C. Armstrong & Son, New York, 1882. Quotations from Sealsfield. Charles Sealsfield, *Samtliche Werke,* Hildesheim, Olms Presse, New York, 1972-74, 9 volumes, edited by Karl J. R. Arndt. Vol. II includes *The United States of North America As they Are* (ed. Arndt). Volumes IV and V include *The Indian Chief; or, Tokeah and the White Rose* (ed. John Krumpelmann). Charles Sealsfield, *Die Schonsten Abenteurer—*geschichten von Sealsfield, Ausgewahlt und eingeleitet von Walter von Molo, Munchen, 1918 (includes *Nathan der Squatter-Regulator).*

[2]Fussell, Edwin, *Frontier: American Literature and the American West,* Princeton, 1965, p.4.

[3]*The Yemassee,* p.299.

[4]*Woodcraft,* pp.298-300.

[5]*The United States of North America As They Are,* pp.118-124 *passim.*

[6]*Ibid.,* pp.109-110.

[7]*Tokeah,* Vol. I, pp.137-145 *passim.*

[9]*Nathan,* p.147.

[10]*Ibid.,* p.21.

[11]*The U.S. of North America,* pp.131-34 *passim.*